PALACE-BURNER

The American Poetry Recovery Series

*A list of books in the series appears at the
end of this book.*

"The End of the Commune—Execution of a Pétroleuse"

PALACE-BURNER

*The Selected Poetry of
Sarah Piatt*

Edited and with an Introduction by

Paula Bernat Bennett

University of Illinois Press

Urbana and Chicago

Library of Congress Cataloging-in-Publication Data
Piatt, Sarah M. B. (Sarah Morgan Bryan), 1836–1919.
Palace-burner : the selected poetry of Sarah Piatt /
edited and with an introduction by Paula Bernat Bennett.
p.   cm. — (The American poetry recovery series)
Includes bibliographical references and index.
ISBN 0-252-02626-8 (alk. paper)
I. Bennett, Paula. II. Title. III. Series.
PS2581.A4   2001
811'.4—dc21   00-010296

C 5 4 3 2 1

To the Lady herself

☙ CONTENTS

CONTENTS

CONTENTS

CONTENTS

⚜ ILLUSTRATIONS

⚝ ABBREVIATIONS

The following abbreviations for manuscript collections and published works are used in this edition.

ARCHIVAL COLLECTIONS

BTC   Bayard Taylor Collection, Division of Rare and Manuscript Collections, Cornell University Library

DCVMC   Dolores C. Venable Memorial Collection, Ohio Historical Society

ECSP   Edmund Clarence Stedman Papers, Rare Book and Manuscript Library, Columbia University

LCMP   Louise Chandler Moulton Papers, Library of Congress

NLC   Newberry Library, Chicago, Illinois

PFP-NY   Piatt Family Papers, Berg Collection of English and American Literature, New York Public Library, Astor, Lenox, and Tilden Foundations

PFP-Y   Piatt Family Papers, Manuscripts and Archives, Yale University Library

EDITIONS OF SARAH PIATT'S BOOKS

COD   *The Children Out-of-Doors: A Book of Verses by Two in One House.* With J. J. Piatt. Cincinnati: Robert Clarke, 1885.

CWB   *Child's-World Ballads and Other Poems.* Second Series. Westminster, England: Archibald Constable, 1895.

DP   *Dramatic Persons and Moods, with Other New Poems.* Boston: Houghton, Osgood, 1880.

EC   *An Enchanted Castle and Other Poems: Pictures, Portraits and People in Ireland.* London: Longmans, Green, 1893.

GT   *The Gift of Tears.* Cincinnati: Western Literary Press, 1906.

IG   *An Irish Garland.* Boston: Houghton, Mifflin, 1885.

IW   *An Irish Wildflower, etc.* London: T. Fisher Unwin, 1891.

NWa   *The Nests at Washington and Other Poems.* With John James Piatt. New York: Walter Low, 1864.

P1	*Poems.* Vol. 1. London: Longmans, Green, 1894.
P2	*Poems.* Vol. 2. London: Longmans, Green, 1894.
PCC	*Poems: In Company with Children.* Boston: D. Lothrop, 1877.
PT	*In Primrose Time: A New Irish Garland.* Boston: Houghton, Mifflin, 1886.
SP	*Mrs. Piatt's Select Poems: A Voyage to the Fortunate Isles and Other Poems.* Boston: Houghton, Mifflin, 1886.
TLE	*Child's-World Ballads: Three Little Emigrants: A Romance of Cork Harbour, 1884, etc.* Cincinnati: Robert Clarke, 1887.
TNW	*That New World and Other Poems.* Boston: James R. Osgood, 1877.
TWG	*The Witch in the Glass.* Boston: Houghton, Mifflin, 1889.
VFI	*A Voyage to the Fortunate Isles, etc.* Boston: James R. Osgood, 1874.
WP	*A Woman's Poems.* Boston: James R. Osgood, 1871.

BOOKS EDITED BY J. J. PIATT

Hesp1	*Hesperian Tree: An Annual of the Ohio Valley.* Cincinnati: George G. Shaw, 1900.
Hesp2	*Hesperian Tree: An Annual of the Ohio Valley.* Columbus, Ohio: S. F. Harriman, 1903.
UAP&A	*Union of American Poetry and Art.* Cincinnati: Dibble, 1880.

ANTHOLOGIES

AAA	*An American Anthology, 1787–1900.* Edited by Edmund Clarence Stedman. Boston: Houghton, Mifflin, 1900.
NAWP	*Nineteenth-Century American Women Poets: An Anthology.* Edited by Paula Bernat Bennett. Oxford: Blackwell, 1997.

PERIODICALS

AM	*Atlantic Monthly*	*L*	*Lippincott's Monthly Magazine*
Cap	*The Capital*	*LJ*	*Louisville Journal*
HB	*Harper's Bazar*	*Mac*	*Mac-A-Cheek Press*
H&H	*Hearth and Home*	*OM*	*Overland Monthly*
HW	*Harper's Weekly*	*SMo*	*Scribner's Monthly*
Ind	*The Independent*	*YC*	*Youth's Companion*

☙ PREFACE

Dismissed after her death as one more in an army of minor poets whose writings helped fill the pages of an endless array of nineteenth-century periodicals, the Kentucky-born poet Sarah Morgan Bryan Piatt is now emerging as, after Emily Dickinson, the nineteenth-century American woman poet most appealing to readers today. Mother of six surviving children, Piatt wrote what is probably the largest single body of poetry *about* motherhood and children in the English language. Yet important as this body of poetry is, it is only one aspect of a complex oeuvre shaped by Piatt's life experience as the descendant of slaveholders and pioneers, as a literary "exile" in Ireland for eleven years, and as a woman deeply invested in the politics of social and national life. Too dark and tough-minded a writer to be taken easily to readers' hearts, Piatt wrote the contradictions of her border-state mentality and her life as Northern bourgeois matron into poetry striking both for the range and complexity of its thematic concerns and for its stylistic anticipations of modernism, in particular, the use of fragmented speakers and pervasive reliance on irony.

Of the 600-odd poems that Piatt published in her lifetime, approximately 350 were collected. Two nonscholarly selections, taken overwhelmingly from this latter poetry, exist: Jessica Roberts's senior honors thesis, "The American Poetry of Sarah Piatt" (Dartmouth College, 1997), and Dr. Larry Michaels's privately printed *That New World: Selected Poems of Sarah Piatt, 1861–1911* (1999). The present edition, the first based on the full range of Piatt's publications, will add considerable depth to what is currently known of the cultural and emotional lives of late nineteenth-century American women. Equally important it will, hopefully, stimulate further attention to Piatt herself, a poet who formally as well as thematically made a unique contribution to the evolution of American poetry. The following introduction sketches what is known to date of Piatt's life and work. It should be stressed, however, that this volume's publication only marks the culmination of the first phase of Piatt's recovery. Both the presentation of her life and the particular selection of poems should be viewed as provisional. Like her life, Piatt's oeuvre is one of great complexity even at a technical level, and much still remains to be done before the full dimensions of her literary achievement and its significance can be assessed.

ACKNOWLEDGMENTS

I wish to express my gratitude to the following individuals and institutions for their support: first, Piatt Castles, West Liberty, Ohio, which opened its archives to me, and Margaret Piatt, especially, who welcomed my endeavors so graciously. It is our shared hope that my entire archive of Piatt materials, including the only extant variorum edition of Sarah Piatt's complete poetry (1854–1911), will be housed at the Castles. Next, my thanks go to Southern Illinois University, Carbondale, for several Office of Research and Development (ORDA) grants providing crucial research assistance; my research assistants at Southern Illinois University, notably April Gentry, for proofreading and double-checking the variants, and Pamela Kincheloe, Ph.D., and Lisa Day, Ph.D., who performed the unenviable task of transcribing the Piatt family's nearly illegible handwriting into readable typescripts. Dr. Kincheloe was largely responsible for putting together the variorum edition now in my possession and for locating and typing out all of Piatt's juvenilia, a mammoth task in itself. Her complete finding list for Piatt's poetry will, hopefully, soon be available on the Sarah Piatt web site, now under construction. Warm thanks also go to various professional colleagues and personal friends who encouraged my obsessive pursuit: Lawrence Buell, Mary Carpenter, Mary de Jong, Paula Geyh, Eric Haralson, Linda Hughes, Karen Kilcup, Paul Lauter, David Leverenz, and last, not least, Edward Brunner, whose judgment in all matters poetical I have so heavily relied on over the past ten years: *il miglior fabbro.* To Cary Nelson, who had to bear with me through the process of transforming this volume from a mad dream into a hard-copy reality, thank you for the wisdom of your advice and the forbearance of your temper.

Born on her maternal grandmother's plantation outside Lexington, Kentucky, on August 11, 1836, Sarah Morgan Bryan Piatt came from one of the state's most illustrious families, the Bryans. Her father, Talbot Nelson Bryan, was a direct descendant of Morgan Bryan, who migrated west from North Carolina with Daniel Boone in the late 1700s. Equally prolific, the Boones and Bryans intermarried over a number of generations, making the mythic "backwoodsman," as Byron once called him, Sarah's kinsman through marriage several times over. Piatt's mother, Mary Ann Spiers, came from less famous but no less well established lines of slaveholders and plantation-owners, the Stocktons and the Simpsons. As a Kentuckian once told to me, without, I fear, any irony, Sarah had a "fine Kentucky pedigree."

In 1844, Piatt's mother died, the first of a number of deaths that would send their shock waves through her poetry, including three children lost in infancy or childhood, in 1873, 1874, and 1884, respectively. After their mother's death, in a custom often followed in the South, the "orphaned" children, Piatt and two younger siblings, were parceled out among relatives, with Piatt and her sister, Ellen, going back to the grandmother's plantation outside Lexington. (The poem, "A Child's Party," is set shortly after her arrival there.) After the grandmother's death, the two girls were placed with family friends and then, briefly, went to live with their father and new stepmother on the latter's plantation in Versailles, Kentucky. For unexplained reasons, this arrangement did not work out[1] and Sarah and Ellen were finally settled with their father's sister, Aunt "Annie" Boone, of New Castle, Kentucky. Through all these changes, the one constant in Piatt's life was her mother's nurse, an elderly slave woman.[2] Piatt celebrates and mourns this relationship, with its double legacy of love and guilt, in a number of poems, but most notably in "The Black Princess," a poem very popular in its own day if problematic in ours.

While in New Castle, Piatt completed her formal education, graduating from Henry Female College in 1855, after a comprehensive four-year course of study covering the sciences and humanities: algebra, geometry, astronomy, botany, meteorology, chemistry, anatomy, and physiology; political economy; ancient, modern, and United States history; grammar, rhetoric, and logic; and natural and moral philosophy.[3] In literature, she gained solid knowledge in poetics through the study of John Milton and Edward Young. Whether on her own time or at school, she also acquired a more-than-passing acquaintance with Shakespeare, Spenser, and the major British romantics, Sir Walter Scott, Percy Bysshe Shelley, Samuel Taylor Coleridge, and above all Lord Byron, whom she, like many another literarily inclined young woman of her day, idolized.[4]

Although Piatt nowhere discusses her experience at Henry, it clearly was formative. In *The Education of the Southern Belle,* Christie Farnham argues that historians have consistently underrated the number and quality of women's colleges in the antebellum South. With its breadth of subjects and devotion to students' intellectual growth, Henry's curriculum supports Farnham's contention. In no way merely a "fashionable school" for belles, as one nineteenth-century anthologist unfortunately chose to call it,[5] Henry, under the leadership of the Reverend S. S. Sumner, cousin of Charles Sumner, the noted Massachusetts senator and outspoken abolitionist, took its mission to educate the school's young charges just as seriously as did its Northern counterparts. Nor does Piatt, whose poetic gift was enthusiastically fostered by the school,[6] ever complain of the quality of her education although she often bemoans other roadblocks in women's way.

In 1854, one of Piatt's cousins sent some of her poems to the *Galveston News,* which promptly printed them. Encouraged, it seems, by this success, Piatt began submitting poetry—yards of it—to her local newspaper, the *Louisville Journal,* where she soon became the much spoiled and petted favorite of George D. Prentice, the *Journal's* waspish publisher and a well-known advocate of women's poetry.[7] In 1857, Piatt's lush, intensely romantic verse also began appearing regularly in the *New York Ledger,* catching the eye of Fitz-Greene Halleck. A well-known literary figure himself, Halleck showed his admiration for the young poetess by sending her his unsolicited autograph together with a brief note of enthusiastic appreciation (Tardy 47). Despite this early work's volume, however—over 150 poems—and the praise it evoked from notable male readers, it is interesting primarily as juvenilia. In its youthful high spirits, romantic naiveté, and relative lack of irony (the distinguishing feature of Piatt's mature poetry), it suggests that Sarah ("Sallie") Bryan still had a great deal to learn.

It was George Prentice who introduced Piatt to her future husband, John James Piatt, a young Ohioan, also from a large pioneering family.[8] A year older than Sarah, J. J., as he was familiarly called, was a newspaper journalist, literateur, and poet of sorts. As promising, seemingly, as he certainly was good-looking, J. J. had by 1859 already placed one poem ("The Morning Street") in the new and highly prestigious northeast literary periodical, the *Atlantic Monthly* (3 [February 1859]: 150–51). Sarah had a lifetime weakness not just for male poets but for beautiful young men (Tynan, *Memories,* 184). If one can trust the internal evidence of her poetry, she was also on the rebound from another relationship.[9] In a courtship custom popular in the antebellum period, she and J. J. began to carry on a public flirtation in the local newspaper, trading poems back and forth.

In 1860, J. J. published his first volume of verse, *Poems of Two Friends,* coauthored with W. D. Howells. First meeting as apprentices at the *Ohio State Journal*—a venture of J. J.'s maternal uncle, Charles Scott—the two young men had reconnected after each had a poem published in the *Atlantic.* Although the volume elicited mixed reviews—Gail Hamilton (Mary Abigail Dodge) gave it the worst drubbing—J. J. undoubtedly believed that authorial success was just around the corner. In a letter to his mother that April, he boasted that he would soon be "the only Piatt *anywhere*" (April 8, 1861, PFP-Y). On June 18, 1861, two months after the Confederate army took Fort Sumter in the opening hostilities of the Civil War, J. J. topped his felicity by marrying Sarah at her Aunt Annie's house. Sarah continued to visit Kentucky intermittently during the war, but with this marriage she broke with the Old South and with the entire way of life for which her ancestors had shed so much blood—their own and others'. The new couple moved north to Washington, D.C., where, with the help of another Ohioan, Salmon P. Chase, President Lincoln's secretary of the treasury, J. J. had snagged a clerkship in the Treasury Department. Against the backdrop of a war in which she could not take sides without betraying someone or something, and in the crucible of a marriage that by her own account brought more grief than joy, Sarah Piatt the poet was formed.

The years between Piatt's marriage to John James and her resumption of publication in 1864 are difficult to document from Sarah's perspective. She and J. J. rented a country home in Georgetown Heights, outside Washington. From here J. J. could walk the two miles separating him from his workplace. Sarah, settling into her new life as wife and mother, stayed at home. For J. J., these were heady years in which he socialized with many of the period's literary luminaries, not just Howells and James Russell Lowell, the editor of the *Atlantic,* but Henry Wadsworth Longfellow, William D. O'Connor, Walt Whitman, E. C. Stedman, and Richard H. Stoddard. For Sarah, on the other hand, they were years of silence. In 1862, Marian, her first child and only daughter, was born; in 1864, her first son, Victor. In "Charity at Home," written in 1862, J. J. celebrates with sublime narcissism the safe, secure retreat that his domestic life represented to him. It is a "closed Fairyland," where "warm within, from our sweet rooms we gaze / Into the dark, and see—our Fireside-blaze" (*NWa* 73). In light of the poetry Sarah would soon begin to write, it is much less certain that this is how she saw it also.[10]

In 1867, for reasons possibly connected with poor job performance and frequent absenteeism, J. J. lost his patronage position at the Treasury.[11] It was only the first of what would become an uninterrupted lifetime of such losses. Unable to secure another position in Washington, J. J. returned to Ohio with Sarah and their rapidly expanding brood—Arthur Donn, born in 1867, followed by Frederick in 1869, and then by three more sons, Guy, Louis, and Cecil, in 1871, 1875, and 1878, respectively. The family settled in North Bend, a rural suburb west of Cincinnati, and J. J. took an editorial job at the *Cincinnati Chronicle,* soon abandoned for the *Cincinnati Commercial.* He and Sarah built a house high on the cliffs overlooking the Ohio River. From this house, J. J. could walk down to the train station where he caught the daily commuter into Cincinnati. For Sarah, with an irony she exploits most forcibly in "Over in Kentucky," the house provided a lifelong view of her old home state, now placed forever on the "other side." "My house looks like a thought of permanence," J. J. wrote E. C. Stedman in November 1869, "and we shall keep it if we can manage to pay for it—for there is a comfortable mortgage sleeping on the house-top" (November 18, 1869, ECSP). It was one of J. J.'s better lines, quickened by a wit that typically was all too heavy-handed,[12] but financially speaking, his levity was out of place.

J. J.'s absolute incompetence as a husband, provider, and poet is too important to his wife's story to gloss over, even in so brief an introduction as this. Determined from the beginning to make a name for himself as an author, J. J. put bread on the family table by garnering a series of patronage positions that kept him and his family shuttling between Washington, D.C., and their home in North Bend, to which J. J. would repair whenever between government jobs. Ephemeral as these jobs were—Treasury clerk, librarian for the United States House of Representatives, a brief, unhappy time in the postal service, and his most successful venture, an eleven-year stint as American consul in Ireland—obtaining them meant constantly begging favors. As resentful as he was dependent, J. J. developed a positive knack for alienating or else wearing out those to whom he turned for help, even, in the end, his oldest, most loyal friends, E. C. Stedman and W. D. Howells.[13]

But while J. J. sacrificed much to pursue his literary career, the career itself never took off. J. J. Piatt was in truth what his wife has been called—a minor "magazine" poet (Hanawalt 43–48). Whatever creative urge he possessed, he expended it fully by 1872 with the publication of *Landmarks and Other Poems,* his third solo volume. Thereafter, his books were primarily reprints of old poems, their titles sometimes changed and a sprinkling of new poems added. Far less admired—as well as distinctly less productive—than his wife, he nevertheless struggled to maintain the appearance of parity with her, publishing his books with hers, sending his poems out with hers, begging reviews for himself as well as for her.[14] Legal owner, as he informed Mary Stuart McKinney, of his wife's writing (June 28, 1900, ECSP), he maintained complete control over it, selecting which poems were sent out and where they were sent (Farman, in Stoddard, 67).[15] For both of them, the results were not good. Sarah, already with one strike against her as a Southerner, was indissolubly linked in the minds of the northeast literary establishment with a man whom most people found annoying. J. J., eternally preoccupied with maintaining his image as author, was less and less able to provide. By 1902, Howells reported to his friend John Hay that he had heard that J. J. was "quite pathetically poor" (*Selected Letters* 5:20). In the final years of their very long lives together both he and Sarah were dependent on the generosity of others to survive.

At the same time, however, Sarah Piatt's marriage should not be viewed simply as the sum of her husband's failures. If J. J. was not half the writer his wife was, he was also, by that token, unable to overwhelm her or to silence her with his own genius, which easily might have happened had he been a writer of equal or greater strength. On the contrary, aware that editors and publishers preferred Sarah's work to his own (Sarah, for example, had thirty poems in the *Atlantic*, to J. J.'s nine),[16] he did all he could to promote her career. So also with their moving. Although it was undoubtedly hard on Sarah to pick up stakes so often, *where* she moved (Washington, D.C., Cork, Dublin, with visits to New York, Boston, London, Edinburgh, Paris, and other major European cities) brought her into centers of cultural power to which otherwise she might never have had access. And so also with the people whom she met. A tepid poetaster himself, J. J. was an assiduous collector of "stars" (Farman, in Stoddard, 62–63; Howells, *Selected Letters*, 1:361); and through him, Sarah came to know—and be known by—many of the most important figures in late-nineteenth-century letters in the United States and in the British Isles: Henry Wadsworth Longfellow, W. D. Howells, James R. Lowell, Bayard Taylor, Walt Whitman, Thomas B. Aldrich, R. H. Stoddard, E. C. Stedman, Emerson Venable, Bret Harte, Louise Chandler Moulton, Andrew Lang, Katherine Tynan, Padraic Colum, Lady Wilde, and Dora Sigerson, into whose highly political family Piatt's son, Donn, married. W. B. Yeats was also among these acquaintances and wrote a positive review of Piatt's most substantial Irish volume, *An Enchanted Castle*, in 1893 (Hanawalt 255).

If none of these advantages fed the family, they did enrich Sarah Piatt's art. Indeed, because of the extraordinary circumstances of her life, and the long span of time over which her poems appeared, Piatt was able to refract in her poetry the principal social, national, and artistic concerns of over fifty years of American culture and American women's history. If she paid, as she says many times, a hefty price in "tears" for the privilege (see, for example, "The

Coming of Eve"), still, I doubt that she would have abandoned the one in order to spare herself the other. In a way quite unlike Emily Dickinson, Sarah Piatt gave her life to art. "My name and my [pen?] have gone . . . wherever the English language is spoken," she told her son Guy, in an undated, frequently incoherent letter written sometime around 1900, when the family's perpetual financial crisis had reached its apogee (PFP-Y). In 1914, J. J. was seriously injured in a carriage accident, and he never regained competence. After his death in 1917, her own increasing ill-health forced Sarah to leave North Bend for the last time. She died of old age at her son Cecil's New Jersey home in 1919, taking the knowledge of her failures and her accomplishments with her to what one can only hope was a quiet grave.

PUBLICATION AND RECEPTION

Piatt's publishing career spanned the years 1854 to 1911 and consisted of eighteen titles,[17] two of which she coauthored with her husband, along with multiple appearances in leading British, Irish, and American literary periodicals and children's magazines—*Atlantic Monthly, Galaxy, Harper's Monthly, Scribner's Monthly, The Independent, Windsor Magazine, Irish Monthly, St. Nicholas,* and *Wide-Awake*—thirty-seven in all. After 1861, with one exception, the *Capital,* published by Donn Piatt, J. J.'s rambunctious cousin and one of the few editors to encourage Piatt's political poetry, she never wrote seriously for newspapers again.[18] Nevertheless, despite this impressive periodical record, and having all her major books save one come out under the imprint of the best Boston and New York publishing houses, Piatt's reviews were typically mixed—when, that is, they were not downright hostile.

To understand the trajectory of Piatt's career both in her lifetime and after her death one must begin with this contradiction, a contradiction that springs directly from splits in Piatt's own poetic. As her more positive reviews make clear, what nineteenth-century readers (and publishers) valued in Piatt's poetry was not her originality—of which her reviewers deemed she had a overplus—but her unusually competent handling of the genteel style, a style that, according to F. Brett Cox, mixed "aesthetic idealism" with "cultural conservatism" (212). Indeed, as Piatt's thirty *Atlantic* publications attest, she ranks among the genteel style's most successful practitioners, male or female.[19] Her poetry, Howells enthused in an 1874 review of *A Voyage to the Fortunate Isles,* is "as delicate and purely poetic as ever was given to the world." The "range [was] not great," to be sure, but, Howells insists, "from chords few and simple" Piatt waked "a pathetic music that is never monotonous, never cloys or wearies" (*AM* 34 [July 1874]: 104).

A poem such as "The Witch in the Glass" (1880) vividly illustrates the kind of "freshness," as William Spengemann calls it, that Piatt could bring to genteel conventions, allowing her poems to "remain alive in ways that those of her far more famous contemporaries simply do not" (xxiii). Using an utmost economy of means, Piatt captures in this poem that moment in a girl-child's life when she first begins her transition to adult sexuality, her innocence still intact. Deploying the sparest of imagery—the mirror, the witch, and the "red, red mouth" of the speaker who seeks "the very thing [she] should not know"—Piatt establishes the status and voice of her prepubescent subject even while conceding the overriding role that fairy tales play in the developing psyches of little girls, a role that even the most determined of mothers can never fully counter:

> "My mother says I must not pass
>   Too near that glass;
> She is afraid that I will see
> A little witch that looks like me,
> With a red, red mouth, to whisper low
> The very thing I should not know!"

Had Piatt filled all her books with poems like this, she probably would have been adored, J. J.'s gaffs and her own Southern origins notwithstanding. Justly so. Poems such as "The Witch in the Glass," "The Christening," and "Transfigured," all published by the likes of the *Atlantic* and *Scribner's Monthly,* are triumphs of genteel art, exquisitely modeled and widely admired. They were what her period wanted. Insofar as she produced them, she was esteemed by publishers, reviewers, and readers alike.

As E. C. Stedman shrewdly observes, however, one's whole sense of Piatt could change if one read "the wrong volume of her poems or the wrong poem" (*Poets of America,* 446). The same poet who wrote "The Witch in the Glass," published by *Scribner's Monthly,* also wrote poems of quite another sort, published in other venues, in particular, the *Capital, Galaxy,* and the *Independent.* In these poems, Piatt covered topics and achieved tonal ranges outside what the genteel style could support. Even worse from some reviewers' point of view, she did so in rhythms so rough these poems could not be read aloud, let alone sung—for many nineteenth-century readers the sine qua non of "poeticalness" itself. If poems like "The Witch in the Glass" won Piatt praise, the nagging presence in her books of these other kinds of poems brought critical chastisement. Unable to dismiss her because she was such a gifted genteel stylist, yet deeply unsettled by her "experiments," reviewers sought to rein her in instead, urging her in the direction that they believed she should go, and warning her of the perils lying in wait on the road she was choosing to travel.

"She is the poet of rhythms as distinguished from metres, for her metrical sense is often at fault while her rhythmical feeling is highly cultivated. More difficult poetry to read aloud could hardly have been written except by Browning, the master of the elocutionist's difficulties," complains one critic in an 1886 review of the reissue of *A Voyage to the Fortunate Isles* (*Critic* 5 [February 13, 1886]: 80). "Had Mrs. Piatt adopted [a sexless *nom de plume*]," another reviewer observes, "she would probably have perplexed her critics. . . . She is studied and hard, and more dramatic in intention than her subject warrants. . . . Her mind, like the mind of most women, is subjective; but she is not satisfied with it, so she tries to make it objective" (*SMo* 14 [May 1877]: 118). A *Harper's* reviewer, speaking of *Poems: In Company with Children*, is briefer but no kinder: "some of [her poems] are so subtle as to be not only incomprehensible to the reader, but to awaken a suspicion that the author did not quite comprehend what she meant herself" (56 [March 1878]: 628). Speaking of *A Voyage*, an *Overland Monthly* reviewer finds her "possibly a little too original" (13 [September 1874]: 295); and in an 1877 review of *That New World and Other Poems*, Howells, among Piatt's warmest supporters, is no less put off by her obscurities and "mannerisms." "Our geniuses," he declares, in a clear warning to the errant poetess, "are not so many that we can afford to have any of them fall a prey to eccentricity or self-conceit—which way madness and Browningism lie (*AM* 39 (January 1877): 89).

It was, however, an 1880 *Scribner's* review of *Dramatic Persons and Moods*, Piatt's fifth volume—and the one in which her deviant poetics are most explicitly on display—that made the most astute case against her verse. Indeed, this review provides the most accurate contemporary description I have found of Piatt's distinctive writing style. Dispensing with any attempt to soften the blows by finding something good to say, this reviewer gets straight to the point. Piatt is hard, she's obscure, she's overly mannered, she asks more of her readers than they can give. Effectively (*pace* Howells), she has gone the way of "Browningism:"

> She is nothing if not dramatic, and nothing if not subtle. Her method is a profound one, in that it works from within outward, and a faulty one, in that it implies more sympathy than she is likely to obtain, and more intelligence than is possessed by one reader in a hundred. Her conceptions are no doubt clear to her, but they are frequently obscure to others. Her situations may be striking from a psychological point of view, but they are not such as to commend themselves to the eyes of common men; the stage upon which her tragedies are played is of the

soul, not of the senses. She not only demands an apprehension which is denied to the many, but she demands also that they forget the language which is natural to them, and learn the language which is natural to her—a primitive speech, so to speak, because it leaves so much to be supplied by intuition and imagination. It is wayward, abrupt, enigmatic, and prolific in hints and innuendoes, and questions it neglects to answer. (*SMo* 19 [February 1880]: 635)

Whoever wrote this review was no fan, but neither was he or she a fool.[20] In choosing to publish poems that were "wayward, abrupt, [and] enigmatic," Piatt was asking more than "one reader in a hundred" would be willing to give. Modernists would eventually solve this dilemma by making textual difficulty itself a prized literary quality, thus "rewarding" with elite status readers willing to put up with it. But even highly trained readers in Piatt's day ranked poetry's music and its power to elicit high-minded sentiment as or more important than its ability to encourage thought. Longfellow, as scholars are fond of reminding us, was the century's most revered and best loved poet, not Emerson, Fuller, Whitman, Melville, or Dickinson. Piatt was not the only writer—even the only woman writer ex-Dickinson—to thematically or formally challenge genteel norms. Poets such as A. D. T. Whitney, Phoebe Cary, Rose Terry Cooke, Elizabeth Stoddard, Harriet P. Spofford, and Elizabeth Stuart Phelps, to name only some of the more prominent, did also. But none, nor most male poets, either, carried their challenge to Piatt's rhetorically twisted extremes; and, bluntly, reviewers roasted her for it.

Gender, let me stress, was not the issue here, despite appearances to the contrary. The same individuals who took Piatt to task for "unwomanliness" treated idiosyncratic male poetry just as, or more, harshly. Indeed, in the much-maligned *Pierre* (1852), Melville, stung by his own encounters with the literary establishment's genteel expectations, savages reviewers who expect "euphonious construction of sentences . . . judicious smoothness and genteelness of . . . sentiments and fancies," and something they called "'Perfect Taste,'" which Melville's narrator identifies with avoiding anything "coarse or new . . . assured that whatever astonishes is vulgar, and whatever is new must be crude" (245). Nor does one have to read far into nineteenth-century reviews to sympathize with Melville's frustration. The *Harper's* reviewer who found Piatt "incomprehensible" writes of Stedman, postbellum dean of the genteel style, that "delicacy of feeling, purity of sentiment, and grace of expression . . . without either remarkable strength or remarkable imagination, have made Mr. Stedman a deserved favorite among a large host of readers" (56 [March 1878]: 628). It was a back-handed compliment, to be sure, but indicative. Forced to choose between a somewhat tepid conventionality and being, as one reviewer put it, "possibly a little too original," poets who wished to prosper were advised to take the road more traveled by. Nineteenth-century reviewers and readers wanted some freshness or originality; they didn't want too much.

In compiling Sarah's books, J. J. apparently tried to compensate for his wife's lapses by shoring up her "womanliness," introducing poems to/on/or about children into what were ostensibly "adult" volumes. But since most of these poems were written *about* not *for* children and had adult themes, their presence simply added to the reviewers' confusion. "Many of Mrs. Piatt poems are very childish, both in sentiment and construction," one reviewer complained, speaking of poems in *A Voyage to the Fortunate Isles* (*OM* 13 [September 1874]: 295). Another reviewer took the opposite tack. "She is not enough a child with children," he or she said, referring to the "poems with children" section in *That New World and Other Poems* (*SMo* 14 [May 1877]: 118). In his troubled review of *Poems: In Company with Children,* Howells—with no small amount of justice—refers to Piatt's child speakers as "infantile undertakers" and bids Piatt lighten up (*AM* 41 [May 1878]: 632).

In coming down so hard on Piatt, these reviewers were not, on the whole, challenging her right to premier publication. Even those reviewers who liked her least treated her by and large as a serious writer. But they were clearly uncomfortable with the direction many of her poems were taking, poems that seemed to go too far to "originality's" other side. And this constant litany of criticism may help explain, therefore, why many of her most important and individuated poems never appear in her books: "Giving Back the Flower," "A Hundred Years Ago," "Mock Diamonds," "Her Chosen Lord," "Old Slave Music," "Another War," "The Grave at Frankfort," "Sour Grapes," "One from the Dead," "Her Blindness in Grief," "Her Rescue," "Shoulder-Rank," "Sorrows of Charlotte," and "My Other Gods" among them. Difficult though it is to get access to these poems, they lie at the heart of Piatt's mature achievement and no judgment of her can have merit that does not take them into account. With Piatt, it does indeed matter, as Stedman said, which poem (as well as volume) one reads. As put together by her husband, Piatt's books are slippery guides at best to the kind of writer she actually was.

PIATT AND THE POETICS OF DRAMATIC REALISM

Given this reception history, one of the saddest yet most predictable ironies of Piatt's career is that insofar as she has been remembered at all, it has been as—what else?—a genteel poet. She was, James B. Colvert (1971) declares in *Notable American Women,* a writer whose poems "reflect joy in her home and family and deep devotion between husband and wife" (64). To Jean Hanawalt (1981), the only scholar to date who has written a full-length study of the Piatts, she, like her husband, can be firmly placed as a "minor" magazine writer whose work exhibits the middle-class "Victorian" values of her time: "the satisfactions of home and family with an occasional look at the attendant anxieties . . . the role of woman as sweetheart, wife, and mother . . . [the sentimentalization of] children and childhood" (1, 27). Virginia Terris (1981) differs from these assessments only by giving this same story an explicitly feminist twist. Attributing Piatt's "melancholy tone and modesty of scope" to "the female literary conventions of her time," Terris nonetheless asserts that the poems "express . . . the unhappiness of a woman of talent and intelligence restricted by her role as the wife of another poet, who received acclaim and satisfaction that was denied her" (388).

Stripped of their thin veneer of fairness, these modern evaluations of Piatt's literary achievement leave her precisely where earlier twentieth-century literary scholars such as Frank Luther Mott (1938) and Carlin T. Kindilien (1956) placed her, side by side with J. J. among the ranks of the deservedly long forgotten.[21] Even Spengemann in his quite laudable attempt to reevaluate Piatt, presents her as, basically, a genteel writer, one whose freshness lies in her consummate ability to give polish to "commonplace themes and forms," making "the most conventional sentiments believable" (xxiii). Unaware, apparently, of the bulk of Piatt's periodical poetry, in particular, all the poems in the *Capital* and all but five in the *Independent,* Spengemann bases his evaluation of Piatt, like his selection and dating of poems, on her books. But it is only when one grasps the full range of her periodical publication, and especially the uncollected political poems, that Piatt becomes something more than the good minor poet whom Spengemann describes.[22]

In this selection of her poetry, I hope first and foremost therefore to put Piatt's reputation as a genteel poet (and nothing more) permanently to rest. Popular though her genteel poems were, I have, accordingly, limited their number here, including only those I view as unusually successful, many of them, poems on children or child death. Otherwise, this edition emphasizes those poems in which Piatt's challenges to gentility as a way of writing and thinking dominate the whole. In these poems, Piatt, abjuring the genteel style's ideality, together with its emphasis on refined sentiment and delicate expression, plunges into the "real," carving out a political vision in poem after poem dedicated to the everyday dramas of family and social life and the life of the nation. Except in her early poem "The Fancy Ball" (1866), of which I will say more later, Piatt nowhere that I have found explains her "new" poetic. However, comments made by J. J. and others make it possible to piece at least some of its history together. In the next few paragraphs I briefly sketch its evolution as I understand it.

In Stoddard's *Poets' Homes,* Ella Farman comments that Piatt's "more in-dividual characteristics of style have manifested themselves, especially that dramatic element," only after her marriage in 1861 (65). This is not entirely true. Anticipations of Piatt's mature poetic can be found in some juvenile pieces, most notably, "The Indian's Inquiry" and "Waiting at the Party," both reprint-ed here. But if the roots of Piatt's mature poetic can be traced to her antebel-lum poetry, it was only in the late 1860s that this way of writing became visi-ble enough to be noticed. "Sallie is writing now-a-days some very good poems. . . . Nearly everything she writes has a sort of dramatic play in it," J. J. told Stedman in 1869 (February 13, 1869, ECSP). In an 1871 letter to Stedman, J. J. firms up his take on "Sallie's" new "style:" "I think you'll like the poems; they seem [illegible] new in measure and individual in their tone—not following of any school or favorite. Their subjects are often taken directly from some experience of life, or suggestion of experience" (January 16, 1871, ECSP). While not all of Piatt's strongest postbellum poetry involves this kind of "dramatic play," the poems that do form the core of her mature work. In them Piatt moves toward a species of dramatic realism or realist dialogue that effective-ly strips away both her juvenilia's romantic excess and the idealism of the gen-teel style itself, grounding her poems, as J. J. puts it, in the "expression of life" instead.

In shifting to this new poetic, Piatt was obviously taking Robert and Eliza-beth Barrett Browning as her guides, along, possibly, with the British poet Augusta Webster, whose 1866 collection of dramatic monologues (*Dramatic Studies*) features the words of "ordinary women."[23] United States political poetry, especially abolitionist poetry, which often used American cant on free-dom and equality against itself, may also have provided Piatt with models. As I have discussed elsewhere, nineteenth-century women's political poetry gen-erally challenged conventional gender norms, including those embedded in genteel expectations ("'The Descent,'" 591–610, and "Introduction," in *NAWP,* xxxiv–xlv). And then there was Gail Hamilton's wickedly funny 1860 review of *Poems of Two Friends.* Given how close this review hit to home, it hardly seems possible that it did not play some role in Sarah's determination to purge her poetry of the kind of vague romantic effects that Hamilton found—and flays—in J. J. himself.

Making hay of J. J. and Howells's midwestern origins, Hamilton imagines the two young authors as "a pair of stout-limbed, ruddy-cheeked, corn-fed country boys." "Yes," she writes, "amid the smoke of chimneys, the din of machinery, and the ceaseless hum of business, 'two friends' have caught the echo of a divine song, and voiced it on sweet-toned lyres to the multitudes that would otherwise have passed on unheeding" (*National Era* [February 16, 1860]:

26). J. J. never got the point, maintaining his "dreamily romantic" brand of Tennysonianism to the bitter end of his career, despite increasingly lackluster reviews. But Sarah apparently did. Well done, the genteel aesthetic ("delicacy of feeling, purity of sentiment, and grace of expression") could win her, like Stedman, a "host of readers." Poorly done, it left her no worse off than her husband. But Sarah Piatt did neither. Resituating her poetry in the real, or what J. J. calls "experience," she chose, as she rather melodramatically put it in a late—and very angry—letter to Stedman, to "stand alone" instead (December 20 [1890?], ECSP).[24]

FROM POETIC TO POEM: THE DRAMATIC OR DIALOGUE POEM

The importance of Piatt's shift to dialogue-based realist lyrics can not be over-estimated. As her reviewers' woes testify, neither can the difficulties that this mode of writing introduces into her work. As reviewers frequently complained, Piatt is a subtle writer, subtle enough sometimes to make Emily Dickinson look like she wields a two-by-four. Piatt's decision to displace her own words by introducing those of alternative speakers greatly exacerbates the problem. The present edition contains (literally) dozens of poems I have read, re-read, and read again, sometimes over many years, before getting their point. Most, if not all, of these poems contain dialogue in one form or another: words remembered as well as spoken, read as well as overheard—poems such as "A Lily of the Nile" and "Her Rescue," both of which I now read as allegories of the Old South; "Beatrice Cenci," "Sad Wisdom—Four Years Old," "Two Visions of Fairy-Land," "A Tragedy of the Night," and "A Mistake in the Bird-Market." One of the things that haunts me in doing this edition is knowing that there are undoubtedly poems I "missed," poems that look "vague" (to use one of Piatt's favorite—and most irritating—words), but aren't.

Beyond compounding the difficulties caused by her subtlety, Piatt's use of dialogue created other problems as well. As J. J. recognized, Piatt used dialogue to root her poems in time and place, taking her subjects "directly from some experience of life, or suggestion of experience." As J. J. explains elsewhere, she would often incorporate words people actually said, in particular, those of her children, directly into her poems (August 2, 1874, ECSP), making them jumping-off places for her speakers' ruminations, or else simply making whole poems out of them. But Piatt apparently did not believe that this obligated her to further contextualization. On the contrary, as in the opening lines of "Sad Wisdom—Four Years Old"—"'Well, but some time I will be dead; / Then you will love me, too!'"—these quotes often seem to materialize out of thin air in ways deliberately designed to shock, mystify, or both. With only this for a handle, readers are then left to piece out the rest for themselves, from, as the *Scrib-*

ner's Monthly reviewer put it, "hints and innuendoes." Is the child whose words are recalled here dead? Did another child die before him? Is the speaker, probably the mother, treating these deaths as some sort of grim joke, one played both on her and on her children? What is Piatt saying here about maternity? about God? about life's little ironies? These are indeed "questions she neglects to answer." And because of the way in which the speaker's initial recall of her child's words plunges you immediately into the poem's situation, readers may find themselves playing a losing game of catchup throughout. If such a strategy undermines any possibility for tendentiousness or, I might add, sentimentality, it can also make her poems singularly hard to read.

In other poems ("Mock Diamonds," "Playing Beggars," "Two Visions of Fairy-Land"), Piatt structures the poem entirely or almost entirely through dialogue, leaving readers to deduce what they can of the speakers' identities and concerns, along with the poem's point, from hints dropped in conversation. In the gently playful "Two Visions of Fairy-Land," for example, one hears a boy and girl talking as they pass each other on the house stairs. The girl is a romantic who lies abed late dreaming of a fairyland Prince Charming. The boy is an empiricist who "wanted things to touch." "Rosily sun-stained" from early morning play outside, he was "'wide awake in time to see / All Fairy-land!'" When his sister asks "'Where?'" Piatt, probably to the despair of more than one reader, tucks his answer into a periphrasis: "'Why, the moon went down on one / Side and upon the other rose the sun!'" (i.e., the earth). If you miss the periphrasis then the poem is a jumble. If you "get it," however, and appreciate the delicacy of the chiasmus that structures the lines and mimics the rising and setting of the sun and moon as well as the reverse positioning of the speakers themselves (the boy going up the stairs, while the girl goes down), then the poem is not only clear, but an absolute delight. It is not a "great" poem; but its neatness typifies those poems that Piatt's more discerning nineteenth-century reviewers, from Howells to Yeats, called "perfect after [their] kind" (as quoted by Hanawalt, 255).

For all the problems they create, these elliptical strategies have other substantial values also. If they belie Piatt's (highly disingenuous) claim in "The Fancy Ball" to abandon "art"—she says she will go to the "Ball" as herself, not in disguise—they possess a riddling quality that keeps willing readers alert. Equally important, they keep her poetry from monovocality—to Mikhail Bakhtin, poetry's besetting limitation. Reading Piatt's poems, one is constantly exposed to divergent voices in debate, not one of which is necessarily Piatt's "own." Finally, at a time when literary mandarins like Lowell were insisting that the poet should find "his ideal somewhere outside of the life that lay immediately about him" (*North American Review* [October 1868]: 660), Piatt's use of dialogue roots her speakers in time and place: "'This is the smokiest city in the world," opines the child voice opening "Over in Kentucky;" "'Yes, yes! It is nine years ago, you say?'" the Southern grandmother in "One from the Dead" agrees, speaking of her soldier-grandson, killed in the Civil War. In illustrating this edition with engravings from *Harper's Weekly* and *Harper's Bazar*, both periodicals in which Piatt published, I have tried to underscore how closely Piatt reproduced the life around her, drawing the inspiration for many of her poems, not least "The Palace-Burner," from newspaper and magazine stories and illustrations. No less than these sources, her poems can be viewed as "speaking-pictures" of her day. In them, "high art" and "popular art" work cooperatively to fructify each other.

METRICS, DICTION, STYLE

Piatt's decision to build poems out of dialogue is better situated to receive a warm welcome from readers today than it was in her own period if only because it introduces into her poetry the very kind of intellectual challenges that modernism has taught us to value. Her handling of other formal elements, especially metrics and language, may not fare so well, especially regarding the latter, should her irony be missed. Like almost all publishing poets in her period, Piatt was a skilled metrist who wrote in a wide variety of stanzaic patterns, from the most difficult to the most common. Like many of her peers she preferred tetrameter to pentameter and abjured free verse. Interestingly and, in light of her reliance on the spoken voice, understandably, she also avoided the sonnet, a form that, she told Louise Chandler Moulton, she disliked and was poor at.[25] But overall, from a metrical standpoint, Piatt's writing falls well within conventional nineteenth-century parameters—or would have had it not been, as one reviewer put it, for her reliance on "rhythm" rather than the metronome.

If, as that reader complained, "[m]ore difficult poetry to read aloud could hardly have been written except by Browning," it was of course Browning whose precedent Piatt followed. In taking him as her model, Piatt wanted, I believe, to disrupt her period's automatic association of poetry with song, stressing poetry as a form of communicative action—to use Jürgen Habermas's term—instead. Reconceptualizing poetry as a vehicle for intersubjective debate, she created a kind of poetry that even in tetrameter, that most singable of meters, could not be sung. Whatever else they did, the actual bits of spoken dialogue that Piatt incorporated into her poems roughened her rhythms, producing in some instances—"Mock Diamonds," for example—a give-and-take washboard effect that even the presence of feminine rhymes did nothing to diminish, indeed, if anything, heightened:

FIGURE 1. *"The Mask-Ball at the New York Academy of Music"*

The handsome man there with the scar?—
   (Who bow'd to me? Yes, slightly)—
A ghastly favor of the War,
   Nor does he wear it lightly.

Such brigand-looking men as these
   Might hide behind a dagger
In—ah, "the fellow, if I please,
   With the low Southern swagger?"

To nineteenth-century readers, who liked their poetry "euphonious," as Melville put it, such lines must have been torture to read. But it remains moot whether the tension that Piatt creates by thus opposing speech stress to meter will be sufficient to rescue her among readers reared largely on free verse. Some readers, I suspect, will still view her meters as too recognizably "Victorian," especially since Piatt, unlike Dickinson, fails to carry her quarrel with regularity into a rejection of perfect rhymes. And this same problem of Victorian veneer may have an even more off-putting effect when it comes to the evaluation of her language, if readers do not credit her irony at the same time.

Before examining this latter issue, however, let me be clear. Piatt could and did write figuratively dense poetry of great power. "Giving Back the Flower," "A Hundred Years Ago," and "The Grave at Frankfort"—not one of which, I might note, made it into her books—all work at every level. In these poems, Piatt's figural power fully matches the complexity of her perceptions. But in other poems of similar intellectual depth and emotional complexity, the language itself may seem little more than a pastiche of Victoriana. In these poems, Piatt's reliance on parentheticals ("I know," "Ah me!" etc.)[26] and on a rhetoric saturated with "tears," "sighs," "wails," "roses" and "dim dews," and all the other verbal paraphernalia of nineteenth-century bourgeois emotionalism seems to belie the ostensible polyvocality of her verse. Worse, such diction may make it all but impossible for readers committed to the "revolution of the word" to see through the apparently flat "feminine" surface of her writing to the complex subjectivity and startling originality of perception beneath.

In the final stanza of "The Fancy Ball," Piatt declares that she intends to strip her poetry of the kind of dense figurative effects characterizing her juvenilia. Even if not as voluntary as she claims (word choice is not always within one's control), this decision had a radical impact on her poetry, planing it down to what Piatt calls "wom[e]n's word[s]."[27] In taking this highly conventional language, which nineteenth-century readers identified as "feminine," even when used by men, and making it the vehicle for the expression of a full range of complex emotions and perspectives, Piatt was following in the steps of a notable line of British and American women poets, in particular, Barrett Browning, Christina Rossetti, Julia Ward Howe, and Rose Terry Cooke. No woman poet of the period, however, stressed the disjunction between this language and women's subjectivity at Piatt's extreme. From the tragic irony and extravagant intensity—even blasphemy—of "We Two," "Her Blindness in Grief," and "A New Thanksgiving," to the tightly controlled and bitterly sophisticated wit of poems such as "Hearing the Battle," "There Was a Rose," and "Heart's-Ease Over Henry Heine," to the playfulness of "Two Visions of Fairy-Land," to the overt sentimental nostalgia of "Old Slave Music," to the powerful political protest of "A Night-Scene from the Rock of Cashel," Piatt pushed the limits of Victorian language and the Victorian female persona as hard as she could, staging in her language a multiply fractured persona instead, a persona divided not just between North and South, but between love and anger, dove and tiger, romanticism and cynicism, piety and apostasy, submissiveness and rank rebellion. In one of her strongest poems, "We Two," her speaker takes on God himself, venting her rage at a deity who asks of flesh more than flesh can bear:

> God's will unto me is not music or wine.
> With helpless reproaching, with desolate tears
> God's will I resist, for God's will is divine;
> And I—shall be dust to the end of my years.
>
> God's will is—not mine. Yet one night I shall lie
> Very still at his feet, where the stars may not shine.
> "Lo! I am well pleased" I shall hear from the sky;
> Because—it is God's will I do, and not mine.

"[M]usic" and "wine" and "desolate tears" may have been standard coin in "genteel" Victorian poetry but there is nothing genteel in the bitter sarcasm of this poem's final stanzas, paraphrasable as: "I'll do God's 'will' all right, when I'm dead." And in forcing this conventional (feminized) discourse to bear, as she does, these singularly unconventional sentiments, Piatt was broadening the range of available emotions for all women poets, collapsing popular notions of what women "were" or could write into the tension-filled high art that she herself, indisputably a woman, nevertheless produced, an art that exhibits the very kind of "remarkable strength and remarkable imagination" that, as the *Harper's* review acknowledged, genteel writers like Stedman lacked. But she did so by yoking antithetical extremes together. For nineteenth-century readers this kind of ironization simply didn't make sense. Given their own inability to go beyond the genteel, they had no way to read her, and reading even a limited number of her reviews makes clear just how thoroughly they misread her instead.

xl

THEMATICS

Leaving aside juvenilia, the bulk of Sarah Piatt's poetry can be divided into five thematic categories: poems on the Civil War and its aftermath, North and South; poems on gender (romance and marriage); poems about motherhood and to/on children; poems inspired by the Piatts' stay in Ireland (1882–93) and travels on the continent; and poems on set cultural themes: religion, dead heroes, moral or political allegories, art and artists, and so on. Except for the religious poetry and an odd poem here or there, such as "Heart's-Ease Over Henry Heine," the last group of poems tends to be Piatt's most conventional; and I will not discuss these poems as a separate category here. For the rest, like her wedding of presumably genteel speakers with radical political critique, and "women's" words with so-called "masculine" thought, Piatt's thematic categories are actually fluid and overlapping and this needs to be understood throughout the discussion below. Finally, there are no hard divisions of any kind in Piatt's oeuvre. Indeed, such divisions would run flatly against the border-state temper of her mind and art.

CIVIL WAR POEMS

As a native-born Kentuckian and daughter of slaveholders, Piatt brought to her Civil War poetry a political subjectivity formed and articulated in the borderland separating North from South. Highly intelligent and fiercely honest, she used this poetry to explore a set of concerns that ran the gamut of the principal social issues of her day: slavery, the war itself, the myth of the Lost Cause, the displacement of Southern blacks, bourgeois corruption in the North, social and economic inequities in the postbellum period, changing gender and social values, and the dubious judgments of God. Driven by her searing knowledge of the war's waste, Piatt was a profoundly political poet for whom issues of social justice (in heaven as well as on earth) were central. At the same time, what makes so much of this poetry peculiarly hers is that despite its strong antiwar stance, it subsists thematically as well as structurally in the in-between world of her borderland mentality, a mentality that, like the speaker's in her signature poem, "The Palace-Burner," is never at home in its own contradictions and never able to ignore its complicity in the evil it condemns.

It was from this last realization—that as neither Southern "belle" or Northern bourgeois matron could she escape the consequences of her white skin and class privilege—that Piatt's most individuated poems on the Civil War come, including "Giving Back the Flower," "A Hundred Years Ago," "The Grave at Frankfort," "Over in Kentucky," "Mock Diamonds," "One for the Dead," "Another War," "A Ghost at the Opera," "There Was a Rose," and "A Child's

Party." In these poems, as through much of her work, neither past nor present provides a safe refuge since in both the speaker must confront the reality of her own involvement in evil. Like the recovered memories of an incest survivor that radically alter the present, Piatt's adult understanding of the corruption on which her "fairy-tale" Southern childhood was based ironized all that came after it, leaving her no stable point on which to stand.

And it may be for this reason that Piatt, alone among Civil War poets, concentrates on the war's aftermath instead of on the war itself. Piatt wrote a number of poems on the war as it occurred. "Hearing the Battle," which blatantly parodizes one of J. J.'s more egregious paeans to domesticity, "The First Fire," is probably the most effective as well as the most cynical of these poems. (Knowing that men close by are dying in battle only increases the bliss J. J.'s speaker experiences when contemplating his own safe, snug home.)[28] But it was actually the war's aftermath that elicited Piatt's strongest response, and it was in the war's aftermath that she located its deepest and most troubling meaning. Unlike Melville, who focuses on the price of the battles themselves, or Whitman, who finds the war's redemption in the sacrificial suffering of soldiers, Piatt looks at what the war destroyed for those who *did not* fight as well as for those who did. Thus she finds her themes in the devastation of Southern lives and lands, which she figures in "A Hundred Years Ago," "From North and South," and "One from the Dead"; in the massive poverty and homelessness caused by governmental indifference in the North to the needs of veterans and the widows and children of the slain ("Giving Back the Flower," "Playing Beggars," "His Mother's Way"); and in the destruction of cohesive community that led some newly emancipated blacks to wonder if they had not lost as much as they had gained in freedom ("Over in Kentucky," "The Old Slave Music," "A Child in the Park").

By focusing on these issues, Piatt wanted, I believe, to accomplish three things. First, she wanted to avoid the romantic drive that inevitably attached to a treatment of the war itself, a drive even Melville's fiercely antiwar poetry has trouble escaping and Whitman's (in my opinion) falls victim to. Second, by writing specifically of the aftermath from a *woman's* perspective, she wanted to demystify war's traditional (and highly perverse) allure for women. And finally, she wanted to suggest (as she does throughout her poetry) that the past subtends both the present and the future. In poems such as "Giving Back the Flower," "The Grave at Frankfort," and "Another War," Piatt treats the past as if it were always with her, writing in multiple time frames at once. In the complicated perspective enjoined on her by this three-dimensional view of time, not just her home state of Kentucky but all of America was a "Dark and Bloody ground"; and at its center stood Piatt's enigmatic kinsman, Daniel Boone, pioneer, Indian-killer, slaveholder, the quintessential American, the man with a gun. She could not escape this relationship; it was written into the past and into her living blood and into the blood of her sons and daughter as well.

POETRY ON GENDER ISSUES

The same kind of liminal positioning that characterizes Piatt's Civil War poetry also structures her poetry on gender issues, in particular, those poems that explore how different societies produce gendered social subjects in the first place. Succinctly, for Piatt, who lived intimately in two very different gender cultures, neither Southern romanticism (the perspective dominating her juvenilia) nor Northern bourgeois domesticity (the perspective of her mature poetry) offered viable gender positions for men and women. Juxtaposing one culture against the other, she exposes the ideological burdens of each and in the process demystifies them both.

The complexity of female subjectivity in Piatt's poetry can be seen everywhere in her handling of the three major roles that women have traditionally played in Western culture: lover, wife, and, as I shall discuss in relation to Piatt's poetry on children, mother. Not surprisingly, Piatt's critique of romantic love is closely allied to her poetry on the South and on the Civil War, even when she is not explicitly dealing with the American South itself. Thus, for instance, in "A Lily of the Nile" and "Her Rescue," she identifies her speaker with Cleopatra, another "Southern" woman deeply implicated in a war that destroys her country, her lover, and herself. In other poems, including "Beatrice Cenci," "Leaving Love," and "Her Snowdrops," southern Europe (Italy) or South America is identified as the geographical site of romantic passion. In these and other poems, Piatt's speakers seem to mock the folly of their own romantic attachment to men who leave them, either for war or for some other dubiously adventurous purpose. Never returning home, these men die on distant battlefields or under alien "palms" in "tropic woods" ("Aunt Annie," "Her Snowdrops," "A Party in a Dream," "My Other Gods").[29] In the late Victorian tradition plumbed by the Pre-Raphaelites, the lover who comes to the waiting woman is death instead ("Her Well-known Story," "Her Rescue").

Equally interesting (and more unusual) are those poems in which the speaker's antebellum romantic fantasies are used as measures against which the "real" worth of Southern romanticism is tested. For all its masquerade of heterosexual desire, Southern romanticism turns out in these poems to be little more than a veil disguising the economic motives that drove (landless) men and women to pursue (landed) members of the opposite sex in an economy in which land, fortune, and status were one. (Piatt's father appears to have availed himself of this strategy twice, but most notably in his second marriage.)

FIGURE 2. *"The Ladder of Love"*

In such poems, as the title of "Mock Diamonds" indicates, the fraudulent nature of the South's commitment to romance (still alive today gratis *Gone with the Wind*) is rawly exposed.

But if Piatt presents Southern romanticism as she does in this poem as a deceit and a mystification of gold-digging motives and brigandish behavior,[30] her view of Northern bourgeois marriage was no more positive. The loveless-ness hidden by the complacencies of the North's (bad-faith) concept of do-mestic love forms one of the principal themes of Piatt's mature work. In these poems, Piatt resurrects romanticism, deliberately using her speakers' faded memories of their earlier (Southern) loves to destabilize their present situa-tions as bourgeois wives and mothers ("Giving Back the Flower," "Siempre," "A Party in a Dream"). Far from finding fulfillment in domesticity, these wom-en spend most of their lives as "slaves of the ring." In poem after poem ("Shapes of a Soul," "The Sorrows of Charlotte," "Two Veils," "The Lament of My Lady"), she suggests not only that men have absolutely no idea what goes on inside women—a favorite theme for nineteenth-century American wom-en poets generally—but that the one true gift God gave women was their "tears" ("The Coming of Eve"). In many poems, Piatt suggests that to live a woman's life was to be trapped within a mirror of self-reflecting narcissism from which death was the only release and misery the sum of experience ("A Life in a Mirror," "A Swallow in the Hall of Mirror).

It is impossible to tell whether Piatt was addressing her own marriage in these sometimes excessively bitter poems; nor does it matter. What counts is that she has almost nothing good to say about this institution that lay at the heart of Northern social life and gender expectations, not to mention at the heart of much of her husband's poetry. Not only are marital relationships not romantic in Piatt's poetry, but, given the gap between what husbands want and women need, they are often close to farcical. By leading men to expect that marriage will provide them with an *angel* to warm their hearths as well as to do their dishes, domestic ideology set both sexes up for a fall. The woman cannot be what her husband wants, for, as Julia Ward Howe observes in "Wom-an" (1848), no flesh-and-blood woman could be (in *NAWP*, 83). Nor can the husband see her for what she "really" is: her multiple conflicting desires, her restlessness, her anger, her pain, and her longing for something beside suffer-ing and routine.

POETRY ABOUT CHILDREN

As the mother of six surviving children, all of whom she educated to some extent at home, Piatt knew children very well; and many of her most refresh-ing poems are those in which she takes tender aim at their foibles: "Some

Morning Orders," for example, and "Out of Tune." I have included a number of these poems in this edition precisely because they show a side of her—tender, playful, and often very funny—that her largely tragic and ironic vision tends to obscure. But as so often is the case with Piatt, even when writing of children, her strongest poems are also her darkest, and nowhere is this darkness more disturbing than in her obsession with child death, understandable as this obsession may be in light of her own experience.

Piatt's elegies for her dead children contain some of her riskiest and—even in her own day—controversial writing, but they are not the only game afoot in this poetry. As mentioned earlier, Piatt opens many poems with a child voice asking a question or making an observation. Because these questions and observations come from the mouths of babes, they often have a direct penetrating force that adult queries and conclusions lack. Very much like Fanny Osgood and Emily Dickinson, that is, Piatt uses "naive" speakers to make "sensitive" adult points, nowhere more successfully than in "The Palace-Burner," the title poem of the edition. In this poem, a young child's naive query to his mother (would she, like the executed Parisian communard, "burn palaces") forces the speaker into a contemplation of her own moral confusion and corruption. As a self-reflexive representation of the female bourgeois subject's complicity in social evil, "Palace-Burner" has, to my knowledge, no counterpart in its time, except in other Piatt poems ("The House below the Hill," "When Saw We Thee?"). The fact that it has been selected so consistently by recent anthologists (Hollander only excepted) suggests it may well distill the essence of what Piatt as a poet is all about, at least for readers today (see Gray, Kilcup, and Spengemann).

In other poems, Piatt reverses this theme, depicting parents who are forced to stand helplessly by as their children are inculcated into the dominant culture's value system through the gendered roles they learn to play. In poems such as "Funeral of a Doll," "Her Grown-Up Doll's Needs," and "Playing Beggars," Piatt has her children play not only "undertaker" but a variety of other middle-class adult roles as well: romantic lovers, soldiers, matrons, and so on. In all this "play," these children mimick the adult behaviors around them, even to parroting the words they hear adults say. If the pathos of their games is striking, the ultimately corrupting effect of their various activities appalls. Children do indeed die physically with great regularity in Piatt's poetry, but they die morally as well. Their ignorance, which is not innocence, cannot protect them from the social ideology that calls them into being as the self-seeking bourgeois men and women they will eventually become.

Piatt's awareness of the less-than-cherubic nature of her children is strikingly evident not just in the poems that represent them alive but, even more noteworthy, in the poems presenting them as dead. "Real" children, as Piatt is at pains to point out, are trouble—one does nothing but complain ("Somebody's Trouble"), another pulls "all the pigeon's feathers out / To see how it will look with none" ("The Little Boy I Dreamed About"). Only when they die do they become "angels"—or so, we are told. But for Piatt, this very traditional consolation in no way compensated for the loss of the child itself. Nothing enraged her more, therefore, than having this particular comfort thrown her way, and it is from this rage, I believe, that Piatt's most controversial poetry on children springs. Turning elegy into confessional, she sends up howls of pain ("Her Blindness in Grief," "Comfort—By a Coffin," "We Two," "A Butterfly's Message") not to be matched again in women's poetry until Sylvia Plath. To Piatt, grief, anger, and lack of understanding were all part of the human condition, indeed, define us as human—as she makes clear in the concluding stanzas of "We Two." She absolutely refused therefore to give them up, or to give up cherished memories of the children who died, and she never stopped resenting God for taking them from her.

Rampant in its self-destructive emotionalism, Piatt's absolute refusal to shed her grief and accept God's will radically differentiates her child elegies from those of her peers; and she was roundly criticized for them. In a very agitated letter to Bayard Taylor, J. J. defends *That New World* (1877)—the volume that contains many of her most overtly agnostic poems—after its apostasy was chastised by E. P. Whipple in the *Boston Globe:* "To be sure," J. J. writes, "there is little of the mouthing of commonplace religious [forms?] of [worship?] characteristic of New England male & female verse writers—'Thy will be done,' 'All is well,' etc. Nor is there the selfish [illegible] encouraged to [illegible] forget ones friends with the consolation that our loss is their gain be [illegible] as to go as quickly as possible about our own personal eating, drinking & merry-making" (November 21, 1876, BTC).[31] For once J. J. held firm on Sarah's right to radicalize. Although she did write a number of poignant, tender poems on the mystery of child death and the pain of maternal loss ("Thought of Astyanax," "Watching the Cow," "Trumpet Flowers," "In a Round Tower at Cloyne," "A Bid for the Crown Jewels") to her very last poems, in particular, the ruthlessly nihilistic "A New Thanksgiving," Sarah Piatt refused to "kiss the chastening rod."

THE IRISH POETRY

Between 1883 and 1911, Piatt published roughly 130 poems, of which approximately half are related one way or another to Ireland or to her family's travels on the continent. As is typical in Piatt's oeuvre, these poems approach their subject from a number of directions, picking up on different problems and refracting them in different ways. Some may seem standard "tourist" pieces, the distanced observations of a white bourgeois American woman bent on admiring the monuments of the past; but even here, as Pamela Kincheloe has ably demonstrated in her dissertation on Piatt's Irish poetry, the impression can be deceptive (91–161; see also "Two Visions of Fairyland," 41–50). Drawing once again on a concept of time as three-dimensional, Piatt proves herself adept at giving twists to these poems that bring the horrors of the past directly into the present. Thus, for example, in "A Child's Cry," she uses a standard tourist visit to Kilcolman Castle, former home of the Elizabethan poet Edmund Spenser, the highly regarded author of *The Faerie Queen*, to remind readers obliquely of the 1598 rebellion that caused Spenser to flee back to England. Claiming to hear the ghostly cry of a child killed during the insurrection, Piatt targets not just the British but artists (like Spenser) who focus on ideal "fairylands" while ignoring the misery crowding at their feet, misery on which they themselves batten. "[A]ll the music Spenser writ," she avers in the poem's blistering final lines, "Is as a whisper now to it [the child's cry]!" In the very different context of "In Primrose Time," Piatt performs an even more outrageous last-minute wipe-out. After three-plus stanzas transforming Ireland's horrors into what one disgusted reviewer labels "a gala out-door love feast" (*AM* 59 [March 1887]: 413), Piatt merrily concludes: "A thousand years of crime / May all be melted in a drop of honey / In Primrose time!" If one has remained alert enough to catch it, the effect is scorching. The reviewer, who chastises Piatt for failing to take Ireland's woes seriously, apparently missed the point; but he is hardly alone in doing so.

Is Piatt playing games with such strategies? Certainly. But they are familiar games, the games she plays throughout her oeuvre, encoding politics and protest in a multitude of guises that subvert incontestable rule—whether men's, Britain's, or God's—in women's poems written in "women's words" and in children's verses with gamboling meters and merrily tinkling rhymes. ("In Primrose Time" was first published in *St. Nicholas* as was the somewhat less scathing, but overtly more political, "The Dance of the Daisies.") Perhaps this kind of absurdist approach was the only way she could make what she saw and sought to convey tolerable to herself. Certainly there is an element of "I dare you," in these late poems that helps (somewhat at least) to undercut their otherwise increasingly despairing drive. By 1890, Piatt's vision, never optimistic, had become bleaker than ever, shot through as it was with child deaths or what Farman calls "the Rachel-sorrow" (in Stoddard, 68), her identification with the grieving mother.[32]

It was this identification—not just her long familiarity with the evils of civil war and the unjust oppression of others (whether Indians, blacks, Irish, or Southerners themselves)—that, I believe, set off the rage that lay at the core of Sarah Piatt's Irish response: rage that God—or the British—could let such conditions exist, rage that children were sacrificed to adult power games, rage that the hungry looked up and were not fed. In the astonishingly powerful "A Night-Scene from the Rock of Cashel," a woman and child starve to death while sheep serenely graze on picturesque Irish meadows. This was Sarah Piatt's vision of Ireland, a view her antebellum experience in the Old South and her postbellum experience in the indifferent North had prepared her to see. Her view of economic and class oppression in England itself as on the continent was hardly less severe. Only "A Prayer to Osiris" engages a different personal register. The sad fate of the Egyptian pharaoh entombed in an Edinburgh museum, so far from his warm sands and waving palms, apparently spoke directly to Piatt's own sense of exile not just as an American in Europe but as

FIGURE 3. *"The Distress in Ireland—Interior of a Cabin"*

a Southerner doomed to live out her life in the North; and she tenderly mocks his stone-inscribed prayer to the god who failed him—"Guide thou my bark." Such prayers did neither of them much good.

CONCLUSION

Of all literary figures, irony is the slipperiest, the hardest often to detect. Indeed, for irony to work, it must, in the very nature of things, be slippery, be capable of misreading, of misrecognition. That is what irony by definition is about, the gap between what we expect and what is, what we think we hear and what is actually said, what we want and what we get. Confronting Sarah Piatt's oeuvre one has two choices: "You will read, or you will not read," she says in "An After-Poem." You will hear the irony or you will not. If you do not, then she will probably seem precisely what literary histories have presented her as: a minor magazine poet, a Victorian sentimentalist, a domestic woman writer who wrote "pleasing, conventional volumes" that were fit companions to those her husband produced (Herzberg 877).

Read ironically, however, Sarah Piatt becomes a very different poet—one who, had it not been for Dickinson, would arguably have fulfilled George Prentice's 1855 prediction for her, that she would be "the first poet of [her] sex in the United States," should she survive, and remain "true" to herself (as quoted in J. J. Piatt, "Biographical Sketch," xxiv). But Piatt will rise to this measure only if she is read as the political poet she actually was, and that may present difficulties in itself that Dickinson never had to confront. Piatt's kind of poetry—poetry wedded to social commitment, to politics—could not be more antithetical to Dickinson's largely insular and language-oriented art and should not be compared to it. In concerns and emphases, these two powerful women writers, born a scant six years apart, lived worlds apart.

In Europe in the nineteenth century, writers such as Victor Hugo, Henrik Ibsen, Charles Dickens, George Eliot, and Robert and Elizabeth Barrett Browning did not diminish their prestige by trying to make serious art out of social commitments and political positions. But in the United States, political art has never enjoyed the same legitimacy. This did not prevent many fine writers, Piatt among them, from treating political themes anyway, but until recently the bulk of such literature has gone entirely untaught, even when penned, as much has been, by long-standing canonical favorites—Emerson's recently recovered writings on slavery, for example, or Melville's *Battle-Pieces*. As defined by *non-political* readings of Emerson, Poe, Hawthorne, Whitman, Melville, Thoreau, James, and Dickinson, the formalist tradition of "high" American literary culture has purled on, largely immune to the demystifying attacks of politically oriented revisionists.

Piatt can never be recuperated as part of this formalist "high art" tradition. Her strongest poetry is too rooted in her own ground, her own time, her own set of desperate and particular concerns: child death, Civil War, bad-faith marriages and bad-faith politics, romanticism gone sour, poetry and art that gild over the truth or exploit it for their own ends, children who lose their innocence before they even know they have it in a society that from its origins was saturated in violence and blood. No white writer of her period had better credentials to take apart the "Dark and Bloody ground" that served as this nation's foundational landscape—and she did, poem after poem, situating her writing in the now, not the (literary) hereafter, speaking to her culture, not for all time.

To read Sarah Piatt as she should be read will mean, therefore, not only grasping her irony. It will also mean becoming considerably more open in what we look for and value in poetry itself. It will mean, that is, learning to read for values beside the word. With the rise of new schools of criticism that are socially engaged—in particular, the "new" historicism and cultural studies—Piatt's poetry, which is so deeply committed both to history and culture, may finally get the audience it deserves. If so, American women's literary culture will be the richer for a poet of unusual complexity and depth. Without attempting to transcend her own time, Piatt, with a courage that verged on blindness, opened her poetry not only to the divergent voices of her period and culture but to those constituting her own fractured and multiple "self," a self that in its very contradictions, its liminality and its disguises, gave rise to a body of poetry that this introduction and this edition have only begun to explore.

NOTES

1. In a letter to Louise Chandler Moulton, January 7 [1890], Piatt expresses undiluted rage at "second" wives: "I hate a man's second wife as far as I can see her" (LCMP). The vehemence suggests tremendous residual anger at her father for remarrying as she goes on to trash men generally for narcissism and inconstancy.

2. Piatt's preference for "nurse" over the Southern favorite, "mammy," may reflect family custom, or may arise from her desire to separate her family from other (crueler) slaveholders. See "Heredity in Death." Farman asserts that Piatt's love for her nurse, who accompanied her north in 1861, was "real and genuine" (in Stoddard, 64). In chapter 5 of her dissertation, Gray provides an interesting discussion of Piatt's relationship to her nurse in the context of postbellum women poets' handling of racial modernity.

3. My information on Henry is based on the school's 1859 catalog, giving the school's philosophy and course of study. Piatt's last name appears among the 1855 graduates as "Bryant," a common alternate spelling for Bryan but one that, to my knowledge, she never used thereafter. Piatt adopts a constantly changing set of signatures throughout

her career: "S.," "S.M.B.," "Mrs. S.M.B. Piatt," "Sallie M. B. Piatt," "Mrs. John James Piatt," "Sarah Piatt," and so on. In response to a query from Francis Browne (NLC), she told the publisher to spell her name any way he liked. She had no preference.

4. Byron's appeal to well-educated young women caused much concern among the older folk of Piatt's day. George Prentice, who played a crucial role in her life as a surrogate father, warned her against him: "Read Byron, if you will, but do not yield yourself up to the fascinations of the deadly serpent that coils among the beautiful and glorious flowers upon his page" (as cited in J. J. Piatt, "Biographical Sketch," xxv). Piatt's use of this same imagery in "Prevented Choice" and "Her Chosen Lord" suggests that she may have been dealing with similar anxieties over her attraction to dangerous but beautiful men (the "Byronic" male) in both poems. In turn, this might help explain why she would end up marrying someone like J. J. on the rebound, who seemed, at least, to be artistic and safe at once. See note 9, below.

5. Venable, in Alderman and Harris, 4003. In a striking instance of class and regional bias, all Piatt's modern biographers—Colvert, Hanawalt, Terris, Roberts, and Michaels—accept Venable's descriptor without inquiring further. Ironically, Henry probably provided an intellectual environment superior to that of many better-known Northern colleges—Mount Holyoke, for instance, whose unrelenting evangelical pressure forced Dickinson to drop out after a year. Schools like Holyoke hoped to turn out good Christian wives for bourgeois males or, better yet, missionaries. Southern women's colleges were designed to produce sophisticated mates for the planter class. The latter mission enabled Southern schools to focus on a strong, secularly based liberal arts curriculum. The real problem with antebellum women's higher education in the South was lack of access. Only the daughters of the landed gentry went to such schools. See Rable (17–22) and Farnham (passim).

6. For example, Piatt was invited at least twice to read poems at graduation exercises at Henry, once at her own commencement, and again in 1858. See "Nobility and Ignobility of Queen Elizabeth" (*LJ*, September 13, 1855) and "A Parting Tribute to the Graduates" (*LJ*, July 1, 1858). I want to thank Dr. Larry Michaels for alerting me to these poems.

7. Prentice also sponsored Amelia Welby, Emma Alice Browne, and Rose Vertner Johnson. Many of Piatt's *Louisville Journal* poems come with his editorial notes, lauding them to the skies, e.g., "A sweet flash from the star-soul of a true poetess (May 17, 1858, 2); "Seldom in all our editorial life have we published so glorious a piece of poetry as this. It is beautiful and lofty and sublime" (October 30, 1858, 2); and "A Magnificent Poem—The most thrilling and glorious poem, that the great crisis of the age has called forth from the depths of human genius and human patriotism, is the following, the production of one whose soul glitters, like God's firmament, with stars" (March 20, 1861, 2). This last was for "If Freedom's Miracle Should Fail," reprinted in the appendix.

8. John James Piatt was born at James' Mills (later Milton) Indiana, but his family moved to the Columbus, Ohio, area when he was ten, and Ohio remained his home base thereafter. Of French Huguenot stock, the Piatt family first took root in the colonies in the eighteenth-century. By J. J.'s day, the family had branches in Indiana, Illi-

nois, Ohio, and Pennsylvania. See Hanawalt (60–62). I wish to thank Piatt family historians, in particular, David H. Boysel and Richard O. Piatt, for such information as they could supply me. To date, I have yet to locate direct descendants of Sarah and J. J. themselves.

9. See, for example, the following in the *Louisville Journal*: "I Dreamed that I Was Free" (September 21, 1858, 82); "The Flowers You Gave" (October 25, 1858, 2); "One Year Tonight" (May 18, 1859, 2); and in the *New York Ledger*: "Memorials" (June 30, 1860,7), "Three Years To-Night" (December 8, 1860, 3), and "A Dirge by the Sea" (December 29, 1860, 6); and the following adult poems, among others: "Mock Diamonds," "Thorns," "A Party in a Dream," and "Confession." How biographical these poems actually are is unclear. However, whatever their biographical value, poetically speaking Piatt never let go of her early infatuations. Throughout her career, her speakers regularly refer to premarital affairs, and sometimes—most importantly in "Giving Back the Flower"—she weaves into her mature texts explicit verbal allusions to past poems and situations. See "Memorials" in the appendix.

10. My dating is based on J. J.'s notes in the copy of *Western Windows* owned by Castle Mac-A-Cheek, West Liberty, Ohio. In a letter to E. C. Stedman (January 29, 1865), J. J. writes that Sarah "has been imprisoned here at Washington (and most of the time in the country) for nearly three years"; and he is eager to get her out and about (PFP-NY). Piatt's discontent in this period surfaces years later in "Descent of the Angel" (1879), which lists "romance and travel" among marriage's immediate casualties.

11. Hanawalt (153). Also see J. J.'s January 29, 1865, letter to Stedman: "You perhaps know the fiend that troubles me. Lazy in disposition to attempt earnestly what I want to do. I think this Thing . . . has kept me from either fortune or fame thus far." He then adds that he is "tired of the kicks we get here from these Congressional asses who propose and dispose for us" (PFP-NY). These same sorts of work habits and attitudes plagued J. J. throughout his career.

12. In *Memories,* Katherine Tynan, the most sensitive and intelligent of Piatt's contemporary biographers, wonders how Sarah can survive living with the totally humorless J. J. (184–85). In an 1870 letter to his father, W. D. Howells characterizes J. J. as perpetually "gloomy" (*Selected Letters* 1:360).

13. In a letter to E. C. Stedman of February 3, 1869 (ECSP), J. J. acknowledges that he goes "a little beyond [the] feeling of proper reserve" in such matters, and that he "hurts and shames" himself by doing so. But when Stedman in his next letter agrees, J. J. immediately becomes defensive: "You are right about my faults—but Lord—think of my virtues! . . . burn this self-seeking epistle. Do not fail. And do not think me perfectly shameless" (February 26, 1869, ECSP). In a letter of 1872, Stedman's patience for this sort of thing apparently ran out, at least temporarily. In an angry and bitter letter to J. J., which sheds great light on just how difficult it was for these men to succeed at their literary endeavors, he comments that his own books "*have not sold 100 copies in five years.*" He then tells J. J., "I need help, instead of helping others, but do not ask help from anyone—not having your ambition & faculty of 'pushing'" (May 25, 1872, ECSP). Also see W. D. Howells to John Milton Hay, March 27, 1902 (*Selected Letters* 5:19–

20); and J. J. Piatt to E. C. Stedman, March 11, 1871, October 27, 1888, and June 20, 1896 (ECSP). Sarah was apparently dismayed by this kind of behavior but in the March 11 letter to Stedman, J. J. says that being "of baser metal" than "Sallie," he is ready to ask for assistance. Also see Sarah's own very revealing and angry letter to Stedman, wherein she describes herself as "deeply mortified" by J. J.'s pushiness (December 20 [1890?], ECSP). Stedman and Howells never abandoned the Piatts entirely, however. Indeed, Howells was primarily responsible for getting the Authors' Club Fund to give the Piatts financial aid after J. J. was permanently disabled in a carriage accident in 1914 (see M. Howells 346–47).

14. In a rare moment of candor, J. J. expressed a number of entirely justified doubts about his poems in an early letter to R. Stoddard: "Sometimes they have looked up at me, when I have read them, with pretty faces like children—encouraging me to do something for them, at other times they have seemed very dull indeed" (March 4, 1863, Richard H. and Elizabeth B. Stoddard Papers, Manuscripts and Archives Division, New York Public Library, Astor, Lenox, and Tilden Foundations). Tellingly, by 1872 Howells was already noting in his reviews J. J.'s failure to develop and his tendency to recirculate old poems. See "Recent Literature," *AM* (March 1872: 367, and April 1879: 546). At the same time, some of J. J.'s letters suggest that he found it difficult to control his envy at Sarah's greater success. On April 3, 1870, he complains to Stedman that *Hearth and Home* took two of her poems but none of his; and in May 22, 1872, he complains that Osgood's edition of Sarah's *A Woman's Poems* sold more in six months than his book, published by Hurd and Houghton, sold in six years (ECSP).

15. Piatt's disinterest in the mechanics of publication has been read conventionally by early biographers (Farman, Tynan, et al.) as a sign of womanly disinterest in professional matters—an interpretation she herself fostered (see, for example, her letter to Stedman, December 20 [1890?], ECSP, and J. J.'s letter to Moulton, December 8, 1888, LCMP). This impression has led some scholars to assume that J. J. was the driving force behind her career, offering her, as Colvert puts it, "stimulus and critical advice" (64). Piatt's voluminous juvenile production and J. J.'s comments to his father on Sarah's "insane notion that she must pay, herself, for the children's clothing and school" (February 5, 1874, PFP-Y) both contradict this impression. A likelier explanation is that the pragmatic Sarah knew wresting control of her poetry out of J. J.'s hands was a lost cause and didn't try.

16. Hanawalt identifies only seven poems of J. J.'s in the *Atlantic* (188). The *Atlantic Monthly* cumulative index (1857–88) lists eight, but it inaccurately attributes one of J. J.'s poems, "A Flower in a Book," to Sarah. To my knowledge neither J. J. nor Sarah published in the *Atlantic* after 1888.

17. This number is highly deceptive. Not only did J. J. recirculate old poems in Sarah's books as well as in his own (albeit far less often); but while in Ireland, he developed a taste for elegant little volumes containing anywhere from eight (*GT*) to seventeen poems (*IW*), which he would then reprint in other more substantial collections. Finally, one title, *A Book About Baby* (1882), is a reissue of an old book (*PCC*, 1877), under a new name. Roberts cites two spurious titles: *Songs of a Year* (1879) and *Songs*

and Satires (1886). The first, listed in the *National Union Catalog,* is actually an anthology in which one of Piatt's poems ("September") appears. The other title, which Hanawalt and Spengemann also cite, is not listed in the *NUC,* nor have I found hard evidence that it ever existed.

18. To my knowledge the only newspaper to which Piatt submitted poetry after 1861, other than the *Capital,* was the *Pilot,* the organ of the Boston Archdiocese, to which J. J. sent a handful of poems in the 1880s. One, "The Ivy of Ireland," won third prize in a poetry contest in 1885. Why J. J. submitted this very weak poem is beyond me but it got what it deserved. Piatt's newspaper and periodical publication is the key to her oeuvre. Three periodicals—the *Capital* (72 poems, including five overlaps with the *Independent*), the *Independent* (69 poems) and *Galaxy* (16 poems)—account for a third of her entire mature production, including 44 of her approximately 90 uncollected poems. These three outlets also published the bulk of her political poetry. Conversely, although the *Atlantic Monthly* also took quite a number (30), the poems it chose are, on the whole, more conventional—helping account, perhaps, for the wide-spread impression that Piatt never escaped the genteel. Including duplicates, Piatt's poems appeared approximately 400 times in periodicals of one sort or another between 1866 and 1911. The 90-odd uncollected poems represent close to a quarter of her entire mature output of, approximately, 440 poems.

19. Hanawalt suggests that Sarah's periodical success was due to Howells's running interference for her (189–90). However, as Sarah astutely observes to Stedman (January 9 [19??] ECSP), all these writers succeeded by scratching each other's backs. The "favors" Sarah received were a pittance compared to those that men did for each other. Howells's admiration for Sarah's (more genteel) poetry appears, moreover, to have been genuine, not simply gentlemanly. In a letter to Bayard Taylor, J. J. says that Howells had written him privately, expressing admiration for Sarah's work: "'She is by far the subtlest genius of her sex who has written poetry in this time; and I don't see, either, why I specify the sex. Her work always deeply affects me'" (November 5, 1876, BTC). In a letter to George Warner, May 28, 1875, Howells calls Sarah "a woman of genius" (*Selected Letters* 2:96). Like Howells, Tynan views Sarah as the poet in the family: "she much more sensible and distinguished than he, with a real poetic gift. He was the simpler of the two" (*Memories* 192). To judge by the Piatts' widely differing acceptance rates, virtually all contemporary editors and publishers saw Sarah as the superior poet also. It was left to twentieth-century literary historians like Dowler, Colvert, Hanawalt, and Terris to reverse this judgment, probably because J. J.'s close connection with Howells kept his name alive long after Sarah's was erased, making him, in history's eyes at least, seem the stronger writer.

20. It is possible that Stedman wrote this review. In 1877, J. J. accused him of writing an earlier *Scribner's Monthly* review criticizing Sarah's lack of womanliness: "I could hardly have expected you to criticize her poems as not *distinctly womanly* (feminine I mean) or that they were artificial . . . and lacked tenderness. So you didn't write it! I fancy some hapless old maid did. . . . if ever a *woman's* poems were womanly, those in my wife's three books are" (May 1, 1877, ECSP). If Stedman did write the 1877 review,

then similarities of tone and complaint make it virtually certain he wrote the later review also, his close friendship with the Piatts notwithstanding. Stedman's own definition of poetry as the "rhythmical expression of emotion and ideality" (*AAA* xxix) is quintessentially genteel.

21. See Mott (3:229) and Kindilien (32). These assessments derive from the way in which late nineteenth-century genteel anthologists like Stedman, Venable, Townsend, and Tardy presented Sarah. When, for example, J. J. provided Stedman with a list of poems for Sarah's contribution to *An American Anthology* (1900), he mingled her safe poetry—"The Witch in the Glass," "Broken Promise," etc.—with some that suggested a harder edge: "A Sea-Gull Wounded" and "A Prayer to Osiris," in particular. These latter poems never made the final cut, however (April 28, 1897, ECSP). Prior to the 1990s, only Watts and Steiner gave Piatt fresh readings.

22. Spengemann does not explain his choice of Piatt poems. However, extrapolating, I hope not unfairly, from the introductory matter and compilation of Piatt's poems made by his student (and coeditor), Jessica Roberts, in her Dartmouth honors thesis, it seems clear that he was unaware of the vast bulk of Piatt's periodical poetry, including all the poetry in Piatt family publications. Certainly he, like Roberts, misdates many poems.

23. In their introduction to the poetry of Augusta Webster, Leighton and Reynolds distinguish Webster's handling of the dramatic monologue from Browning's, noting that where he used the form to explore the consciousness of aberrant personalities, Webster used it to give "ordinary, humble, downtrodden women" a voice (418). Neither Browning nor Webster, however, have their characters actually engage with others in debate; nor do they make their own personas part of the conversation.

24. The long, complicated letter in which Piatt issues this otherwise very conventional assertion of romantic isolation makes it, perhaps, something more than mere convention. By the early 1890s, when the letter was written, Piatt had become fully aware that she and J. J. were "finished" where the Northeast literary establishment was concerned. At different points in the letter she sounds confused, desperate, and enraged. What she seems to be holding onto here is simply her pride. But Roberts is absolutely right to insist that the statement also reflects a real difference in Piatt's art. At her quintessential best, Piatt truly does not sound like anyone else (Roberts xxvi). Where I disagree with both Spengemann and Roberts is why. They locate the source of her difference in her "unaffected" artlessness (Roberts xxvi), or what Spengemann calls her "freshness." I place it in her addiction to highly mannered "realist" strategies. Indeed, Piatt's very assertion of difference in this letter is a case in point since it could not be more archly stated: "*You*, dear Mr. Stedman, have once or twice been blessed (or otherwise) to mention me among the 'fifty thousand Women Poets of America' who so grieve the dear soul of Mr. Andrew Lang (who is, perhaps apart from a painful effort to be 'too clever by half' a charming fellow) but I have been, in most cases, the most hopelessly————of the lot. I don't use the dash in a *swearing* sense! Frankly, I am sorry for it—that is, I am sorry you took the trouble to speak of me at all. I do not belong to the animals that go in herds. Whether my place be on the height or elsewhere,

I choose to stand alone" (December 20 [1890?], ECSP). Piatt's coy denial to the contrary, her dash clearly stands for "damned." Piatt must have been furious indeed to reveal so much of her hand in this way.

25. See LCMP (January 7 [1890]). Piatt wrote only two sonnets, "A Parting" (*Cap* 7 [September 23, 1877]: 6), signed "S.M.B.," and "Oh, Singer at My Window," written in Queenstown in 1890. The latter, the only unpublished poem found to date, was discovered by Lucy Frank, to whom I owe a debt of thanks for sharing it with me (DCVMC). Piatt dedicated the sonnet to Emerson Venable and in the accompanying note again expresses her distaste for the form.

26. A British reviewer of *VFI* chastised Piatt severely (and quite correctly, in my opinion) for her excessive reliance on parentheticals. See "Mrs. Piatt's Poems," *Westminster Review* 70 (July 1886): n.p. One wishes more reviewers had, earlier on.

27. In a letter to W. T. Howe, Piatt apologizes for using the word "lovely," which she dismisses as a "woman's word." But the fact is she still used it and many words like it, suggesting that such diction was natural to her, not simply adopted for effect. The comment also suggests, however, that she was keenly aware how gendered her language was and used it against itself (May 3 [1916?], William Conant Church Papers, New York Public Library). The irony of course is that although this language was gendered as "female," it was also used by male writers, especially by weaker ones like J. J., who, according to Farman, expressed "a man's thought . . . with a woman's grace and sweetness" (in Stoddard, 73). J. J. and Sarah's vocabularies were in fact almost the same; it was their visions that differed, and their rhetorical strategies. See, for example, J. J.'s "New Grass," "The First Tryst," "His Dream," and "The Birthplace," all of which I thought might be Sarah's on first encountering them anonymously in the *Mac* and *Cap*. When Sarah was writing badly, she could sound disconcertingly like her spouse.

28. J. J. himself was aware of the inappropriateness of his strategy in this poem, calling it an "ill-timed gay conceit," but this did not stop him. Self-chastised for a moment, he then proceeds as before, crediting "the Fairy's minstrel," i.e., a cricket, with singing "Away the ghosts of saddest things!" (*NWa* 28).

29. Three principal (Southern) male figures haunt Piatt's poetry: the first, apparently modeled on James, "Aunt Annie" Boone's son, leaves home for southern climes (possibly South America, possibly California) and is never heard of again; the second, a soldier, is said to have died of a breast wound in the war; the third is a gold-digger, possibly modeled on her father, who survives the war, and whom Piatt's speaker continues to find attractive despite what she knows of him. The second and third figures sometimes blend and occasionally one or the other seems ambiguously positioned as a Northerner ("Giving Back the Flower," "Siempre"). Piatt's teasing treatment of the romance narrative that she threads through her poetry might help shed light on Dickinson's similar strategy. The love narrative is a point off which they write but its real-life verifiability is moot, and the poets themselves deliberately scramble many of the clues.

30. In "The Custom House" introduction to *The Scarlet Letter* (1850), Hawthorne makes his oft-quoted claim to situate his writing in a "neutral territory somewhere

between the real world and fairy-land." This "neutral territory" is the realm of "Romance." Piatt, I believe, is saying that Romance in itself is the greatest, most persistent, and ultimately most destructive of "fairy-tales," whether encoded in the "Myth of the Lost Cause" or the dreams of a young girl. In poems such as "Mock Diamonds" and "Counsel—in the South" she treats the Old South effectively as a mass delusion that led Southerners to believe they were doing something noble when in fact (in the "real world"), they were behaving like brigands, murderers, and Christ-killers.

31. This letter is also of interest insofar it indicates that J. J. and Sarah knew that her poetry failed to meet the criteria for domestic elegies set by northeast bourgeois women: e.g., Lydia Sigourney and Harriet Beecher Stowe. Piatt also ran into trouble with her elegies in Ireland, however. "What is the use of talking about the grave?" queries one reviewer. "Of each of the redeemed as of the Redeemer it may be . . . said: *Surrexit non est hic*" (*Irish Monthly* 22 [November 1894]: 613). To Piatt, offers of redemption and resurrection just weren't good enough, not when children were involved.

32. Piatt not only identified with Rachel herself but wrote a number of poems stressing her identification with other women similarly afflicted ("The Thought of Astyanax," "A Tragedy in Western Woods," "The Prince Imperial," "Rachel at the Lodge"). For Piatt, no less than for earlier abolitionists, the "universality" of child death had the power to create political solidarity between women at every social level and over time and culture—from French royalty to the Irish peasant to the pioneer woman of the West to bourgeois Northern matrons such as herself. Insofar as she was a tragic poet as well as a political one, the central (political) tragedy at the core of her poetry was the dead child, and to my knowledge her exploration of this tragedy on both a personal and a social level has no counterpart in anglophonic poetry to this day. Nor, I think, should we be surprised to find that Piatt's strongest claim to "universality" would lie precisely in her relentless probing of an issue so specifically tied to her position as both bourgeois mother and nineteenth-century woman.

♨ NOTE ON EDITING
AND ARRANGEMENT

This edition arranges Piatt's poems by date and place of first publication, or by date of composition, if that is known. In order to bring some sort of principle of consistency to this project, where hundreds of choices had to be made, most texts are also based on first published versions. A source line following each poem gives the first known place of publication; if the text in the present collection was drawn from a later source, that is noted in the line following. In every case where there are variant wordings known to me, I have supplied them in the notes accompanying the texts. With only a few exceptions (in particular, "There Was a Rose"), I have not supplied punctuation variants since they number in the thousands and I have no idea who in any particular case is responsible for them. Not only J. J. but a host of editors had their hands in Sarah's work.

The problem of multiple hands has led me to take a conservative approach generally to Piatt's texts since attempts to regularize can potentially affect the readings of particular poems. For example, in "A Child's Party," Piatt refers to an old black slave first as "uncle Sam" and then as "Uncle Sam," an inconsistency in capitalization one could easily, and probably correctly, ascribe to typographer error. But there is also the possibility of a sly allusion here, especially when one looks at the inconsistency in context. Is this elderly black man a figure for national law and order imposing "his" will on two little girls who, by their joint play, challenge the racialized patriarchal regime for which the speaker's Bible-reading grandmother—and her shawl—also stand? Or is he, as he is first introduced, simply old uncle Sam, the illiterate slave, who goes above himself in his outrage on the grandmother's behalf? This kind of slyness was certainly not beyond Piatt. In most cases therefore I have opted to leave inconsistencies, including irregular spellings and grammar, as I found them, preferring that to silent corrections where meaning might be lost.

My reasoning for privileging periodical provenance is twofold. First, poems published in books cannot be securely dated. For example, Piatt published "Waiting at the Party" in the *Louisville Journal* in 1860; the poem was then republished twice, first in the *Capital* in 1874, then, in 1894, in the second volume of her collected *Poems*. Without knowledge of this periodical history, the poem, whose peculiar importance rests in its early date, would have to be grouped among the poems of her late maturity.

Beyond this, however, periodicals provide essential cultural context for Piatt's poems as a whole. My ten-year pursuit of her poetry has convinced me that, from Piatt's *Louisville Journal* days on, she was basically a niche poet, writing polished genteel verse for the *Atlantic Monthly,* society verse for *Harper's Bazar,* political poetry for the *Capital* and the *Independent,* and so on. Although the arrangement of her books helps illuminate how J. J. sought to market her to the largely genteel audience of nineteenth-century book buyers and reviewers, everything suggests that when Piatt wrote, it was primarily with the more varied and unpredictable audiences of periodicals in mind.

PALACE-BURNER

WAITING AT THE PARTY[1]

The lamp-flowers wreathe the walls below,
　And drop their tremulous golden bloom
On gem and smile—and I must go
　From this dim, lonesome room.

It is not long;—but oh, it seems,
　Since those bright girls went down the stair
I've crossed a thousand years of dreams,
　And landed everywhere.

In tropic palms I've caught strange birds
　With summer painted on their plumes;
I've feigned the south wind's music-words
　To woo his wild-rose blooms.

I've watched great mirage-buds break through
　Their sand-leaves in red desert-noons;
And gathered pearly bells and blue
　By pallid northern moons.

Yet most I've seen a lily-band
　Of buried visions I should know
Rise from that misty fairy land
　We call the Long Ago.

These wear death's snow-calms in their breasts,
　Like great, white flowers—and linger near:
Oh, beautiful—oh pale, still guests!
　Who did invite *you* here?

. . . Once more I hear the music start
    And murmur through its veil of light,
And the deep fountains of my heart
    Are broken up to-night.

. . . But—you are waiting at the door,
    With half a frown and half a smile,
Thinking, no doubt, I've stayed before
    The mirror all this while.

And, as your delicate fingers twine
    Unrestful through your curls of brown,
You lift your dark, cold eyes to mine,
    And ask: "shall we go down?"

Yes, if you will. A funeral chime,
    You say, is in my voice. 'Tis true.
What have I thought of all this time?
    Ah, sir, I have not thought of—you!

Louisville Journal (1860)
Text from *Poems 2*, 1894

HEARING THE BATTLE.—JULY 21, 1861.[2]

One day in the dreamy summer,
    On the Sabbath hills, from afar
We heard the solemn echoes
    Of the first fierce words of war.

Ah, tell me, thou veilèd Watcher
    Of the storm and the calm to come,
How long by the sun or shadow
    Till these noises again are dumb.

And soon in a hush and glimmer
    We thought of the dark, strange fight,
Whose close in a ghastly quiet
    Lay dim in the beautiful night.

Then we talk'd of coldness and pallor,
    And of things with blinded eyes

2

FIGURE 4. *"Uncared For"*

That stared at the golden stillness
  Of the moon in those lighted skies;

And of souls, at morning wrestling
  In the dust with passion and moan,
So far away at evening
  In the silence of worlds unknown.

But a delicate wind beside us
  Was rustling the dusky hours,
As it gather'd the dewy odors
  Of the snowy jessamine-flowers.

And I gave you a spray of the blossoms,
  And said: "I shall never know
How the hearts in the land are breaking,
  My dearest, unless you go."

Text from *Nests at Washington,* 1864

THE FANCY BALL[3]

As Morning you'd have me rise
  On that shining world of art;
You forget: I have too much dark in my eyes—
  And too much dark in my heart.

"Then go as the Night—in June:
  Pass, dreamily, by the crowd,
With jewels to mock the stars and the moon,
  And shadowy robes like cloud.

"Or as Spring, with a spray in your hair
  Of blossoms as yet unblown;
It will suit you well, for our youth should wear
  The bloom in the bud alone.

"Or drift from the outer gloom
  With the soft white silence of Snow:"
I should melt myself with the warm, close room—
  Or my own life's burning. No.

"Then fly through the glitter and mirth
  As a Bird of Paradise:"
Nay, the waters I drink have touch'd the earth:
  I breathe no summer of spice.

"Then——" Hush: if I go at all,
  (It will make them stare and shrink,
It will look so strange at a Fancy Ball,)
  I will go as——Myself, I think!

Galaxy (1866)

Text from *A Woman's Poems*, 1871

ARMY OF OCCUPATION[4]
At Arlington, 1866.

The summer blew its little drifts of sound—
  Tangled with wet leaf-shadows and the light
Small breath of scattered morning buds—around
The yellow path through which our footsteps wound.
  Below, the Capitol rose glittering white.

There stretched a sleeping army. One by one,
  They took their places until thousands met;
No leader's stars flashed on before, and none
Leaned on his sword or stagg[e]r'd with his gun—
  I wonder if their feet have rested yet!

They saw the dust, they joined the moving mass,
  They answer'd the fierce music's cry for blood,
Then straggled here and lay down in the grass:—
Wear flowers for such, shores whence their feet did pass;
  Sing tenderly; O river's haunted flood!

They had been sick, and worn, and weary, when
  They stopp'd on this calm hill beneath the trees:
Yet if, in some red-clouded dawn, again
The country should be calling to her men,
  Shall the r[e]veill[e] not remember these?

UNKNOWN SOLDIERS' MONUMENT AT ARLINGTON.

ORPHAN CHILDREN STREWING FLOWERS ON THE GRAVES AT ARLINGTON.

DECORATING THE SOLDIERS' GRAVES—CEREMONIES AT ARLINGTON, VIRGINIA.—[SKETCHED BY C. M. THOMAS.]

DECORATION OF SOLDIERS' GRAVES.

THE order of General JOHN A. LOGAN to the Grand Army of the Republic, setting apart May 30 as an occasion on which to honor the memory of the dead soldiers of the Union Army, was generally observed, not only by that organization but by our citizens in general.

Our illustrations are from several sources. The ceremonies at Arlington, Virginia, the former home of the rebel General LEE, but now a cemetery, were of a most interesting character. Arlington House was decorated with flags and crape and presented a strange and unusual appearance; an oration was delivered by Mr. GARFIELD of Ohio, and an original poem read. After this a procession was formed which moved to the tomb of the unknown soldiers who fell in Virginia during the early part of the war. This tomb is a massive granite structure, bearing an inscription to the effect that beneath the stone reposes 2111 unknown soldiers gathered after the war from the fields of Bull Run and the route to the Rappahannock, whose remains could not be identified by the names and dates of record in the archives. The tomb was tastefully decorated with flags and evergreens. Subsequently the children of the orphan asylum deployed and took positions at the different flower-

DECORATING GENERAL LANDER'S GRAVE AT SALEM, MASS.—[SKETCHED BY J. W. TRYNO.]

stands, where they were provided with baskets of flowers, and then proceeded through the cemetery, strewing the flowers upon the mounds as they passed. The ceremony was simple, yet impressive, and many of the spectators followed the procession and added their floral offerings. The scene impressed one more fully with its solemnity as there broke upon the ear at intervals the low booming of a cannon.

Another illustration represents the scene at Salem, Massachusetts, showing more particularly the decoration of the grave of General FREDERICK W. LANDER. The other graves having been decorated, the line was drawn up before the General's resting-place, the band playing a dirge, and after Commander PERKINS had placed upon the tomb several beautiful emblems prepared by the hands of Mrs. LANDER, the hero's widow, the members of the Grand Army and the soldiers and sailors, uncovered, passed by and each one threw upon the tomb a floral offering.

There are over three thousand Union soldiers buried in Cypress Hill Cemetery, near Brooklyn, Long Island, and the scene which here occurred on May 30 was most impressive and yet pleasing. Several thousand old soldiers and citizens marched to the ground, and after listening to an oration, engaged, as our illustration represents them, in the work of decorating the mounds under which the soldiers repose.

DECORATING THE THREE THOUSAND SOLDIERS' GRAVES IN CYPRESS HILL CEMETERY, NEAR BROOKLYN, LONG ISLAND.—[SKETCHED BY STANLEY FOX.]

FIGURE 5. *"Decoration of Soldiers' Graves"*

Around them underneath the mid-day skies
   The dreadful phantoms of the living walk,
And by low moons and darkness with their cries—
The mothers, sisters, wives with faded eyes,
   Who call still names amid their broken talk.

And there is one who comes alone and stands
   At his dim fireless hearth—chill'd and oppress'd
By Something he has summon'd to his lands,
While the weird pallor of its many hands
   Points to his rusted sword in his own breast!

Harper's Weekly (1866)

Text from *Mac-A-Cheek Press,* 1867

GIVING BACK THE FLOWER[5]

So, because you chose to follow me into the subtle sadness of night,
   And to stand in the half-set moon with the weird fall-light on your
      glimmering hair,
Till your presence hid all of the earth and all of the sky from my sight,
   And to give me a little scarlet bud, that was dying of frost, to wear,

Say, must you taunt me forever, forever? You looked at my hand and you knew
   That I was the slave of the Ring, while you were as free as the wind is free.
When I saw your corpse in your coffin, I flung back your flower to you;
   It was all of yours that I ever had; you may keep it, and—keep from me.

Ah? so God is your witness. Has God, then, no world to look after but ours?
   May He not have been searching for that wild star, with the trailing plumage,
      that flew
Far over a part of our darkness while we were there by the freezing flowers,
   Or else brightening some planet's luminous rings, instead of thinking of you?

Or, if He was near us at all, do you think that He would sit listening there
   Because you sang "Hear me, Norma," to a woman in jewels and lace,
While, so close to us, down in another street, in the wet, unlighted air,
   There were children crying for bread and fire, and mothers who questioned
      His grace?

Or perhaps He had gone to the ghastly field where the fight had been that day,
   To number the bloody stabs that were there, to look at and judge the dead;

7

Or else to the place full of fever and moans where the wretched wounded lay;
   At least I do not believe that He cares to remember a word that you said.

So take back your flower, I tell you—of its sweetness I now have no need;
   Yes; take back your flower down into the stillness and mystery to keep;
When you wake I will take it, and God, then, perhaps will witness indeed,
   But go, now, and tell Death he must watch you, and not let you walk in your
      sleep.

Text from Galaxy, 1867

SHAPES OF A SOUL[6]

White with the starlight folded in its wings,
   And nestling timidly against your love,
For this soft time of hushed and glimmering things,
   You call my soul a dove, a snowy dove.

If I shall ask you in some shining hour,
   When bees and odors through the clear air pass,
You'll say my soul buds as a small flush'd flower,
   Far off, half hiding, in the old home-grass.

Ah, pretty names for pretty moods; and you,
   Who love me, such sweet shapes as these can see;
But, take it from its sphere of bloom and dew,
   And where will then your bird or blossom be?

Could you but see it, by life's torrid light,
   Crouch in its sands and glare with fire-red wrath,
My soul would seem a tiger, fierce and bright
   Among the trembling passions in its path.

And, could you sometimes watch it coil and slide,
   And drag its colors through the dust a while,
And hiss its poison under foot, and hide,
   My soul would seem a snake—ah, do not smile!

Yet fiercer forms and viler it can wear;
   No matter, though, when these are of the Past,
If as a lamb in the Good Shepherd's care
   By the still waters it lie down at last.

Text from Galaxy, 1867

A LILY OF THE NILE[7]

Who was the beautiful woman whose lover
   Once left her this dead old flower, did you say?
Well, perhaps that is she in the picture over
   The blossoms you brought me to-day.

The one with the deep strange dress that is flowing,
   All purple and pearls, through each stiffen'd fold,
And the band on her forehead, whose dusk-red glowing
   Shoots into great sharp thorns of gold.

Never mind the light. You will see, to-morrow,
   That, with eyes raised darkly and lips close-prest,
She is giving away her awful sorrow
   To the snake she keeps at her breast!

"And who was her lover?" Why, that may be he, there,
   In the other picture glimmering nigh—
Yes, the handsome and wretched man you see there,
   Falling against his sword to die.

Will he die for *her,* do you say? (Ah, will he?)
   No doubt he has often told her so.
"Did it bloom far away, this crumbling lily?"
   Very far——and so long ago.

"And who gave it to me?" . . So the wither'd story
   I've dream'd by the twilight all this while
For some vanished blossom's day of glory
   Is your truth, my Lily of the Nile.

For the beautiful woman *is* slowly dying
   Of a snake as plain as this to my sight;
And her lover who gave her this flower is lying
   On the edge of a sword to-night.

Text from *Galaxy,* 1869

QUESTIONS OF THE HOUR[8]

"Do angels wear white dresses, say?
  Always, or only in the summer? Do
Their birthdays have to come like mine, in May?
  Do they have scarlet sashes then, or blue?

"When little Jessie died last night,
  How could she walk to Heaven—it is so far?
How did she find the way without a light?
  There was n't even any moon or star.

"Will she have red or golden wings?
  Then will she have to be a bird, and fly?
Do they take men like presidents and kings,
  In hearses with black plumes clear to the sky?

"How old is God? Has he gray hair?
  Can He see yet? Where did He have to stay
Before—you know—he had made—Anywhere?
  Who does He pray to—when He has to pray?

"How many drops are in the sea?
  How many stars?—well, then, you ought to know
How many flowers are on an apple-tree?
  How does the wind look when it does n't blow?

"Where does the rainbow end? And why
  Did—Captain Kidd—bury the gold there? When
Will this world burn? And will the firemen try
  To put the fire out with the engines then?

"If you should ever die, may we
  Have pumpkins growing in the garden, so
My fairy godmother can come for me
  When there's a prince's ball, and let me go?

"Read Cinderella just once more——
  What makes—men's other wives—so mean?" I know
That I was tired, it may be cross, before
  I shut the painted book for her to go.

Hours later, from a child's white bed
   I heard the timid, last queer question start:
"Mamma, are you—my stepmother?" it said.
   The innocent reproof crept to my heart.

Hearth and Home (1869)

Text from *A Woman's Poems*, 1871

PLAYING BEGGARS[9]

"Let us pretend we are two beggars." "No,
   For beggars are im——something, something bad!
You know they are, because Papa says so,
   And Papa when he calls them that looks mad:
You should have seen him, how he frown'd, one day,
When Mamma gave his wedding-coat away."

"Well, now he can't get married any more,
   Because he has no wedding-coat to wear.
But that poor ragged soldier at the door
   Was starved to death in prison once somewhere,
And shot dead somewhere else, and it was right
To give him coats—because he had to fight.

"Now let's be beggars." "They're im—postors. Yes,
   That's what they are, im—postors: and that means
Rich people, for they all *are* rich, I guess,
   Richer than we are, rich as Jews, or queens,
And *they're* just playing beggars when they cry——"
"Then let us play like they do, you and I."

"Well, we'll be rich and wear old naughty clothes."
   "But they're *not* rich. If they were rich they'd buy
All the fine horses at the fairs and shows
   To give to General Grant. I'll *tell* you why:
Once when the rebels wanted to kill all
The men in this *world*—*he* let Richmond fall!

"*That* broke them up! I like the rebels, though,
   Because they have the curliest kind of hair.

11

One time, so many years and years ago,
　　I saw one over in Kentucky there.
It show'd me such a shabby sword and said
It wanted to cut off—Somebody's head!

"But—*do* play beggar. You be one; and, mind,
　　Shut up one eye, and get all over dust,
And say this:
　　　'Lady, be so very kind
　　As to give me some water. Well, I must
Rest on your step, I think, ma'am, for a while—
I've walked full twenty if I've walked one mile.

"'Lady, this is your little girl, I know:
　　She is a beautiful child—and just like you;
You look too young to be her mother, though.
　　This handsome boy is like his father, too;
The gentleman was he who passed this way
And look'd so cross?—so pleasant I *should* say.

"'But trouble, Lady, trouble puts me wrong.
　　Lady, I'm sure you'll spare a dress or two—
You look so stylish. (Oh, if I was strong.)
　　And shoes? Yours are too small. I need them new.
The money——thank you. Now, you have some tea,
And flour and sugar, you'll not miss for me?

"'Ah, I forgot to tell you that my house
　　Was burn'd last night. My baby has no bread,
And I'm as poor, ma'am, as a cellar-mouse.
　　My husband died once; my grandmother's dead;
She was a good soul (but she's gone, that's true—
You have some coffee, madam?)—so are you.'"

"Oh, it's too long. I can't say half of *that*.
　　I'll not be an im—postor, anyhow.
(But I *should* like to give one my torn hat,
　　So I could get a prettier one, just now.)
They're worse than Christians, ghosts, or—anything!
I'll play that I'm a great man or a king."

Text from *Galaxy*, 1870

12

A HUNDRED YEARS AGO

You wrong that lovely time to smile and say
    Sharp desolation shivered in the snow,
And bright sands nursed bright serpents, as to-day,
    A hundred years ago.

The world was full of dew and very fair,
    Before I saw it scarr'd and blacken'd so;
There was wide beauty and flush'd silence there,
    A hundred years ago.

No child's sweet grave, with rose-buds torn away
    By the most bitter winds the falls can blow,
Before my tears in freezing loneness lay
    A hundred years ago.

No phantom stars, one night in every Spring,
    Saw my faint hands, with pallor wavering slow,
Give back the glimmering fragment of a ring,
    A hundred years ago.

I did not feel this dim far-trembling doubt
    Of Christ's love in the sky, or man's below,
And hold my heart to keep one Terror out,
    A hundred years ago.

The shadow Life may wither from the grass,
    Back to God's hand the unresting seas may flow;
But what shall take me where I dream I was
    A hundred years ago?

Ah, would I care to look beyond the shine
    Of this weird-setting moon, if I could know
The peace that made my nothingness divine
    A hundred years ago?

Text from *Galaxy,* 1870

DEATH BEFORE DEATH[10]

Are mine the empty eyes
That stare toward the little new grave on the beautiful burial-hill?
　　Was mine the last wet kiss that lies
Shut up in his coffin, kissing him still,
　　　　Kissing him still?

Is mine the hollow room?
Was it not cruel to take all the pretty small furniture, say?
　　The fairy pictures and heaps of bloom,
And music of mock-harps—so far away,
　　　　So far away?

Is mine the hidden face
That one night's sudden dread watching has thinned and faded so much?
　　Mine the lonesome hands through bitter space,
Yearning for something they never can touch,
　　　　Never can touch?

Is mine the passionate pain
That will hearken the trembling wind and feel the wide still snow,
　　And sob at night with the sobbing rain,
And only feel that I cannot know,
　　　　I cannot know?

Was mine that lovely child?
Did he drop from my heart and go where the Powers of the Dust can destroy?
　　Can I see the very way he smiled—
"Let God keep his angels"? Do I want my boy—
　　　　I want my boy?

Is he gone from his air,
From his sun, from his voice, his motion, his mother, his world, and his skies,
　　From the unshorn light in his sweet hair,
From the elusion of his butterflies,
　　　　His butterflies?

If not, why let me go
Where another sorrow is watching a small, cold bed alone,
　　And whisper how I have loved her so,
That to save her darling I gave my own,
　　　　I gave my own?

14

Ah! if I learned her part,
If such dark Fancies can play in despair like tragedy queens,
   Then my only audience was my heart,
And my tears, that *were* tears, were behind the scenes,
      Behind the scenes.

Text from *Hearth and Home*, 1870

OUR OLD AND NEW LANDLORDS—1869/70[11]

"Perhaps," one kindly said, through his gray smile,
   "I've been a generous Landlord, on the whole;
My tenants will remember me a while,
   And pay for some sweet masses for my soul.

"They have had warm-dyed wool and linens fine;
   My fair wide harvests gave them daily bread;
I sent them, for their weddings, fruits and wine,
   And—flowers, too, for the coffins of their dead.

"For Travel I have done some handsome things;
   The old East has her grand Canal at last,
Whose plan winds vaguely to her spice-sealed kings;
   The West on her new Railway journeys fast.

"There has been trouble that I could not reach:
   God pity this—to Him I leave the rest,
And Church and State——but I'll not make a speech!
   For Church and State are bitter at the best.

"Now as for Spain and all her castles—well,
   I've advertised her royal residence,
Which for good reasons was to let, or sell:
   An Occupant will come—no matter whence.

"Then, Rome—why should I worry about Rome?
   The Holy Father is—infirm, I say,
And needs grave Council at St. Peter's dome,
   Where let him keep his Chamber while he may.

"Make ready now for greeting and good cheer—
   (And let your tears for me be few, at most);

Enjoy yourselves with this Young Fellow here,
     And pledge with laugh and song my worthy Ghost!"

The Other, springing boyish on the scene,
     Salutes with careless grace high Guests around;
Nods to the Emperor, the Sultan, the Queen,
     And makes our President a bow profound!

"Your Excellency, let's have a cigar,
     (His Majesty, there, can no longer smoke,)
And talk of—horses, or of the late War.
     Your pardon—you do n't talk." Grant never spoke.

Perhaps he had not time to speak, before
     A charming clamor spread from East to West;
Sublime in furs and jewels, at the door
     Broke brightly in earth's beautiful Oppressed!

"You want your New Year presents, do you not?—
     Ribbons and rings, and lots of baby toys?"
"We want the Right of Suffrage, that is what!"
     They answered, with a scornful, mighty noise.

"With Train, the chivalrous, and precious Mill,
     Woman, the great Superior of Man"——
"Hush, pretty dears, you shall have what you will—
     That is, I mean, I'll help you if I can!"

Date of Composition 1870?

Text from *Voyage to the Fortunate Isles,* 1874

PARIS[12]
(January, 1871.)

Speak! Dying, that never can be dead!
     Speak! O wounded, and wan, and wasted!
"Blood is better than wine," she said—
     "Famine the sweetest food I have tasted.

"Pallor is brighter than bloom, and scars
     Than my old jewels have made me fairer.

When the Vapor put out my lamps, the stars
    Gave me a surer light and a rarer.

"My flowers were false, my glory was shame,
    My Life was Death, in my years of pleasure.
Divine from my sorrow my Beauty came—
    Safe in my ashes shall shine my treasure."

Capital (1871)
Text from *A Woman's Poems,* 1871

HER SNOWDROPS

"The woman who sits in the firelight here,
    Kissing her child to its lovely sleep,
Has the faith of a soul more tender and clear,
    In its higher beauty, than yours, to keep.

"Ah, she does not love you lying alone,
    A thing of the past, a phantom at most—
The roof of your grave all overgrown
    With the wild, thick sands of a distant coast.

"Sometimes she is sad at a rustling sound—
    Like radiant wings in the palms, it seems;
She can feel the shining Equator wound,
    Like a chain of gold, through her shadowy dreams.

"She can see the Night above you make
    The sign of the Cross on her Catholic breast,
And the passionate storms, by their lightnings, break
    In the shaken dark o'er your lonesome rest.

"And this is all. But the girl who stood,
    Her young eyes drooping with timid tears,
By one she loved, in the vague Spring wood,
    Will love him only through all the years.

"And sometimes yet, from the dewy air
    Of that blossoming morning of long ago,
He puts these cold, white buds in her hair,
    And says: 'They will melt in its sunny glow.'"

Text from the *Capital,* 1871

AN AFTER-POEM

You will read, or you will not read,
  That the lilies are whitest after they wither;
That the fairest buds stay shut in the seed,
  Though the bee in the dew say "Come you up hither."

You have seen, if you were not blind,
  That the moon can be crowded into a crescent,
And promise us light that we never can find
  When the midnights are wide and yellow and pleasant.

You will know, or you will not know,
  That the seas to the sun can fling their foam only,
And keep all their terrible waters below
  With the jewels and dead men quiet and lonely.

Capital (1871)
Text from *A Woman's Poems,* 1871

SHOULDER-RANK[13]

"West Point?" Yes, that was the one grand argument ever so long
  At the capital, I remember now, in our far-back battledays:
If the hour's great Leader blundered and war, therefore, went wrong,
  West Point would give a subtle faith in that great Leader's ways.

West Point—Ah, well, no doubt they can graduate generals there,
  Why, I wonder they do not send them out, plumed, sworded, and ready-
    scarr'd,
And just because one when a boy has happened somehow to wear
  The uniform of their cadets, let his shoulders be splendidly starr'd!

And if he in such starlight should grope on a little ahead
  Of the failures of two or three others and fall in some shining high place,
Does that go to prove that not one in the dusty dim legions he led
  Could give him his orders in secret and point him the way to your grace?

Oh, you fancy you honor where honor is due? But I feel
  You may shake the hand that finished your work, nor guess at the head that
    planned;

What if I tell you that one, who studied the science of steel,
   In the nameless name of a Private commanded his chief to command!

If I say that he passed, through a wound in his breast, up the hill,
   And lies buried where grave-marks by thousands at Arlington whiten the
      air—
Why—you will go on and believe that our very first warrior still
   Sits smoking his pipe of Peace in the Presidential easy chair!

Text from The Capital, 1871

MY DEAD FAIRIES

"Do the Fairies ever die?"
   Why, yes, they are always dying.
There, in the freezing dark close by,
   A thousand, dead, are lying.

Of the time they made so fair
   But the fading shadow lingers;
Oh, how the light gold of my hair
   Curled on their airy fingers!

I shall not see them again.
   They fell in the Sun's fierce bright'ning;
They were drowned in drops of——"Rain?"
   They were burned to death with lightning.

With bloom, as the bee-songs pass,
   Our sweet-briar keeps its promise;
The fireflies shine in the grass;
   Winds blow our butterflies from us!

Yet under that thin gray tree,
   With the moonrise in its stillness,
They keep hidden away from me,
   Forever, in dusty [ch]illness.

Text from The Independent, 1871

THORNS

You must not tear them from the Tree!
   They make a language sharp and sad—
A fierce sign-language, that to me
   Tells all the life it ever had;
   Tells why it never grows too glad
At the little murmur of the bee,
   Or tender touch of bud or root,
Or thrill of wing in lifted leaves.
   Poor Tree! It holds nor flower or fruit,
Yet not for flower or fruit it grieves.

Veil it with climbing roses? No.
   Were not its blood-marked Thorns left plain
It might not have the grace to grow;
   Might fancy fain still stars were vain,
   Nor yearn for dew nor reach for rain,
Nor bear that white reproof, the snow,
   Nor tremble at some shadowy crime,
Some wound made over eyes divine,
   In the great gloom of backward time,
By its own dreary sin, or mine.

Leave me the Thorns. I need them, too.
   No priest-watched faith from Holy Land
Keeps one Christ-relic half so true.
   Through them I dimly understand,
   And learn to quiet and command
The passionate pain I bear for you.
   They crown the phantom of a Face
So beautiful with agony
   That at its upward sorrowful grace
Your own fades faint and far from me.

Text from *The Independent*, 1871

A LIFE IN A MIRROR[14]

O, pretty Prisoner, young and sweet,
  And just a little white and worn,
It makes my heart ache when I meet
  Such beauty so forlorn:

To think the lilies in your grass
  Must glimmer out and you not know,
That flocks of butterflies must pass
  And still elude you so;

To think there is a sun by day,
  A moon whose fairness fills the night;
Yet you, a captive, pine—away
  From every lovely sight.

You babble much of foreign things—
  How you have seen the world, perchance;
And how great generals and kings
  Have asked you, once, to dance!

Your peerless face has made you dream!
  For, in your life, you never was
(Though far away you sometimes seem)
  Outside of your own glass!

In it you sleep, in it you wake,
  In it at last your dust will be;
For Death, and only Death, can break
  Your fate, and set you free!

Text from The Independent (1871)

BEATRICE CENCI[15]
(In a City Shop-Window.)

Out of low light an exquisite, faint face
  Suddenly started. Goldenness of hair,
A South-look of sweet, sorrowful eyes, a trace
  Of prison paleness—what if these were there

21

FIGURE 6. *"Guido in the Cell of Beatrice Cenci"*

When Guido's hand could never reach the grace
    That glimmered on me from the Italian air—
    Fairness so fierce, or fierceness half so fair?

"Is it some Actress?" a slight school-boy said.
    Some Actress? Yes.——
                            The curtain rolled away,
Dusty and dim. The scene—among the dead—
    In some weird, gloomy, pillared palace lay;
The Tragedy, which we have brokenly read,
    With its two hundred ghastly years was gray:
    None dared applaud with flowers her shadowy way—
Yet, ah! how bitterly well she seemed to play!

—Hush! for a child's quick murmur breaks the charm
    Of terror that was winding round me so.
And, at the white touch of a pretty arm,
    Darkness and Death and Agony crouch low
In old-time dungeons:
                    "Tell me, (is it harm
    To ask you?): is the picture real, though?—
    And why the beautiful ladies all, you know,
Live so far-off, and die so long ago?"

Text from *Overland Monthly*, 1871

ONE FROM THE DEAD[16]

"Yes, yes! It is nine years, you say?
There is his portrait. He was handsome. Yes!"
His mother's mother kept her eyes away,
    But pointed up, and I could guess.

He was remembered in his room:
Of him pet window-flowers, in odors, dreamed;
His shut piano, under their sad bloom,
    The coffin of dead music seemed.

His vain-plumed hat was there; there, too,
The sword, whose bitter cause was never gained;

FIGURE 7. *"Sad Memories—Decoration Day"*

The coat, with glimmering shoulder-leaves, shot through
   The breast, I think, and fiercely stained.

   Yet, till I saw his name—the one
His youth had soiled—above the creeping dew
Thrust high, to whiten in the grave-yard sun:
   I vaguely felt, I darkly knew.

   Oh, coward-praise men give to dust,
Only when it lies motionless and mute
Beneath the shining slander, which it must
   Not, till the Judgment-light, refute!

What more? If one, with voice and breath,
Had given to one a rose-geranium bud,
And changed with moons, and vanished into death
   In far-back feuds of hate and blood;

   If that one, from great after-grief—
In some long, empty, lonesome cry—had said,
"I would believe; help Thou mine unbelief
   With One that was—One from the Dead;"

   And felt a sudden, luminous Face—
Sweet terror, yet divinest quiet, there;
And reached—to find that Thorns were in the place
   Of lovely, worldly-fancied hair;

   That Hands, not such as gave old flowers,
But torn with Nails, had blessed a piteous head:
That Doubt's slow question, from the unlighted hours,
   Was answered by One from the Dead;

   If this had been——You smile, and say to me,
"It were Illusion, shaped of wandering sleep!"
Well, if it were illusion, let it be:
   I have a tender Faith to keep.

Text from *Overland Monthly,* 1871

HER RESCUE[17]
(Related by Her as a Fable.)

He said to me: "Your queenly grief
    At losing me, my lady, is so great
I long to find you some such calm relief
    As suits imperial state:

"Something to draw with child-like breath
    The poison we call life from your fair breast,
And leave the languor of a lovely death
    With you—with God the rest;"

Then walked away. But, as I stood
    With ring and veil upon my wedding night,
A sudden burning tremor shook my blood;
    A Hand put out the light,

And held a glittering casket near,
    In which there was a bridal gift for me.
I opened it with pallor and with fear—
    What therein did I see?

Only a short, sand-colored thing
    With dull dead eyes and hateful hornèd head—
A charming messenger in sooth to bring
    The rosy note I read.

"I send you greeting—by an asp.
    May it, my beautiful, find you in time.
Take it up tenderly, and let it clasp
    Your heart from pain and crime.

"Caesar awaits you. Will you grace
    His triumph-marches through the dust to Rome?
Or keep the desperate glory of your place
    In silent scorn at home?"

No—no, my bosom does not ache.
    Its precious nurseling did not come too late.
With eager, dying lips I kiss the snake—
    I kiss the snake—and wait.

Text from *The Capital,* 1872

26

THE GRAVE AT FRANKFORT[18]

I turned and threw my rose upon the mound
   Beneath whose grass my old, rude kinsman lies,
And thought had from his Dark and Bloody Ground
   The blood secured in the shape of flowers to rise.

I left his dust to dew and dimness then,
   Who did not need the glitter of mock stars
To show his homely generalship to men
   And light his shoulders through his troubled wars.

I passed his rustling wild-cane, reached the gate,
   And heard the city's noisy murmurings;
Forgot the simple hero of my State,
   Looked in the gaslight, thought of other things.

Ah, that was many withered springs ago;
   Yet once, last winter, in the whirl of snows,
A vague half-fever, or, for aught I know,
   A wish to touch the hand that gave my rose,

Showed me a hunter of the wooded West,
   With dog and gun, beside his cabin door;
And, in the strange fringed garments on his breast,
   I recognized at once the rose he wore!

Text from *The Capital*, 1872

ANOTHER WAR

Yes, they are coming from the fort—
   Not weary they, nor dimm'd with dust;
Their march seems but a shining sport,
   Their swords too new for rust.

You think the captains look so fine,
   You like, I know, the long sharp flash,
The fair silk flags above the line,
   The pretty scarlet sash?

You like the horses when they neigh,
  You like the music most of all,
And, if they had to fight to-day,
  You'd like to see them fall.

I wisely think the uniform
  Was made for skeletons to wear,
But your young blood is quick and warm,
  And so—you do not care.

You lift your eager eyes and ask:
  "Could we not have another war?"
As I might give this fearful task
  To armies near and far.

Another war? Perhaps we could,
  Yet, child of mine with sunniest head,
I sometimes wonder if I would
  Bear then to see the dead!

But am I in a dream? For see,
  My pretty boy follows the men—
Surely he did not speak to me,
  Who could have spoken, then?

It was another child, less fair,
  Less young, less innocent, I know,
Who lost the light gold from its hair
  Most bitter years ago!

It was that restless, wavering child
  I call Myself. No other, dear.
Perhaps you knew it when you smiled
  Because none else was near.

Then not my boy, it seems, but I
  Would wage another war?—to see
The shining sights, to hear the cry
  Of ghastly victory?

No—for another war could bring
  No second bloom to wither'd flowers,
No second song to birds that sing,
  Lost tunes in other hours!

But, friend, since time is full of pain,
    Whether men fall by field or hearth,
I want the old war back again,
    And nothing new on earth!

Text from The Capital, 1872

MOCK DIAMONDS[19] — *[handwritten: about the marriage, not the politics]*
(At the Seaside.)

The handsome man there with the scar?— *[handwritten: husband is from the*
    (Who bow'd to me? Yes, slightly)— *north, wife from the*
A ghastly favor of the War, *south]*
    Nor does he wear it lightly.

Such brigand-looking men as these
    Might hide behind a dagger
In—ah, "the fellow, if I please,
    With the low Southern swagger?

[handwritten: husband] "One of the doubtful chivalry,
    The midnight-vengeance meetings,
Who sends, from ghostly company,
    Such fearful queer-spell'd greetings!" — *[handwritten: KKK]*

[handwritten: he] No—but a soldier late to throw
    (I see not where the harm is)
Lost Cause and Conquer'd Flag below
    The dust of Northern armies.

What more? Before the South laid down
    Her insolent false glory,
He was, at this fair seaside town,
    The hero of—a story.

And painted Beauty scheming through *[handwritten: — the speaker]*
    The glare of gilded station,
Long'd for the orange flowers—that grew
    Upon his rich plantation.

I knew him then? Well, he was young
    And I was—what he thought me;
[handwritten: woman seen through poets eyes as aesthetic object]

And there were kisses hidden among
  The thin bud-scents he brought me.

One night I saw a stranger here,—
  "An heiress, you must know her,"
His mother whisper'd, sliding near.
  Perhaps my heart beat lower.

The band play'd on, the hours declined,
  His eyes looked tired and dreamy;
I knew her diamonds flash'd him blind—
  He could no longer see me.

Leave your sweet jealousy unsaid:
  Your bright child's fading mother
And that guerrilla from—the dead?
  Are nothing to each other.

He rose before me on the sand
  Through that damp sky's vague glimmer,
With shadows in his shadow, and
  All the dim sea grew dimmer.

He spoke? He laughed? Men hear of men
  Such words, such laughter never.
He said? *"She wore Mock-Diamonds"*—then,
  Pass'd to the Past forever.

Speaker is also mock-diamonds

Text from *The Capital*, 1872

PREVENTED CHOICE[20]

  A Stranger pass'd my door,
  With beauty sorrowful, not weak;
Great eyes of luminous quiet told me more
  Than any tongue could speak.

  He wore divinest air
  About Him like a garment, while
A white Dove flutter'd at His shoulder,
  Its wing could touch His smile.

The Pinnacle's sharp height,
　The shadow of the Wilderness,
The black and beating Waves He walked at night
　Toward my unborn distress:

These rose and stretched around,
　But, even as with grave-clothes, I
From head to foot with my shroud-dream was bound.
　And could not wake nor cry.

His torn sweet hand unroll'd
　A picture mark'd with burial-stones,
Full of fierce-color'd jewels, fiery gold,
　And scatter'd crowns and thrones.

High banners stained and thin
　Droop'd wide and wearily, half-furled,
And letters made of blood-drops read therein:
　"The Kingdoms of the World."

Beside the picture there
　And circled with an awful charm,
One Phantom from the grandeur of despair
　Reach'd me his scar'd right arm,

And sweetly whisper'd: "These
　And all the glory thereof see.
Mine are the shining lands, the shining seas.
　Fall down and worship me!"

In vain I shook my sleep,
　And tried to fall before his face;
The Master's pity, very calm and deep,
　Lent me an upright grace.

He made the picture dim
　With rays that glimmer'd from the Word
And left my soul, in memory of Him,
　His own white, nestling Bird.

Text from *The Capital*, 1872

THE FUNERAL OF A DOLL[21]

They used to call her Little Nell,
  In memory of that lovely child
Whose story each had learned to tell.
  She, too, was slight and still and mild,
  Blue-eyed and sweet; she always smiled,
And never troubled any one
Until her pretty life was done.
And so they tolled a tiny bell,
  That made a wailing fine and faint,
As fairies ring, and all was well.
  Then she became a waxen saint.

Her funeral it was small and sad.
  Some birds sang bird-hymns in the air.
The humming-bee seemed hardly glad,
  Spite of the honey everywhere.
  The very sunshine seemed to wear
Some thought of death, caught in its gold,
That made it waver wan and cold.
Then, with what broken voice he had,
  The Preacher slowly murmured on
(With many warnings to the bad)
  The virtues of the Doll now gone.

A paper coffin rosily-lined
  Had Little Nell. There, drest in white,
With buds about her, she reclined,
  A very fair and piteous sight—
  Enough to make one sorry, quite.
And, when at last the lid was shut
Under white flowers, I fancied———but
No matter. When I heard the wind
  Scatter Spring-rain that night across
The Doll's wee grave, with tears half-blind
  One child's heart felt a grievous loss.

"It was a funeral, mamma. Oh,
  Poor Little Nell is dead, is dead.

How dark!—and do you hear it blow?
   She is afraid." And, as she said
   These sobbing words, she laid her head
Between her hands and whispered: "Here
Her bed is made, the precious dear—
She cannot sleep in it, I know.
   And there is no one left to wear
Her pretty clothes. *Where did she go?*
————See, this poor ribbon tied her hair!"

The Capital (1872)

Text from *Poems in Company with Children*, 1877

THE SORROWS OF CHARLOTTE[22]

The Sorrows of Werther, that is the Book,
   Little girl of mine. Will I show you what
His sorrows were like? Such a brown-eyed look
   Could hardly see. Never mind, they were not
Such sorrows, I fancy, as yours or mine,
But such as in pictures look so fine,
   And such as can end—in a pistol shot.

"Is any one else in the Book?" (I knew
   She would ask me that.) Yes, Charlotte is there.
["]Then is it the Sorrows of Charlotte too?"
   No, child, for never a man would care
To write such a long sad story, you see,
   As the—cutting of bread-and-butter would be;
   And never a woman had time to dare!

Text from *The Capital*, 1872

LEAVING LOVE[23]

"If one should stay in Italy awhile,
   With bloom to hide the dust beneath her feet,
With birds in love with roses to beguile
   Her life until its sadness grew too sweet;

"If she should slowly see some statue there,
    Divine with whiteness and with coldness keep
A very halo in the hovering air;
    If she should weep—because it could not weep;

"If she should waste each early gift of grace
    In watching it with rapturous despair,
Should kiss her youth out on its stony face,
    And feel the grayness gathering toward her hair;

"Then fancy, though it had till now seemed blind—
    Blind to her little fairness,—it could see
How scarred of soul, how wan and worn of mind,
    How faint of form and faded she must be;

"If she should moan: 'Ah, land of flower and fruit,
    Ah! fiercely languid land, undo your charm!
Ah! song impassioned, make your music mute!
    Ah! bosom, shake away my clinging arm!'

"Then swiftly climb into the mountains near,
    And set her face forever toward the snow,
And feel the North in chasm and cliff, and hear
    No echo from the fairyland below;

"If she should feel her own new loneliness,
    With every deep-marked, freezing step she trod,
Nearing (and in that nearness growing less)
    The vast and utter loneliness of God;

"If back to scented valleys she should call,
    This woman that I fancy—only she;
Would it remind one statue there at all,
    O, cruel Silence in the South, of me?"

Text from *The Independent* (1872)

A WELL-KNOWN STORY[24]

She had waited,
On her soft cheek catching many a winter's snow.
    Very lovely was the heart unmated;

Beauty far too beautiful to show,
  When her dewy days had faded,
    Bloomed below.

  Children brightly
Near her Christmas windows held their toys and passed;
  Mothers kissed their laughing babies lightly;
Heads of girls went, sunny, sweet, and fast,
  Under gifts of bridal blossoms;
      And, at last,

  One green morning,
When small songs were shaking many a pretty nest,
  On her birthday, without any warning,
Came her life-long Lover to her breast,
  Bringing white flowers and a casket
      Full of rest.

Text from The Independent, 1872

LOVE-STORIES[25]

Can I tell any? No:
  I have forgotten all I ever knew.
I am too old. I saw the fairies go
  Forever from the moonshine and the dew
    Before I met with you.

"Rose's grandmother knows
  Love stories?" *She* could tell you one or two?
"*She* is not young?" You wish that you were Rose?
  "*She* hears love-stories? Are they ever true?"
    Some time I may ask you.

I was not living when
  Columbus came here, nor before that? So,
You wonder when I saw the fairies, then?
  The Indians would have killed them all, you know?
    "How *long* is long ago?"

And if I am too old
  To know love-stories, why am I not good?

Why do n't I read the Bible, and not scold?
　Why do n't I pray, as all old ladies should?
　　(I only wish I could.)

Why do n't I buy gray hair?
　And why——
　　　Oh! child, the Sphinx herself might spring
Out of her sands to answer, should you dare
　Her patience with your endless questioning.
　　"Does *she* know any thing?"

Perhaps. "Then, could she tell
　Love-stories?" If her lips were not all stone;
For there is one she must remember well—
　One whose great glitter showed a fiery zone
　　Brightness beyond its own.

One whose long music aches—
　How sharp the sword, how sweet the snake, O Queen!—
Into the last unquiet heart that breaks.
　But the Nile-lily rises faint betwe[e]n——
　　You wonder what I mean?

I mean there is but one
　Love-story in this withered world, forsooth;
And it is brief, and ends, where it begun,
　(What if I tell, in play, the dreary truth?)
　　With something we call Youth.

The Independent (1872)

Text from *Voyage to the Fortunate Isles*, 1874

— takes place in
Cincinnati

OVER IN KENTUCKY[26]

Speaker's daughter

"This is the smokiest city in the world,"
　A slight voice, wise and weary, said, "I know.
My sash is tied, and if my hair was curled,
　I'd like to have my prettiest hat and go
There where some violets had to stay, you said,
Before your torn-up butterflies were dead—
　　Over in Kentucky."

Then one, whose half-sad face still wore the hue
  The North Star loved to light and linger on,
Before the war, looked slowly at me too,
  And darkly whispered: "What is gone is gone.
Yet, though it may be better to be free,
I'd rather have things as they used to be
    Over in Kentucky."

[Handwritten:] black nurse

[Handwritten:] better to be a slave?

Perhaps I thought how fierce the master's hold,
  Spite of all armies, kept the slave within;
How iron chains, when broken, turned to gold,
  In empty cabins, where glad songs had been,
Before the Southern sword knew blood and rust,
Before wild cavalry sprang from the dust,
    Over in Kentucky.

[Handwritten:] master must have hold on her — mother's thoughts

[Handwritten:] physical vs. economic restraint

Perhaps—but, since two eyes, half-full of tears,
  Half-full of sleep, would love to keep awake
With fairy pictures from my fairy years,
  I have a phantom pencil that can make
Shadows of moons, far back and faint, to rise
On dewier grass and in diviner skies,
    Over in Kentucky.

[Handwritten:] realizes she is romanticizing the south - making it an aesthetic object for her daughter

For yonder river, wider than the sea,
  Seems sometimes in the dusk a visible moan
Between two worlds—one fair, one dear to me.
  The fair has forms of ever-glimmering stone,
Weird-whispering ruin, graves where legends hide,
And lies in mist upon the charmèd side,
    Over in Kentucky.

The dear has restless, dimpled, pretty hands,
  Yearning toward unshaped steel, unfancied wars,
Unbuilded cities, and unbroken lands,
  With something sweeter than the faded stars
And dim, dead dews of my lost romance, found
In beauty that has vanished from the ground,
    Over in Kentucky.

[Handwritten:] realizes she created an ideal picture of Kentucky

Cincinnati, *Ohio*.

           The Independent (1872)
    Text from *Voyage to the Fortunate Isles* (1874)

THE BLACK PRINCESS[27]
(A True Fable of My Old Kentucky Nurse.)

I knew a Princess: she was old,
   Crisp-haired, flat-featured, with a look
Such as no dainty pen of gold
   Would write of in a fairy book.

So bent she almost crouched, her face
   Was like the Sphinx's face, to me,
Touched with vast patience, desert grace,
   And lonesome, brooding mystery.

What wonder that a faith so strong
   As hers, so sorrowful, so still,
Should watch in bitter sands so long,
   Obedient to a burdening will!

This Princess was a slave—like one
   I read of in a painted tale;
Yet free enough to see the sun,
   And all the flowers, without a vail.

Not of the lamp, not of the ring,
   The helpless, powerful slave was she;
But of a subtler, fiercer thing—
   She was the slave of Slavery.

Court lace nor jewels had she seen:
   She wore a precious smile, so rare
That at her side the whitest queen
   Were dark—her darkness was so fair.

Nothing of loveliest loveliness
   This strange, sad Princess seemed to lack;
Majestic with her calm distress
   She was, and beautiful, though black.

Black, but enchanted black, and shut
   In some vague giant's tower of air,
Built higher than her hope was. But
   The true knight came and found her there.

The Knight of the Pale Horse, he laid
　His shadowy lance against the spell
That hid her self: as if afraid,
　The cruel blackness shrank and fell.

Then, lifting slow her pleasant sleep,
　He took her with him through the night,
And swam a river cold and deep,
　And vanished up an awful hight.

And in her Father's house beyond,
　They gave her beauty, robe, and crown:
On me, I think, far, faint, and fond,
　Her eyes to-day look, yearning, down.

Text from *The Independent*, 1872

THE PALACE-BURNER[28]
(A Picture in a Newspaper.)

She has been burning palaces. "To see
　The sparks look pretty in the wind?" Well, yes—
And something more. But women brave as she
　Leave much for cowards such as I to guess.

But this is old, so old that everything
　Is ashes here—the woman and the rest.
Two years are oh! so long. Now you may bring
　Some newer pictures. You like this one best?

You wish that you had lived in Paris then?
　You would have loved to burn a palace, too?
But they had guns in France, and Christian men
　Shot wicked little Communists, like you.

You would have burned the palace? Just because
　You did not live in it yourself! Oh! why?
Have I not taught you to respect the laws?
　You would have burned the palace. Would not *I*?

Would I? Go to your play. Would I, indeed?
　I? Does the boy not know my soul to be

Languid and worldly, with a dainty need
  For light and music? Yet he questions me.

Can he have seen my soul more near than I?
  Ah! in the dusk and distance sweet she seems,
With lips to kiss away a baby's cry,
  Hands fit for flowers, and eyes for tears and dreams.

Can he have seen my soul? And could she wear
  Such utter life upon a dying face,
Such unappealing, beautiful despair,
  Such garments—soon to be a shroud—with grace?

Has she a charm so calm that it could breathe
  In damp, low places till some frightened hour;
Then start, like a fair, subtle snake, and wreathe
  A stinging poison with a shadowy power?

Would *I* burn palaces? The child has seen
  In this fierce creature of the Commune here,
So bright with bitterness and so serene,
  A being finer than my soul, I fear.

Text from The Independent, 1872

WHY SHOULD WE CARE?[29]

Well, if the bee should sting the flower to death,
  With just one drop of honey for the stinging;
If the high bird should break its airy breath,
  And lose the song forever with the singing,
    Why should we care?

If in our magic-books no charm is found
  To call back last night's moon from last night's distance;
If violets cannot stay the whole year round,
  Spite of their odor and the dew's resistance,
    Why should we care?

If hands nor hearts like ours have strength to hold
  Fierce shining toys, nor treasures sweet and simple;

If nothing can be held for love or gold;
   If kisses cannot keep a baby's dimple,
      Why should we care?

If sand is in the south, frost in the north,
   And sorrow everywhere, and passionate yearning;
If stars fade from the skies; if men go forth
   From their own thresholds and make no returning,
      Why should we care?

If this same world can never be the same
   After this instant, but grows grayer, older,
And nearer to the silence whence it came;
   If faith itself is fainter, stiller, colder,
      Why should we care?

And if the grass is but a pretty vail
   Spread on our graves to hide them when we enter;
And, after we are gone, if light should fail,
   And fires should eat the green world to its center,
      Why should we care?

If tears were dry, and laughter should seem strange;
   And if the soul should doubt itself and falter;
Since God is God, and He can never change,
   The fashions of the earth and Heaven may alter,
      Why should we care?

Text from The Independent, 1872

THERE WAS A ROSE[30]

"There was a Rose," she said,
   "Like other roses, perhaps, to you.
Nine years ago it was faint and red
   Away in the cold dark dew,
   On the dwarf bush where it grew.

"Never any rose before
   Was like that rose, very well I know;

Never another rose any more
   Will blow as that rose did blow
   When the wet wind shook it so.

"'What do I want?'—Ah, what?
   Why, I want that rose, that wee one rose,
Only that rose. And that rose is not
   Anywhere just now? God knows
   Where all the old sweetness goes.

"I want that rose so much:
   I would take the world back there to the night
Where I saw it blush in the grass, to touch
   It once in that fair fall light,
   And only once, if I might.

"But a million marching men
   From the North and the South would arise?
And the dead—would have to die again?
   And the women's widowed cries
   Would trouble anew the skies?

"No matter. I would not care?
   Were it not better that this should be?
The sorrow of many the many bear,—
   Mine is too heavy for me.
   And I want that rose, you see!"

                 Text from *Atlantic Monthly,* 1872

THE OLD SLAVE-MUSIC[31]

Blow back the breath of the bird,
   Scatter the song through the air;
There was music you never heard, *Northerners*
   And cannot hear anywhere.

It was not the sob of the vain
   In the old, old dark so sweet,
(I shall never hear it again,)
   Nor the coming of fairy feet.

It was music and music alone,
    Not a sigh from a lover's mouth;
Now it comes in a phantom moan
    From the dead and buried South.

It was savage and fierce and glad,
    It played with the heart at will;
Oh, what a wizard touch it had—
    Oh, if I could hear it still!

Were they slaves? They were not then;
    The music had made them free.
They were happy women and men—
    What more do we care to be?

There is blood and blackness and dust,
    There are terrible things to see,
There are stories of swords that rust,
    Between that music and me.

Dark ghosts with your ghostly tunes
    Come back till I laugh through tears;
Dance under the sunken moons,
    Dance over the grassy years!
Hush, hush—I know it, I say,
    Your armies were bright and brave,
But the music they took away
    Was worth—whatever they gave.

recognizes that music takes place in the past

past becomes fantasy

addressing and once

argument breaks down

Text from *The Capital*, 1873

A GHOST AT THE OPERA[32]

It was, I think, the Lover of the play:
    He, from stage-incantations, turned his head,
And one remembered motion shook away
    The whole mock fairyland and raised the dead.

I, in an instant, saw the scenery change.
    Old trees before me by enchantment grew.
Late roses shivered, beautiful and strange.
    One red geranium scented all the dew.

43

A sudden comet flung its awful vail
    Around the frightened stars. A sudden light
Stood, moon-shaped, in the East. A sudden wail
    From troubled music smote the spectral night.

Then blue sweet shadows fell from flower-like eyes,
    And purplish darkness drooped on careless hair,
And lips most lovely—ah, what empty sighs,
    Breathed to the air, for something less than air!

Oh, beauty such as no man ever wore
    In this wan world outside of Eden's shine,
Save he who vanished from the sun before
    Youth learned that youth itself was not divine!

I might have touched that fair and real ghost,
    He laughed so lightly, looked so bright and brave—
So all unlike that thin and wavering host
    Who walk unquiet from the quiet grave.

Myself another ghost as vain and young,
    And nearer Heaven than now by years and years,
My heart, like some quick bird of morning, sung
    On fluttering wings above all dust and tears.

But some great lightning made a long red glare:
    Black-plumed and brigand-like I saw him stand—
What ghastly sights, what noises in the air!
    How sharp the sword seemed in his lifted hand!

He looked at me across the fading field.
    The South was in his blood, his soul, his face.
Imperious despair, too lost to yield,
    Gave a quick glory to a desperate grace.

I saw him fall. I saw the deadly stain
    Upon his breast—he cared not what was won.
The ghost was in the land of ghosts again.
    The curtain fell, the phantom play was done.

The Capital (1873)
Text from *Dramatic Persons and Moods,* 1879

SOUR GRAPES[33]

They are purple enough, I know,
   And the frost has made them sweet, you say.
Did the fox in the fable find them so?
   Do not look at them so, I pray.

Why? Because in a Book I've read
   There's a story of grapes that haunts me so.
They poisoned men, so the story said,
   Hundreds of misty falls ago.

And the men? were our Fathers, child.
   They went to the woods one bitter day,
When the grapes were sour and the winds were wild,
   And our teeth are set on edge to-day!

Text from The Capital, 1873

HER CHOSEN LORD[34]

Ah, this subtle purple is sweet—
   Let His fair Bird moan and flutter;
My kingdoms lie at my feet,
   And the glory thereof is utter.

My crown is ethereal gold,
   And fiercer than fire it flashes.
My jewels are precious and cold,
   And my heart is ashes, ashes.

Sometimes in the empty night
   He looks at me from a vision.
His face is troubled and white,
   And mine is black with derision.

The world that I shine in is sand.
   My soul at His shadow catches—
His garment's hem from my hand
   The wind of the Wilderness snatches.

Yea, my subtle purple is sweet—
   Let His fair Bird moan and flutter;

My kingdoms lie at my feet,
 And the glory thereof is utter.

The other burns like a star
 In a desert of darkness lonely.
When he calls me, near or afar,
 I answer—"I love you only."

At his breast, like a brooding mail,
 See the Serpent of Eden glitter.
In Heaven it is high to fail;
 Outside the bitter is bitter.

Oh, a thousand times a day
 In his scorned despair of beauty
He will waver across my way,
 Till my worship seems but duty.

"My Lord, the King," I moan,
 "Whose right arm holds me ever
Fast on his own sweet throne—
 I am his queen forever."

So, let this one burn like a star
 In his desert of darkness lonely:
When he calls me, near or afar,
 I answer—"I love you only."

Text from The Capital, 1873

[SONG]³⁵

When the full moon's light is burning
 At its brightest, it is pleasant,
Sometimes, blindly to sit yearning
 For the slightness of the crescent;

When the finished rose is shining
 In the sun with flushed completeness,
For the vanished bud repining,
 Willfully to miss its sweetness.

The Capital (1873)
Text from Voyage to the Fortunate Isles, 1874

AT THE PLAY[36]

I have been to the play, my child.
  Night after night I go.
What if the weather be wild?—
  I am used to rain and snow.

Shakespeare's Poor Player is there.
  The stage is wide and dim.
The music is old, and rare
  Are the flowers I fling to him.

And the Play keeps wavering. But,
  Through forest and desert and sea,
By palace and temple and hut,
  The charm is the same to me.

The gods stand by in stone,
  With calm in their awful eyes;
Christ clings to his cross, alone
  In the bitter world, and dies.

The Player wears all the while,
  As soldier, or priest, or king,
Or peasant, the same sad smile;
  And the Play is—the same sad thing.

With jewels the boxes shine;
  Fierce eyes look out of the pit;
All whisper: "The Play is fine,"
  And all are weary of it.

But the Player is at his best
  In the shadow-scene—you shrink?—
Where he falls on his Brother's breast,
  (His Brother is Death,) I think.

The Independent (1873)
Text from Voyage to the Fortunate Isles, 1874

HIS FAIRY GODMOTHER[37]
(Cinderella Speaks.)

Who felt the quaint light subtly shining in?
  Who heard that other wind within the wind?
Who saw the Little Lady, wild and thin,
  Pale with the spirits and the spells behind?

I see her now. I take this withered wand,
  A weird Egyptian lily, when I choose,
And wave her to and fro, and back beyond
  That lonesome moonshine and those charmèd dews.

I see her now—if I but shut my eyes—
  Dressed in the frosty green of leaves half-dead:
Ah! still witch-smile; ah! old and wise replies
  To all the precious words—you never said!

How queer you both looked as she rose and shook
  Her ancient, shrunken, clinched hand in your face;
Then laid her finger on your lip and took
  Beside you in the dance her sudden place!

You play the Prince. Princes grow gray like you
  'Tis the worn story, slightly changed in truth.
Poor Cinderella never found her shoe;
  She is left out—a fable of your youth.

You have the citrons and the wines of life,
  Its lights, its honors: what has it beside?
Her Majesty, the Queen, your worthy wife,
  Has plumes and pearls and garments purple dyed.

She, in a peasant's cottage, built low down,
  Kisses gold heads and waits a twilight voice;
Nor envies you the palace and the crown,
  But finds her own in your godmother's choice.

Still she finds time, in dreaming, evermore,
  To wonder if, in flying sleep, you pass,
Handsome and young, sometimes, from your great door,
  To kiss and keep—a Slipper made of Glass.

Text from *The Independent,* 1873

HER BLINDNESS IN GRIEF[38]

What if my soul is left to me?
Oh! sweeter than my soul was he.
  Its breast broods on a coffin lid;
Its empty eyes stare at the dust.
  Tears follow tears, for treasure hid
Forevermore from moth and rust.

The sky a shadow is; how much
I long for something I can touch!
  God is a silence: could I hear
Him whisper once, "Poor child," to me!
  God is a dream, a hope, a fear,
A vision—that the seraphs see,

— Christ's words to Mary

"Woman, why weepest thou?" One said,
To His own mother, from the dead.
  If He should come to mock me now,
Here in my utter loneliness,
  And say to me, "Why weepest thou?"
I wonder would I weep the less.

Or, could I, through these endless tears,
Look high into the lovely spheres
  And see him there—my little child—
Nursed tenderly at Mary's breast,
  Would not my sorrow be as wild?
Christ help me. Who shall say the rest?

There is no comfort anywhere.
My baby's clothes, my baby's hair,
  My baby's grave are all I know.
What could have hurt my baby? Why,
  Why did he come; why did he go?
And shall I have him by and by? *meter breaks down*

Poor grave of mine, so strange, so small,
You cover all, you cover all!
  The flush of every flower, the dew,

49

FIGURE 8. *"The Empty Cradle"*

The bird's old song, the heart's old trust,
    The star's fair light, the darkness, too,
Are hidden in your heavy dust.

Oh! but to kiss his little feet,
And say to them, "So sweet, so sweet,"
    I would give up whatever pain
(What else is there to give, I say?)
    This wide world holds. Again, again,
I yearn to follow him away.

My cry is but a human cry.
Who grieves for angels? Do they die?
    Oh! precious hands, as still as snows,
How your white fingers hold my heart!
    Yet keep your buried buds of rose,
Though earth and Heaven are far apart.

The grief is bitter. Let me be.
He lies beneath that lonesome tree.
    I've heard the fierce rain beating there.
Night covers it with cold moonshine.
    Despair can only be despair.
God has his will. I have not mine.

*— no consolation for
her grief
— there are no connections
to her community —
she is alone*

*her version
of "God is a Mastiff"*

Text from *The Independent*, 1873

WE TWO[39]

God's will is—the bud of the rose for your hair,
    The ring for your hand and the pearl for your breast;
God's will is—the mirror that makes you look fair.
    No wonder you whisper: "God's will is the best."

But what if God's will were the famine, the flood?
    And were God's will the coffin shut down in your face?
And were God's will the worm in the fold of the bud,
    Instead of the picture, the light, and the lace?

Were God's will the arrow that flieth by night,
    Were God's will the pestilence walking by day,

The clod in the valley, the rock on the hight—
    I fancy "God's will" would be harder to say.

God's will is—your own will. What honor have you
    For having your own will, awake or asleep?
Who praises the lily for keeping the dew,
    When the dew is so sweet for the lily to keep?

God's will unto me is not music or wine.
    With helpless reproaching, with desolate tears
God's will I resist, for God's will is divine;
    And I—shall be dust to the end of my years.

God's will is—not mine. Yet one night I shall lie
    Very still at his feet, where the stars may not shine.
"Lo! I am well pleased" I shall hear from the sky;
    Because—it is God's will I do, and not mine.

Text from The Independent, 1874

UNHEEDED GIFTS[40]

The song no bird should sing in vain,
The song no bird will sing again,
I did not hear before the fleet
Air-singer lost it at my feet.

The lily that was in my grass—
(White as a child's sweet shroud it was)—
Shook down forlornest leaves before
I thought that it would bloom no more.

The moon that had a charmèd light
(Oh! never after that one night
Will any eye such shining see)
Went out—before it shone for me.

The ship that anchored at my door,
With treasure from a fairy shore—
Which was to be and is not mine—
Full fathom five lies lost in brine.

The wind, that blew the enchanted scent
From some divine still continent
Beat long against my window, but
It passed away—the window shut.

The bee that brought the one sweet drop,
The cure for bitterness, could stop
To offer in its golden haste
The honey—which I did not taste.

The king's fair son, who came in state,
With my lost slipper, for its mate,
I only saw through my regret—
Oh! I am in the ashes yet!

Text from The Independent (1874)

COUNSEL—IN THE SOUTH[41]

My boy, not of your will nor mine
   You keep the mountain pass and wait,
Restless, for evil gold to shine
   And hold you to your fate.

A stronger Hand than yours gave you
   The lawless sword—you know not why.
That you must live is all too true,
   And other men must die.

My boy, be brigand if you must,
   But face the traveller in your track:
Stand one to one, and never thrust
   The dagger in his back.

Nay, make no ambush of the dark.
   Look straight into your victim's eyes;
Then—let his free soul, like a lark,
   Fly, singing, toward the skies.

My boy, if Christ must be betrayed,
   And you must the betrayer be,

Oh, marked before the worlds were made!
  What help is there for me?

Ah, if the prophets from their graves
  Demand such blood of you as this,
Take Him, I say, with swords and staves,
  But—never with a kiss!

Text from Galaxy, 1874

AUNT ANNIE[42]

The old house has, for being sweet,
  Some sweeter reason than the rose
Which, red or white, about the feet
  Of many a nested home-bird grows.

And sadder reason than the rain
  On the quaint porch, for being sad,
(Oh, human pity, human pain!)
  The old house, in its shadows, had.

I sat within it as a guest,
  I who went from it as a wife;—
The young days there, though not the best,
  Had been the fairest of my life:

For love itself must ever seem
  More precious, to our restless youth,
When hovering subtly in its dream
  Than when we touch its nestling truth.

I sat there as a guest, I said—
  Holding the loveliest boy on earth,
With his fair, sleepy, yellow head
  Close to the pleasant shining hearth.

He laughed out in his sleep, and I
  Laughed too, and kissed him—when I heard
A wise and very cautious sigh;
  And once again the dimples stirred.

Aunt Annie looked at him awhile;
    Then shook her head at her own fears,
With more of sorrow in her smile
    Than I could ever put in tears.

"He is a pretty boy I know—
    The prettiest in the world? Ah, me!
One other, fifty years ago,
    Was quite as pretty, dear, as he.

"Now I am eighty. Twenty-five
    Are gone since last we heard from James.
I sometimes think he is alive."
    She hushed, and looked into the flames.

"He used to tell me, when a child,
    Of far, strange countries, where they say
The flowers bloom all the year"—she smiled—
    "I can't believe it, to this day!

"And still I think he may have crossed
    The sea—and stayed the other side.
His letters may have all been lost—
    Who knows? Who knows? The world is wide.

"I often think, if you could know
    How much he makes me think of *him*,
You'd guess why I love Victor so."
    Again the troubled eyes were dim.

"If your child, such a night, were out
    Lost in this dark and snow and sleet,
You would go wild, I do not doubt."
    I almost heard her own heart beat.

"Yet long, on stormier nights than this,
    Mine has been out—why should I care
How many a winter now it is?
    Mine has been out—and God knows where."

Text from *Voyage to the Fortunate Isles*, 1874

A BUTTERFLY'S MESSAGE[43]

Out in the dark, imploring hands I wrung,
  And reached for pity yearningly and high,
While my own soul, with fierce fever stung,
  Answered him, cry for cry—
  "Come in, and see him die."

Come in and see him die? That was not he
  So white and strange, so like the very dead.
Far back in dew and flowers could I not see
  His pretty glimmering head,
  And torn straw hat, instead?

I moaned and moaned: "Oh, give me back my child!"
  An Angel laid a small white garment by,
And looked at me through tears. I only smiled,
  To see him fly and fly
  Alone through God's fair sky.

"I will be very patient now and sweet,"
  I whispered to the Angel as he flew,
"And lead—through thorns, it must be—little feet
  Forever nearer you."
  But—what I was he knew!

"If I forget, send me some silent sign—
  That butterfly he used to follow so,
Or its next summer-ghost, shall seem divine
  Reproof, and I shall know.
  Oh! hear me as you go."

To-day, when some small want had made me fret,
  A sudden butterfly wavered around.
Blown from another world it was, and yet
  I felt a subtle wound.
  It would not touch the ground.

The passionate words, "Give back my child," the vow
  To the still Angel which last year I made,

And broke, were bitterly remembered now;
  And I was sore afraid
  There in the haunted shade.

Because no phantom child is following you,
  Come to me often, phantom butterfly!
Help me to keep my tearful promise true;
  For when you tremble by,
  My guilty heart knows why.

Text from Voyage to the Fortunate Isles, 1874

THE FAVORITE CHILD[44]

Which of five snowdrops would the moon
  Think whitest, if the moon could see?
Which of five rosebuds flushed with June
  Were reddest to the mother-tree?
Which of five birds, that play one tune
  On their soft-shining throats, may be
  Chief singer? Who will answer me?

Would not the moon know, if around
  One snowdrop any shadow lay?—
Would not the rose-tree, if the ground
  Should let one blossom droop a day?
Does not the one bird take a sound
  Into the cloud, when caught away,
  Finer than all the sounds that stay?

Oh, little, quiet boy of mine,
  Whose yellow head lies languid here—
Poor yellow head, its restless shine
  Brightened the butterflies last year!—
Whose pretty hands may intertwine
  With paler hands unseen but near:
  You are my favorite now, I fear!

Text from Voyage to the Fortunate Isles, 1874

WORTHLESS TREASURE

If one with a sick, whispering heart should yield
   To its faint fever, brokenly, and scorn
To furrow some low, pleasant, narrow field,
   To whose sweet labor he was born;

If he should have it hold him violets
   Enough to make the fairest wreath on earth,
But with cold thanks and very dim regrets
   Refuse their humble, precious worth;

If, fiercely held by some strange gathering thought,
   Within whose doubtful darkness he could see
A thousand stars with fiery meanings caught,
   His weird and restless life should be;

If he to that great breathless light which lies
   Under the ground descended, dreaming there
To find the fearful charm that gave his eyes
   Their glittering, ever-downward stare;

If, year by year, shut from the sun, he tried
   To gather riches from the cruel mine,
Whose Slave his Soul was, still to be denied
   And still to feel them shine and shine;

If, gray and ghastly, heat last should break,
   As from the dead, into the dew, and bring
Diamonds enough to light a grave, or make,
   Twice-told, the glory of a king;

If he should have his jewels cut and set
   After some beautiful and worldly rule—
Then find himself, when in his coronet,
   Only a crowned and laughed-at Fool:

I know, to-day, how bitter it would be
   For him to learn his treasure was not true,
Because (as even you through love might see,)
   Because—I wear mock-jewels too!

Text from *The Capital,* 1875

"SIEMPRE" [45]

They stood in the southern tower
   To look on the vale below,
And watch, in the weird moon light,
   The carriages come and go.

From the distant halls of revel
   Swelled music upon the air,
Laughter and lights and perfume,
   And flowers were everywhere.

No light but the moon's pale glimmer
   Shone here; in a trance they seemed.
He could feel the breath of her sighing,
   And his eyes in the darkness gleamed.

"Have you thought of me, love," he whispered,
   "All these lonely weeks gone past?"
She could only murmur "siempre,"
   But her heart beat loud and fast.

His arms were about her tightly,
   (O to *die* in those arms were bliss!)
And their lips for one mad, sweet moment,
   Close clung in a lingering kiss.

Ah! why did they go to the tower
   The moonlit valley to see?
And why did she whisper "siempre"
   When he said "have you thought of me?"

For a word was hastily spoken,
   A cloud passed over the moon,
And the sweet love-spell now broken,
   They returned to the gay saloon.

And she went back to duty
   By an unloved husband's side;
And he to his worldly pleasures
   And his search for a wealthy bride.

Yet oft in the dreary future
  She will look from the tower again,
Seeing naught of the lovely valley
  For her tears, that fall like rain.

And under her breath she will murmur
  That musical word, as of yore—
"Siempre! O darling, siempre!
  I will love the[e] forevermore."

And perhaps he will sometimes remember,
  When sorrow his eyes may dim,
One heart that is true and tender,
  Tho' breaking, *still throbs for him.*

Text from *The Capital,* 1875

ANSWERING A CHILD

But if I should ask the king?
  He could if he would? Ah! no.
Though he took from his hand the ring,
  Though he took from his head the crown—
  In the dust I should lay them down.

If I sat at a fairy's feet?
  A fairy could if she would?
(Oh! the fairy-faith is sweet.)
  Though she gave me her wand and her wings,
  To me they were pitiful things.

Ask God? He can if He will?
  He is better than fairies or kings?
(Ask God? He would whisper: "Be still.")
  Though He gave me each star I can see
  Through my tears, it were nothing to me.

"He can do"———But He cannot undo
  The terrible darkened gate

Which the fire of His will went through,
  Leading the Dead away;
  For the Past it is vain to pray.

Text from *The Independent,* 1875

THAT NEW WORLD[46]

How gracious we are to grant to the dead
  Those wide, vague lands in the foreign sky,
Reserving this world for ourselves instead;
  For we must live, though others must die!

And what is the world that we keep, I pray?
  True, it has glimpses of dews and flowers;
Then youth and love are here and away,
  Like mated birds,—but nothing is ours.

Ah, nothing indeed, but we cling to it all.
  It is nothing to hear one's own heart beat,
It is nothing to see one's own tears fall;
  Yet surely the breath of our life is sweet.

Yes, the breath of our life is so sweet, I fear
  We were loath to give it for all we know
Of that charmèd country we hold so dear,
  Far into whose beauty the breathless go.

Yet certain we are, when we see them fade
  Out of the pleasant light of the sun,
Of the sands of gold in the palm-leaf's shade,
  And the strange, high jewels all these have won.

You dare not doubt it, O soul of mine!
  And yet, if these vacant eyes could see
One, only one, from that voyage divine,
  With something, anything, sure for me!

Ah, blow me the scent of one lily, to tell
  That it grew outside of the world, at most;
Ah, show me a plume to touch, or a shell
  That whispers of some unearthly coast!

Text from *The Atlantic Monthly,* 1875

LADY FRANKLIN[47]

In shadowy ships that freeze
We think of men who sail, the frozen-fated.
   Tears, if you will, for these.
  But, oh! the truest searcher of the seas
In the blown breath of English daisies waited.

   And that forlornest [f]rost,
From the earth's edge (for years and years slow-creeping),
   Where something sweet was lost,
  Where something brave too bitterly was crossed,
Has touched the poor heart into tender sleeping!

   A pathway here or there
He sought, the old, unlighted Pathway finding;
   Out of the North's despair,
  Out of the South's flower-burdened wastes of air,
Into another world forever winding.

   A sadder pathway she
Sought, seeking him. Pathway to Love! where hidden
   Can that fair Secret be?
  Who wrings from any wave or any tree
The thing most precious—pearl or fruit forbidden?

   Oh, after that vague quest
Among weird winds, in icy deserts lonely,
   Has she lain down to rest
  Under a Palm, whose light leaves on her breast
Drop balms of summer, sun and silence only?

   Has some one whispered, "Why,
O woman faithful, why this dark delaying
   Outside the pleasant sky?—
  How could you seek me in the snows, when I
Here, in the Loveliest Land of all, was staying?"

Text from *Harper's Bazar,* 1875

queen of genteel imagery

IN A QUEEN'S DOMAIN[48]

Ah! my subject, the rose, I know,
    Will give me her breath and her blush;
And my subject, the lily, spreads snow,
    If I pass, for my foot to crush.

My subjects, the lamb and the fawn,
    They hide their heads in my breast;
And my subject, the dove, coos on,
    Though my hand creep close to her nest.

But my subject, the bee, will sting;
    And my subject, the thorn, will tear;
And my subject, the tiger, will spring
    At me, with a cry and a glare.

And my subject, the lion, will shake
    With his anger my loneliest lands;
And my subject, the snake (ah! the snake!)
    Will strike me dead in the sands.

Text from *The Independent*, 1876

GIVING UP THE WORLD[49]

So, from the ruins of the world alone
    Can Heaven be builded? Oh,
What other temples must be overthrown,
    Founded in sand or snow!

But, Heaven cannot be built with jeweled hands?
    Then, from my own I wring
Glitter of gold, the gifts of many lands;
    The seas their pearls I fling.

Heaven must be hung with pictures of the dead?
    The shroud must robe the saint?
Never one halo round a living head
    Did Raphael dare to paint?

Heaven must have flowers:—after the worm has crossed
    Their blush, the wind their breath?
After the utter silence of the frost
    Has made them white with death?

Heaven must have music:—but the birds that sing
    In that divinest nest
Thither must waver, wounded in the wing
    And wounded in the breast?

Heaven must be lighted—at the fallen light
    Of moon and star and sun?
Ah me, since these have made the earth too bright,
    Let the dark Will be done!

Text from *The Atlantic Monthly*, 1876

COMFORT—BY A COFFIN[50]

    Ah, friend of mine,
The old enchanted story!—Oh,
    I cannot hear a word!
Tell some poor child who loved a bird,
And knows he holds it stained and still:
    "It flies—in Fairyland!
Its nest is in a palm-tree, on a hill;
    Go, catch it—if you will."

    Ah, friend of mine,
The music (which ear hath not heard?)
    At best wails from the skies,
Somehow, into our funeral cries!
The flowers (eye hath not seen?) still fail
    To hide the coffin-lid.
Against this face so pitiless now and pale
    Can the high Heavens avail?

    Ah, friend of mine,
I think you mean—to mean it all!
    But then an angel's wing
Is a remote and subtle thing,

FIGURE 9. *"One Year Ago"*

(If you could show me any such
    In air that I can breathe!)
And surely Death's cold hand has much, so much,
    About it we can touch!

    Ah, friend of mine,
Say nothing of the thorns—and then
    Say nothing of the snow.
God's will? It is—that thorns must grow,
Despite our bare and troubled feet,
    To crown Christ on the cross;
The snow keeps white watch on the unrisen wheat,
    And yet—the world is sweet.

    Ah, friend of mine,
I know, I know—all you can know!
    All you can say is—this:
"It is the last time you can kiss
This only one of all the dead,
    Knowing it is the last;
These are the last tears you can ever shed
    On this fair fallen head."

Text from *Scribner's Monthly*, 1876

SAD WISDOM—FOUR YEARS OLD[51]

"Well, but some time I will be dead;
    Then you will love me, too!"
Ah! mouth so wise for mouth so red,
    I wonder how you knew.
(Closer, closer, little brown head—
    Not long can I keep *you!*)

Here, take this one poor bud to hold,
    Take this long kiss and last;
Love cannot loosen one fixed fold
    Of the shroud that holds you fast—
Never, never, oh, cold, so cold!
    All that was sweet is past.

Oh, tears and tears and foolish tears,
　　Dropped on a grave somewhere!
Does not the child laugh in my ears
　　What time I feign despair?
Whisper, whisper—I know he hears.
　　Yet this is hard to bear.

Oh, world with your wet face above
　　One veil of dust, thick-drawn!
Oh, weird voice of the hopeless dove,
　　Broken for something gone!
Tell me, tell me, when will we love
　　The thing the sun shines on?

Text from Appleton's Journal, 1876

A WOMAN'S COUNSEL[52]

It is yourself you love, I say,
My fine Narcissus of to-day;
Your eyes that lift the light divine,
Your hair the sun can not unshine—
　　Not mine, ah me! not mine.

If it were I, you would not sigh,
"I gave you this or that," though I
Had all the world here at my feet
In flowers and jewels—hardly sweet
　　To me, and incomplete.

Had thorn or lightning scarred my face,
Love still could see unearthly grace;
If I lay dead, and love were true,
One heart could hold the life for two—
　　Ah, Sir, good-night to you!

Good-night; and it were well to bring
Yourself a priest and wedding ring:
Through joy and sorrow I should see
That you unto yourself could be
　　Constant till death—ah me!

Good-night! I fear to see you pass
Your charmèd presence in the glass,
Lest that mock face should seem as fair
As yours, and hold you prisoned there,
    To die of love's despair.

Text from *Harper's Bazar,* 1876

THE LITTLE BOY I DREAMED ABOUT[53]

This is the only world I know;
    It is in this same world, no doubt.
Ah me! but I could love him so,
    If I could only find him out,
    The Little Boy I dreamed about!

This Little Boy who never takes
    The prettiest oranges he can see,
The reddest apple, all the cakes
    (When there are *twice* enough for three)—
    Where can the darling ever be?

He does not tease and storm and pout
    To climb the roof in rain and sun,
And pull the pigeon's feathers out
    To see how it will look with none,
    Or fight the hornets, one by one.

He does not hide, and cut his hair,
    And wind the watches wrong, and try
To throw the kitten down the stair
    To see how often it can die.
    (It's strange that you can wonder why.)

He never wakes too late to know
    A bird is singing near his bed;
He tells the tired moon, "You may go
    To sleep yourself." *He* never said,
    When told to do a thing, "Tell Fred."

If I said "Go," *he* would not stay
    To lose his hat or break a toy,

Then hurry like the wind away,
    And whistle like the wind for joy,
    To please himself—this Little Boy.

Let any stranger come who can,
    He will not say—if it *is* true—
"Old Lady" (or "Old Gentleman"),
    "I wish you would go home, I do;
    I think my mamma wants you to!"

——No, Fairy-land is far and dim:
    He does not play in silver sand.
But if I could believe in him,
    I could believe in Fairy-land,
    Because—do you not understand?

Dead? dead? Somehow I do not know.
    The sweetest children die. We may
Miss some poor foot-print from the snow
    That was his very own to-day——
    "God's will" is what the Christians say.

Like you, or you, or you can be,
    When you are good, he looks, no doubt.
I'd give—the goldenest star I see
    In all the dark, to find him out,
    The Little Boy I dreamed about.

Text from Harper's Bazar, 1876

KEEPING THE FAITH[54]

How long must you believe in Fairy-land?
    Forever, child. You must not bear to doubt
That one true country sweeter than this honey,
    Where little people surely go about
And buy and sell with grains of golden sand,
Which they, indeed, the foolish things, call money!

Believe, while out of broken bits of dew,
    For window-panes, something you cannot see—

Something that never *was* a bird—is peeping,
  And whispering what you cannot hear to you,
Shy as a shadow, where some good old tree,
Close by, its friendly watch and ward is keeping.

Who have believed in it? Why, all the men
  In all the world—and all the women, too.
Because it is so pleasant to believe in:
  There are so many pretty things to do,
Such light to laugh and dance in; yes, and then
Such lonesome, rainy woods for one to grieve in.

Believe in it. Until he sailed from Spain
  Columbus did. (But keep it out of sight.)
Yes, he found Fairy-land, and found it surely,
  (And landed there as one who had a right;)
But reached his hand for it, and caught a chain,
  Which in his coffin he can keep securely.

Then captains have believed in it and gone
  With swords and soldiers there to fight for it,
And torn their plumes and spoiled their scarlet sashes,
  But mended matters for us scarce a whit.
Why, Cinderella, her glass slippers on,
  Goes there—yes, now—from kitchen-smoke and ashes!

Did I believe in Fairy-land? I do.
  The young believe in it less than the old.
As eyes grow blind and heads grow white and whiter
  (The heads that dreamed about it in their gold)
We change its name to Heaven. That makes it true,
  And all the light of all the stars grows lighter.

The Capital (1877)

Text from *Poems in Company with Children,* 1877

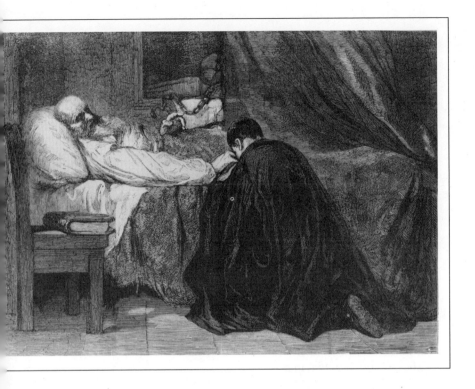

FIGURE 10. *"The Death of Columbus"*

A GREETING[55]

The sun has whispered it everywhere,
   And the whole earth thrills and quivers
With the breath of the tidings strong and fair,
   To the music of winds and rivers;
Over the hills at break of day,
   Linked by a flowery tether,
Spring time and love are coming this way—
   Spring time and love together!

Love the immortal who doth die,
   And spring the deathless mortal!
Their banners are set against the sky,
   They've opened April's portal,
Hark to the r[hy]me of their dancing feet
   Pulsing across the heather,
And the seasons calling all hearts to greet
   Spring time and love together!

Wedded and crowned by God's command,
   (And lo! the frosts are broken!)
The dower of beauty is in her hand,
   The sceptre of youth his token;
They'll rule the world with a smile, a song,
   A kiss, a leaf, a feather,
And wonders and wisdom to them belong,
   Spring time and love together!

O love! O spring! Come fast! Come sure!
   With never a step delaying;
How could our faith through the snows endure,
   If we didn't dream of the Maying?
But love, alas! too soon doth pass,
   And brief is the golden weather,
Here for a day, and then away,
   Spring time and love together!

Text from *The Capital,* 1877

THE LAMENT OF MY LADY[56]

So, it is time to tire of youth
   And my sweet mirror, where I see
That beautiful and bitter truth,
   Myself, reproach and pity me.

Wrong, somehow, have I not my wrongs?
   Better I were if left alone.
One snares me in a net of songs,
   Another changes me to stone!

Another steals my colours rare
   And gives them to some doubtful saint;—
Almost I wish I were not fair,
   Spite of their sonnets, marble, paint.

My beauty stirs within me strife.
   For men to see—am I for this?
Where others suffer death and life;
   Shall I have just a look, a kiss?

Why, any clown can wear a ring
   Of gold my head cannot outshine;
The wild bird in the air can sing
   With what diviner voice than mine.

What is my little sweetness worth?
   Here lies a violet at my feet:
The sweetest woman upon earth
   Was never half so sweetly sweet.

For men to see? If this be all,
   Yon lily, sirs, shows whiter grace;
The rose that climbs your garden wall
   Looks at you with a lovelier face.

The Capital (1877)
Text from *Irish Monthly*, 1887

HER LOVER'S TRIAL

I.

I bade him look at my own face,
   Wan with the agony of tears;
I dared him without other grace
   Than grief might leave forlornest years.

With flowerless hair, unjewelled breast,
   And mourning garments, stood I near.
I took the sun to be my guest
   And show him all he had to fear.

"Well? Love and love and love it was,
   Through last night's moonshine, everywhere."
"But—did not last night's moonshine pass?
   I think—a woman should be fair."

His eyes were farther from my heart
   Than any stars in yon vague sky:
"Sir, I forgive your dream. We part
   In the plain daylight?" "Yes. Good-by."

II.

Round tropic buds I coiled my hair,
   In lovely raiment hid my pain;
And beauty—such as women wear
   By evening lamps—I wore again!

Ah, sudden spell of pearls and lace!
   The slight soul trembled toward my feet;
The faint eyes saw my painted face:
   "Sweet," sighed the wavering voice, and "sweet."

"Nay, sir—this hand you try to touch
   Must drop its diamonds in the dust,
Must bleed with thorns, and reach for much
   Beyond your flowers and wines, I trust.

"Go, catch the butterflies that shine
    Athwart the sun, a little yet.
The darkness of your grave and mine
    Will leave us leisure to forget."

Text from *Galaxy*, 1877

THE HOUSE BELOW THE HILL[57]

You ask me of the farthest star,
    Whither your thought can climb at will,
Forever-questioning child of mine.
I fear it is not half so far
    As is the house below the hill,
Where one poor lamp begins to shine,
The lamp that is of death the sign.

Has it indeed been there for years,
    In rain and snow, with ruined roof
For God to look through, day and night,
At man's despair and woman's tears,
    While with myself I stood aloof,
As one by some enchanted right
Held high from any ghastly sight?

. . . One of my children lightly said,
    "Oh, nothing (Why must we be still?),
Only the people have to cry
Because the woman's child is dead
    There in the house below the hill.
I wish that we could see it fly.
It has gold wings, and that is why!"

Gold wings it *has?* I only know
    What wasted little hands it had,
That reached to me for pity, but
Before I thought to give it—oh,
    On earth's last rose-bud faint and sad,
Less cold than mine had been, they shut.
Sharper than steel some things should cut!

. . . I thought the mother showed to me,
　With something of a subtle scorn
(When morning mocked with bird and dew),
That brief and bitter courtesy
　Which awes us in the lowliest born.
Ah, soul, to thine own self be true;
God's eyes, grown human, look thee through!

"We need no help—we needed it.
　You have not come in time, and so
The women here did everything.
You did not know? You did not know!"
　I surely saw the dark brows knit.
To let the living die for bread,
Then bring fair shrouds to hide the dead!

What time I cried with Rachel's cry,
　I wondered that I could not wring,
While sitting at the grave, forlorn,
Compassion from yon alien sky,
　That knows not death nor anything
That troubles man of woman born,
Save that he wounded Christ with thorn.

My sorrow had the right to find
　Immortal pity? I could sit,
Not hearing at my very feet
The utter wailing of my kind,
　And dream my dream high over it!
O human heart, what need to beat,
If nothing save your own is sweet?

Ah me, that fluttering flower and leaf,
　That weird wan moon and pitiless sun,
And my own shadow in the grass,
Should hide from me this common grief!
　Was I not dust? What had I done?
In that fixed face as in a glass
I saw myself to judgment pass!

Text from *The Atlantic Monthly,* 1877

CAPRICE AT HOME

No, I will not say good-by—
　　Not good-by, nor anything.
He is gone. . . . I wonder why
　　Lilacs are not sweet this spring?—
　　How that tiresome bird will sing!

I might follow him and say
　　Just that he forgot to kiss
Baby, when he went away.
　　Everything I want I miss.
　　Oh, a precious world is this!

. . . . What if night came and not he?
　　Something might mislead his feet.
Does the moon rise late? Ah me!
　　There are things that he might meet.
　　Now the rain begins to beat:

So it will be dark. The bell?
　　Some one some one loves is dead.
Were it he——I cannot tell
　　Half the fretful words I said,
　　Half the fretful tears I shed.

Dead? And but to think of death;
　　Men might bring him through the gate:
Lips that have not any breath,
　　Eyes that stare——And I must wait!
　　Is it time, or is it late?

I was wrong, and wrong, and wrong;
　　I will tell him, oh, be sure!
If the heavens are builded strong,
　　Love shall therein be secure;
　　Love like mine shall there endure.

. . . . Listen, listen—that is he!
　　I'll not speak to him, I say.

If he choose to say to me,
  "I was all to blame to-day;
  Sweet, forgive me," why—I may!

Text from *Appleton's Journal*, 1877

COUNSEL[58]

Others will kiss you while your mouth is red.
  Beauty is brief. Of all the guests who come
While the lamp shines on flowers, and wine, and bread,
  In time of famine who will spare a crumb?

Therefore, oh, next to God, I pray you keep
  Yourself as your own friend, the tried, the true.
Sit your own watch—others will surely sleep.
  Weep your own tears. Ask none to die with you.

Text from *Appleton's Journal*, 1877

SOMEBODY'S TROUBLE[59]

Come, you little maiden, hush a while your fretting;—
  Surely you have trouble with your ribbons and your rings,
And trouble with the rain, which always is forgetting
  That you want to go [to] church—and with many other things.

There *is* trouble with your gloves, and trouble with your dresses;
  There is trouble with your music——You hate music? Does a bird?
There is trouble with your French, which poor Madame half confesses
  Is rather the most foreign that she has ever heard.

Why, the first thing in the morning, if Spring chance to be the season,
  After trouble with awaking, there is trouble with the dew;
Yes, the May-dew *is* the meanest, and there ought to be no reason
  Why, to make your face look fairer, it should have to wet your shoe.

You have trouble with the sun, which, instead of being pleasant—
  Only pleasant, nothing further—is too gracious with his heat;

And there's trouble with the moon, which is sometimes just a crescent
   When it *should* shine full and golden through the
      shadow at your feet.

You have trouble with the blossoms, which keep lying close and curly,—
   Afraid of wind and all that,—although you want to wear
A bud of rose or violet, that's "out" a little early,
   To some beautiful pert party in your muslins and your hair.

You have trouble with the fruit—with the lagging sweet strawberries,
   (And with W[ols]ey's killing frost, which make[s] shrouds of many a flower
For the apples and the peaches, for the pears and plums and cherries;)
   And there's trouble with those grapes which the fable says are sour.

You have trouble with the convent, where each pale and patient sister,
   After trouble with her rosary and trouble with her veil,
Has trouble with your trouble. There was one (I could
      have kissed her!)
   Why, she told me you were lovely. Wasn't that a pretty tale?

You have trouble, through your books, with some hundred thousand cities,
   With a spicy lot of islands and a stormy set of seas,
With your moods, sometimes imperative; and certainly one pities
   A golden head so sadly vexed with unknown quantities.

You have trouble with all nations too, through history or tradition,
   With their manners, dress, religions, with their kings and with their wars,
And (perhaps somewhat remotely, through the telescopic vision
   Of Professor This or That,) you have trouble with the stars.

Now, since you must have trouble, since to bear it you seem able,
   (I fancy even trouble may be made a little sweet,)
Suppose you take your trouble and arrange it on the table;
   Let the China, glass, and silver show that trouble can be neat.

Suppose you try, with trouble, if you cannot please the baby,
   (He has many a pretty failure and many a grievous loss;)
And suppose you dust a chair or two as charmingly as may be,
   And suppose you teach a housemaid just how not to be so cross.

                                        Harper's Bazar (1877)
                        Text from *Poems in Company with Children*, 1877

A COAT OF ARMS[60]

Rose says her family is old,
   Older than yours, perhaps? Ah me!
(How wise she is! Who could have told
   So much to such a child as she?

If those sweet Sisters teach her this,
   Their veils are vanity, I fear.)
Pray what comes next, my lovely miss?
   ——You want a coat of arms, my dear?

Ah?—other people have such things?
   Rose had *ancestors* too—an earl?
Tell Rose *you* have the blood of kings,
   And show it—when you blush, my girl.

I am not jesting; I could name,
   Among the greatest, one or two
Who have the right (divine) to claim
   Remote relationship with you.

Alfred—who never burned a cake.
   Arthur—who had no Table Round,
Nor knight like Lancelot of the Lake,
   Nor ruled one rood of English ground.

Lear, who outraved the storm—at most
   The crown is straw that crowns old age.
And Hamlet's father——He's a ghost?
   A real ghost, though—on the stage.

Edwards and Henries, and of these
   Old Blue-beard Hal, from whom you take
Your own bluff manners, if you please!
   Let's *love* him for Queen Catharine's sake!

Richard from Holy Land, who heard—
   Or did not hear—poor Blondel's song.
The other Richard too, the Third,
   Whom Shakspeare does a grievous wrong;

But——still he smothered in the Tower
    The pretty princes? Charles, whose head
At Cromwell's breath fell as a flower
    Falls at the frost, as I have read.

Another Charles, who had the crown
    Of France and Germany to hold,
But at a cloister laid it down,
    And kept two hollow hands to fold.

Philip the Handsome, who will rise
    From his old grave, the legends say,
And show the sun those Flemish eyes
    That——yes, I mean at Judgment Day.

Louis the Grand——Madam is so
    Like some one at his court, you hear?
These Washington reporters, though,
    Were never at his court, I fear.

Great Frederick, with his snuff (I may
    Say something of Great Peter too);
And one who made kings out of clay,
    And lost the world at Waterloo.

Of others—more than I can write.
    In some still cave scarce known to men
One sleeps, in his long beard's red light,
    A hundred years—then sleeps again.

One—who with all his peerage fell
    By Fontarabia—sits forlorn
In jeweled death at Aix. (Ah, well,
    Who listens now for Roland's horn?)

One—who was half a god, they say—
    Cried for the stars, and died of wine.
One pushed the crown of Rome away—
    And Antony's speech was very fine.

The Shah of Persia, too? Why, yes,
    He and his overcoat, no doubt.

FIGURE 11. *"Hang Yourself for a Pastime"*

——Oh, the Khedive *will* send, I guess,
  Half Egypt—when he finds you out!

That royal lady, late the Queen,
  Now Empress of all space, must own
Your race might give you grace to lean
  Right near her new imperial throne.

Victor of Italy, the Czar,
  Franz-Joseph, the sweet Spanish youth,
And Prussian William—these all are
  Your kinsmen, child, in very truth.

Lilies and lions, new-world stars,
  Damascus swords and Spartan shields,
Crescents and crosses, feuds and scars,
  Meet and confuse in famous fields.

Your coat of arms, then——I forgot
  Some kings—the oldest, wisest, best:
Take Jason's Golden Fleece—why not?
  Put Solomon's seal upon your crest.

There! I can prove your Family's ties
  Bind you to all the Great, I trust:
Its Founder lived in Paradise,
  And his ancestor was—the Dust.

Can Rose say more? Your ancient Tree
  Must hold a sword of fire (its root
Down in the very grave must be),
  With serpent and—Forbidden Fruit.

Text from *Harper's Bazar,* 1877

TWO LITTLE SEXTONS

Two Little Sextons, is your pretty trade
  Its own reward? I fancy it may be
For love of making graves that graves are made
  Under the quiet of that thorny tree,

Whose very thorns to-day were sharply laid
  To rest beside the blue faint flowers you found
  And hurried back into their native ground.

Two Little Sextons, yellow of hair, I fear
  There have been burials of butterflies,
Sudden and secret—many a time this year.
  Ah, brave confession!—merrily one replies,
With young light logic, very fair to hear:
  "We had to kill them, for they would not die,
  So they could turn to angels in the sky."

Text from Poems in the Company of Children, 1877

NO HELP

When will the flowers grow there? I cannot tell.
  Oh, many and many a rain will beat there first,
Stormy and dreary, such as never fell
  Save when the heart was breaking that had nursed
Something most dear a little while, and then
Murmured at giving God his own again.

The woods were full of violets, I know;
  And some wild sweet-briers grew so near the place:
Their time is not yet come. Dead leaves and snow
  Must cover first the darling little face
From these wet eyes, forever fixed upon
Your last still cradle, O most precious one!

Is he not with his Father? So I trust.
  Is he not His? Was he not also mine?
His mother's empty arms yearn toward the dust.
  Heaven lies too high, the soul is too divine.
I wake at night and miss him from my breast,
And—human words can never say the rest.

Safe? But out of the world, out of my sight!
  My way to him through utter darkness lies.

I am gone blind with weeping, and the light—
　　If there be light—is shut inside the skies.
Think you, to give my bosom back his breath,
I would not kiss him from the peace called Death?

And do I want a little Angel? No,
　　I want my Baby—with such piteous pain,
That were this bitter life thrice bitter, oh!
　　I could not choose but take him back again.
God cannot help me, for God cannot break
His own dark Law—for my poor sorrow's sake.

Text from That New World, 1877

ONE OUT-OF-DOORS

A ghost—is he afraid to be a ghost?
　　A ghost? It breaks my heart to think of it.
Something that wavers in the moon, at most;
　　Something that wanders; something that must flit
From morning, from the bird's breath and the dew.
Ah, if I knew,—ah, if I only knew!

Something so weirdly wan, so weirdly still!
　　O yearning lips that our warm blood can flush,
Follow it with your kisses, if you will;
　　O beating heart, think of its helpless hush.
Oh, bitterest of all, to fear we fear
Something that was so near, that was so dear!

No,—no, he is no ghost; he could not be;
　　Something that hides, forlorn, in frost and brier;
Something shut outside in the dark, while we
　　Laugh and forget by the familiar fire;
Something whose moan we call the wind, whose tears
Sound but as rain-drops in our human ears.

Text from The Atlantic Monthly, 1878

AFTER THE QUARREL[61]

Hush, my pretty one. Not yet.
   Wait a little, only wait.
Other blue flowers are as wet
   As your eyes, outside the gate
He has shut forever.—But
Is the gate forever shut?

Just a young man in the rain
   Saying (the last time?) "good-night!"
Should he never come again
   Would the world be ended quite?
Where would all these rose-buds go?—
All these robins? Do you know?

But—he will not come? Why, then,
   Is no other within call?
There are men, and men, and men—
   And these men are brothers all!
Each sweet fault of his you'll find
Just as sweet in all his kind.

None with eyes like his? Oh—oh!
   In diviner ones did I
Look, perhaps, an hour ago.
   Whose? Indeed (you must not cry)
Those I thought of—are not free
To laugh down your tears, you see.

Voice like his was never heard?
   No,—but better ones, I vow;
Did you ever hear a bird?—
   Listen, one is singing now!
And his gloves? His gloves? Ah, well,
There are gloves like his to sell.

At the play to-night you'll see,
   In mock-velvet cloaks, mock earls
With mock-jeweled swords—that he
   Were a clown by!—Now, those curls

86

Are the barber's pride, I say;
Do not cry for them, I pray.

If no one should love you? Why,
   You can love some other still:
Philip Sidney, Shakspere, ay,
   Good King Arthur, if you will;
Raphael—*he* was handsome too.
Love them, one and all. I do.

Text from Scribner's Monthly, 1878

IN DOUBT

Through dream and dusk a frightened whisper said:
"Lay down the world: the one you love is dead."
In the near waters, without any cry,
I sank, therefore, glad—oh, so glad to die!

Far on the shore, with sun and dove and dew
And apple-flowers, I suddenly saw you;
Then—was it kind or cruel that the sea
Held back my hands, and kissed and clung to me?

Text from Appleton's Journal, 1878

"WE WOMEN"

Heart-ache and heart-break—always that or this:
   Sometimes it rains just when the sun should shine;
Sometimes a glove or ribbon goes amiss;
   Sometimes, in youth, your lover should be mine.

Still madam frets at life, through pearls and lace
   (A breath can break her pale heart's measured beat),
And still demands the maid who paints her face
   Shall find the world forever smooth and sweet.

Text from Appleton's Journal, 1878

A HINT FROM HOMER[62]

I let the sun stand still this lonesome day,
    And hardly heard the very baby coo,
(Meanwhile the earth went on—the other way!)
    That I might watch the siege of Troy with you.

The great Achilles (whom we know) was there—
    His shining shield was what we guessed him by;
And Hector with his plume of horse's hair
    Frightened his child and laughed to hear it cry.

Poor Hector! Never sorrow for the dead,
    In these three thousand rather piteous years,
Stole into sweeter words than Helen said
    Beside him through the dropping of her tears.

We grieved with Priam for his gracious son.
    Much-wandering Ulysses with his craft
Cheated us through strange seas—and every one
    Came straight to grief with him upon his raft.

Not one among you but could draw his bow,
    After its rust in Ithaca, and bring
A suitor down!—In the dark backward, oh,
    How sad the swallow-twitter of its string!

Now that it's time to shut the shadowy book—
    (Ah me, they clash together, left and right,
And Greek meets Greek—or Trojan! Only look!)
    What have you learned from it? You say: "To fight!"

Text from Wide-Awake, 1878

FROM NORTH AND SOUTH[63]
(A Lesson from the Newspaper.)

"Some people have the loveliest time.
    I'm tired of learning everything!"
"You have not learned it yet. We climb
    Great mountains slowly, child, and bring

88

Few flowers into the huts below,
When down for bread and sleep we go."

"Just read this letter. Oh, how sweet
    She must have looked;—only one year
Older than I, too." "Very neat
    Her hat and plume may be, my dear."
"'More queenly than a queen'"—"Just so"—
"'In her dark purple habit.'"—("Oh!")

"'Then at the ball that night she wore
    Only one blush-rose in her hair
And one in either cheek.'" "What more
    Needs any charming Miss to wear?
They do not cost like lace and pearls,
You saddest of gold-headed girls."

"That's from the North" "Now turn and read
    A letter from the South, I say."
"'Nothing but Death is here'"—"Indeed!"
    "'And Misery following Death.'" "Ah me!—
    That's of some people, too, you see."

Youth's Companion (1878)

Text from *Dramatic Persons and Moods*, 1879

THE PRINCE IMPERIAL[64]
(Killed in South Africa, June 1, 1879.)

Strange things do come to pass,
    Far from the dews of France, by the sharp glitter
Of torrid suns, alone in the long grass,
    The last imperial Violet dies. Alas,
    This is the end. The end is bitter.

You looked toward kingly years
    For your one gracious boy, oh, regal mother!
You planned the throne for him. Who planned the spears?
    Ah, among women, many send you tears,
    Remembering in him some other.

Poor world to dream in, where
  The purple swathed may be so grayly shrouded;
And poor, dead Prince—as the bird from the snare,
  Escaped. Did he decline thus, unaware,
  The Empire, cruel-starred, fire-clouded?

Text from The Capital, 1879

A TRAGEDY IN WESTERN WOODS[65]
(Woman Speaks.)

Why, we are willing, friend, to end with death;
  Death to begin with is another thing.
Too bitter is it, not to keep our breath
  Until its beat from this brave world we wring.

Confronting dew and briar-rose, pitiless sun,
  And bird that sang not knowing, on her breast
A bud unwithered, damp with blood, lay one
  Who dreamed of life, perhaps—and knew the rest.

The girl's shy lover, through weird, whispering trees
  Walked eagerly, perhaps an instant late;
(That day of all days, feverish to please!)
  He started, stared, and fell against the gate.

Blossom and blush he came to find. He found
  Only the dead—who left an empty earth.
——But, sir, a ploughman's heart can hold a wound
  As deep as if he cared for books or birth.

With tears unfallen, from out the murmurous crowd
  A woman trembled, who was sad and gray.
Lifting the maid she dressed her in her shroud,
  And watched her a long, still, wordless way.

"That boy!" one moaned; "why that could never be."
  Another said: "He owns what he has done."
She was a widow. As they muttered she
  Looked from the door—and saw her only son!

.... Ah, baby laugh and dimple, baby kiss
   And wandering baby hands, that take one's heart
To play with—or let drop and break! Was this
   The end, poor mother, of a mother's part?

We cry for help. God has the Heavens to hold.
   Can He let fall the stars to take us up
And comfort us? He lets our lips grow cold—
   And that is much—after we drink the cup.

And she who saw men lead away that youth
   (The childish gold scarce blown from off his hair,—
More evil for his beauty's sake), in truth
   Saw no more sorrow, surely, anywhere!

If light come ever to the void in eyes
   That, having seen such woe, shut and are sealed,
It is the utter light of Paradise,
   Whereby no thing not fair shall be revealed.

The Capital (1879)

Text from *Dramatic Persons and Moods*, 1879

A PIQUE AT PARTING

Why, sir, as to that——I did not know it was time for the moon to rise,
   (So, the longest day of them all can end, if we will have patience with it.)
One woman can hardly care, I think, to remember another one's eyes,
   And——the bats are beginning to flit.
   .... We hate one another? It may be true.
   That else do you teach us to do?
   Yea, verily, to love you.

My lords—and gentlemen—are you sure that after we love quite all
   There is in your noble selves to be loved, no time on our hands will remain?
Why, an hour a day were enough for this. We may watch the wild leaves fall
   On the graves you forget. .... It is plain
   That you were not pleased when she said——Just so;
   Still, what do we want, after all, you know,
   But room for a rose to grow?

You leave us the baby to kiss, perhaps; the bird in the cage to sing;
The flower on the window, the fire on the hearth (and the fires in the
heart) to tend.
When the wandering hand that would reach somewhere has become the Slave
of the Ring,
You give us—an image to mend;
Then shut with a careless smile, the door—
(There's dew or frost on the path before;)
We are safe inside. What more?

If the baby should moan, or the bird sit hushed, or the flower fade out——what
then?
Ah? the old, old feud of mistress and maid would be left though the sun
went out?
You can number the stars and call them by names, and, as men, you can wring
from men
The world—for they own it, no doubt.
We, not being eagles, are doves? Why, yes,
We must hide in the leaves, I guess,
And coo down our loneliness.

God meant us for saints? Yes—in Heaven. Well, I, for one, am content
To trust Him through darkness and space to the end—if an end there shall
be;
But, as to His meanings, I fancy I never knew quite what He meant.
And——why, what were you saying to me
Of the saints—or *that* saint? It is late;
The lilies look weird by the gate.
. . . . Ah, sir, as to that—we will wait.

The Capital (1879)

Text from *Dramatic Persons and Moods*, 1879

A LESSON IN A PICTURE[66]

So it is whispered, here and there,
   That you are rather pretty? Well?
(Here's matter for a bird of the air
   To drop down from the dusk and tell.)

Let's have no lights, my child. Somehow,
The shadow suits your blushes now.

The blonde young man who called to-day
    (He only rang to leave a book?—
Yes, and a flower or two, I say!)
    Was handsome, look you. Will you look?
You did not know his eyes were fine,—
You did not? Can you look in mine?

What is it in this picture here
    That you should suddenly watch it so?
A maiden leaning, half in fear,
    From her far casement; and, below,
In cap and plumes (or cap and bells!),
Some fairy tale her lover tells.

Suppose this lonesome night could be
    Some night a thousand springs ago,
Dim round that tower; and you were she,
    And your shy friend her lover (Oh!),
And I—her mother! And suppose
I knew just why she wore that rose.

Do you think I'd kiss my girl, and say,
    "Make haste to bid the wedding guest,
And make the wedding garment gay.
    You could not find in East or West
So brave a bridegroom; I rejoice
That you have made so sweet a choice"?

Or say, "To look forever fair,
    Just keep this turret-moonlight wound
About your face; stay in mid-air:
    Rope-ladders lead one to the ground,
Where all things take the touch of tears,
And nothing lasts a thousand years"?

Text from *The Atlantic Monthly*, 1879

ENGAGED TOO LONG[67]

Why do I grieve with summer here?
I want the flower that died last year;
I want the old drops of the dew,
And my old love, sir,—and not you.

Younger than you, nor quite so wise,
Was he who had your hair and eyes,—
Who said, "I love you" first, you see;
This you repeat, and weary me.

Text from *The Atlantic Monthly*, 1879

TRANSFIGURED[68]

Almost afraid they led her in:
 (A dwarf more piteous none could find);
Withered as some weird leaf, and thin,
 The woman was—and wan and blind.

Into his mirror with a smile—
 Not vain to be so fair, but glad—
The South-born painter looked the while,
 With eyes than Christ's alone less sad.

"Mother of God," in pale surprise
 He whispered, "What am I to paint?"
A voice that sounded from the skies
 Said to him: "Raphael, a saint."

She sat before him in the sun;
 He scarce could look at her, and she
Was still and silent. "It is done,"
 He said. "Oh, call the world to see!"

Ah, that was she in veriest truth—
 Transcendent face and haloed hair;
The beauty of divinest youth,
 Divinely beautiful, was there.

Herself into her picture passed—
   Herself and not her poor disguise
Made up of time and dust. At last
   One saw her with the Master's eyes.

Text from *Scribner's Monthly*, 1879

THE DESCENT OF THE ANGEL[69]

"This is the house. Come, take the keys.
   Romance and travel here must end."
Out of the clouds, not quite at ease,
   I saw the pretty bride descend;
With satin sandals, fit alone
   To glide in air, she touched the stone.

A thing to fade through wedding lace,
   From silk and scents, with priest and ring,
Floated across that earthly place
   Where life must be an earthly thing.
An earthly voice was in her ears,
   Her eyes awoke to earthly tears.

Text from *Scribner's Monthly*, 1879

HER REPROOF TO A ROSE[70]

Sad rose, foolish rose,
   Fading on the floor,
Will he love you while he knows
   There are many more
   At the very door?

Sad rose, foolish rose,
   One among the rest:
Each is lovely—each that blows;
   It must be confest
   None is loveliest!

Sad rose, foolish rose,
   Had you known to wait,

And with dead leaves or with snows
   Come alone and late—
   Sweet had been your fate!

Sad rose, foolish rose,
   If no other grew
In the wide world, I suppose,
   My own lover, too,
   Would love—only you!

Text from Scribner's Monthly, 1879

THE STORY OF A SHAWL[71]
(1879.)

My child, is it so strange, indeed,
This tale of the Plague in the East, you read?—

This tale of how a soldier found
A gleaming shawl of silk, close-wound,

(And stained, perhaps, with two-fold red)
About a dead man's careless head?

He took the treasure on his breast
To one he loved. We know the rest.

If Russia shudders near and far,
From peasant's hut to throne of Czar:

If Germany bids an armed guard
By sun and moon keep watch and ward

Along her line, that they who fly
From death, ah me! shall surely die:

This trouble for the world was all
Wrapped in that soldier's sweetheart's shawl.

——Pray God no other lovers bring
Some gift as dread in rose or ring.

Youth's Companion (1879)
Text from The Witch in the Glass, 1888

HER WORD OF REPROACH

We must not quarrel, whatever we do;
   For if I was (but I was not!) wrong,
Here are the tears for it, here are the tears:— *[lear !]*
   What else has a woman to offer you?
Love might not last for a thousand years,
   You know, though the stars should rise so long.

Oh you, you talk in a man's great way!—
   So, love would last though the stars should fall?
Why, yes. If it last to the grave, indeed,
   After the grave last on it may.
But—in the grave? Will its dust take heed
   Of anything sweet—or the sweetest of all?

Ah, death is nothing! It may be so.
   Yet, granting at least that death is death
(Pray look at the rose, and hear the bird),
   Whatever it is—we must die to know!
Sometime we may long to say one word
   Together—and find we have no breath.

Ah me, how divine you are growing again!—
   How coldly sure that the Heavens are sure,
Whither too lightly you always fly
   To hide from the passion of human pain.
Come, grieve that the Earth is not secure,
   For this one night—and forget the sky!

[handwritten note: in thinking of eternal life, the husband fails to appreciate the present]

Text from *Dramatic Persons and Moods*, 1879

BROKEN PROMISE

After strange stars, inscrutable, on high;
   After strange seas beneath his floating feet;
After the glare in many a brooding eye,—
   I wonder if the cry of "Land" was sweet?

Or did the Atlantic gold, the Atlantic palm,
    The Atlantic bird and flower, seem poor, at best,
To the gray Admiral under sun and calm,
    After the passionate doubt and faith of quest?

Text from Dramatic Persons and Moods, 1879

DENIED

I.
(The Lady's Thought.)[72]

It may have been——Who knows, who knows?
    It was too dark for me to see.
The wind that spared this very rose
    Its few last leaves could hardly be
        Sadder of voice than he.

A foreign Prince here in disguise,
    Who asked a shelter from the rain.
(The country that he came from lies
    Above the clouds.) He asked in vain,
        And will not come again.

If I *had* known that it was He
    Who had not where to lay his head:—
"But my Lord Christ, it cannot be;
    My guest-room has too white a bed
        For way-side dust," I had said.

II.
(The Mother's Thought.)[73]

It was my own sweet child—the one
    Whose baby mouth breathes at my breast.
(A fairer and a brighter, none
    Save His own Mother ever prest
        Into diviner rest.)

He had escaped my arms and strayed
    Into the pitiless world that night.

With wounded feet and faith betrayed,
   Charmed backward by a glimmer of light,
     Almost he stood in sight.

Oh, I had let *him* ask in vain,
   (Vague, lonesome, shadowy years ahead,)
My roof to hide him from the rain,
   My lamp to comfort him, my bread,
     Who came as from the dead!

                   Text from *Dramatic Persons and Moods*, 1879

HIS MOTHER'S WAY[74]

"My Mamma just knows how to cry
   About an old glove or a ring,
Or even a stranger going by
   The gate, or—almost anything!

"She cried till both her eyes were red
   About *him,* too. (I saw her, though!)
And he was just a——, Papa said.
   (We have to call them that, you know.)

"She cried about the shabbiest shawl,
   Because it cost too much to buy;
But Papa cannot cry at all,
   For he's a man. And that is why!

"Why, if his coat was not right new,
   And if the yellow bird would die
That sings, and my white kitten too,
   Or even himself, *he* would not cry.

"He said that he would sleep to-night
   With both the pistols at his head,
Because that ragged fellow might
   Come back. That's what my Papa said!

"But Mamma goes and hides her face
   There in the curtains, and peeps out
At him, and almost spoils the lace.
   And he is what she cries about!

FIGURE 12. *"The Tramp"*

"She says he looks so cold, so cold,
    And has no pleasant place to stay!
Why can't he work? He is not old;
    His eyes are blue—they've not turned gray."

So the boy babbled. . . . Well, sweet sirs,
    Flushed with your office-fires, you write
You laugh down at such grief as hers;
    But are these women foolish quite?

I know. But, look you, there may be
    Stains sad as wayside dust, I say.
Upon your own white hands (ah, me!)
    No woman's tears can wash away.

One sees her baby's dimple hold
    More love than you can measure. . . . Then
Nights darken down on heads of gold
    Till wind and frost try wandering men!

But there are prisons made for such,
    Where the strong roof shuts out the snow;
And bread (that you would scorn to touch)
    Is served them there. I know, I know.

Ah! while you have your books, your ease,
    Your lamp-light leisure, jests, and wine,
Fierce outside whispers, if you please,
    Moan, each: "These things are also mine!"

Text from The Independent, 1880

A STRANGE COUNTRY[75]

It's a strange story I must tell
Of a strange country! Well, then—well,
The strangest country that I know
Is one where palm-trees do not grow;
It lies within the very reach
    Of your two hands, and blue-birds flit
Among the flowers of pear and peach,
    In pleasant dews, all over it.

In this strange country, then, last night,
A lady in the gracious light
Of garden-lamps and rising moon
(Hush! you may do your guessing soon),
With bits of stone she chose to wear
　　That elfin queens, perhaps, had lost,
Outflashed the fire-flies in the air,
　　And what a sum her party cost!

This morning, with a beard as white
As his own shroud should be, in sight
Of her high windows' precious lace,
A man—with oh! so sad a face
One scarce could look at it for tears—
　　Stood with a staff, and slowly said:
"It's the first time in all these years;
　　But, Madam, I must ask for bread."

The lady, lily-like, within
Her hands, that did not toil nor spin,
Held all sweet things this world can give;
The man, for just the breath to live,
Early and late, in sun and snow,
　　Had done his best. I thought you knew.
It must be a strange country, though,
　　Where such strange stories can be true.

Text from *The Independent,* 1880

WATCHING THE COW[76]

"Come, look at her, and you will love her.
　　Go, lead her now through pleasant places,
And teach her that our new world's clover
　　Is sweet as Jersey-island daisies.

"Yes, you may do a little playing
　　Close to the gate, my pretty warder,
But, meanwhile, keep your cow from straying
　　Across the elfin-people's border."

So to the boy his mother jested
  About his light task, lightly heeding;
While in the flowering grass he rested
  The magic book that he was reading.

At sundown, for the cow's returning,
  The milkmaid waited long, I'm thinking;
Hours later, by the moonlight's burning,
  Did fairy-folk have cream for drinking?

* * * What of the boy? By hill and hollow,
  Through bloom and briar, till twilight ended,
His book had charmed him on to follow
  The cow—the one that Cadmus tended!

Text from *Scribner's Monthly*, 1880

THE THOUGHT OF ASTYANAX BESIDE IÜLUS[77]
After Reading Virgil's Story of Andromache in Exile.

Yes, all the doves begin to moan,
But it is not the doves alone.
Some trouble, that you never heard
In any tree from breath of bird,
That reaches back to Eden, lies
Between your wind-flower and my eyes.

I fear it was not well, indeed,
Upon so sad a day to read
So sad a story. But the day
Is full of blossoms, do you say,—
And how the sun does shine? I know.
These things do make it sadder, though.

You'd cry, if you were not a boy,
About this mournful tale of Troy?
Then do not laugh at me, if I—
Who am too old, you know, to cry—
Just hide my face awhile from you,
Down here among these drops of dew.

* * * Must I for sorrow look so far?
This baby headed like a star,
Afraid of Hector's horse-hair plume
(His one sweet child, whose bitter doom
So piteous seems)—oh, tears and tears!—
Has he been dust three thousand years?

Yet when I see his mother fold
The pretty cloak she stitched with gold
Around another boy, and say:
"He would be just your age to-day,
With just your hands, your eyes, your hair"—
Her grief is more than I can bear.

Text from Scribner's Monthly, 1880

THE WITCH IN THE GLASS[78]

"My mother says I must not pass
   Too near that glass;
She is afraid that I will see
A little witch that looks like me,
With a red, red mouth, to whisper low
The very thing I should not know!"

Alack for all your mother's care!
   A bird of the air,
A wistful wind, or (I suppose
Sent by some hapless boy) a rose,
With breath too sweet, will whisper low,
The very thing you should not know!

The Union of American Poetry and Art (1880)
Text from Scribner's Monthly, 1881

HER GROWN-UP DOLL'S NEEDS[79]
A Hint to Mamma.

"Now I begin to think it's time that Rose
Should wear a train. She's a young lady now.
You really cannot guess how much she knows.
(She's read some charming novels, anyhow.)

"How sweet she'd look in a commencement dress—
White satin and illusion, and some pearls.
Her gloves must have six buttons, and—I guess
She'd get more flowers than all the other girls.

"I fancy she should have some company.
(One's papa always comes home late and tired.)
And if she only had—some one, you see,
To take her out, she would be much admired.

"Oh, you forget you brought her home to me
Once on my birthday, years and years ago.
She could not be a baby yet, you see;
Why, then I was a child myself, you know!"

Text from *Youth's Companion*, 1880

SOME CHILDREN ASLEEP

Who would believe that, when awake—
Who would believe? Not I, for one!
Yes, God in truth was good to make
The stars to hide the stains of sun.
Somehow the dead sins of the day
At night take wings and fly away.

Divinest of the Masters, Sleep!
What cherubs born of paint and dream,
Old Time has left new Time to keep,
Were ever quite so sweet, as seem
These wayward, wind-wild boys of mine
Beneath your aureole of—moon-shine!

Text from *Youth's Companion*, 1880

A NEIGHBORHOOD INCIDENT⁸⁰

"Did you know, Mamma, that the man was dead
  In that pretty place, there under the hill?"
"So, with only the clouds to cover his head,
  He died down there in that old stone mill;
He died, in the wind and sleet, and—mark
This truth, fair sirs—in the dark.

"(Yes, a pretty place!) In the summer time,
  When the birds sing out of the leaves for joy,
And the blue wild morning-glories climb
  On the broken walls, it is pretty, my boy:
But not when the world around is snow
And the river is ice below.

"Men looked sometimes from the morning cars
  Toward the place where he lay in the winter sun,
And said, through the smoke of their dear cigars,
  That something really ought to be done.
Then talked of—the President, or the play,
Or the war—that was furthest away."

"Do you know when his father wanted some bread,
  One time, by the well there? Wasn't he old!
I mean that day when the blossoms were red
  On the cliffs, and it wasn't so very cold."
"And I gave him the little I well could spare
When I looked at his face and hair.

"Then we met him once—it was almost night—
  Out looking for berries among the briers,
So withered and weird, such a piteous sight,
  And gathering wood for their gypsy fires.
'No, the young man is no better. No, no.'
He would keep on saying, so low."

"But the women there would not work, they say."
  "Why, that is the story; but, if it be true,
There are other women, I think, to-day
  Who will not work, yet, their whole lives through,

106

FIGURE 13. *"Turned Out"*

All lovely things from the seas and lands
Drop into their idle hands.

"But they would not work, so their brother—and ours—
    Deserved to die in that desolate place?
Shall we send regrets and the usual flowers?
    Shall we stop and see the upbraiding face,
As it lies in the roofless room forlorn,
For the sake of a dead man's scorn?

"He did his best, as none will deny,
    At serving the Earth to pay for his breath;
So she gave him early (and why not, why?)
    The one thing merciful men call death.
Ah! gift that must be gracious indeed,
Since it leaves us nothing to need.

"As for us, sweet friends, let us dress and sleep,
    Let us praise our pictures and drink our wine.
Meanwhile, let us drive His starving sheep
    To our good Lord Christ, on the hights divine;
For the flowerless valleys are dim and drear,
And the winds right bitter, down here."

North Bend, O.   Text from *The Independent*, 1881

TWO VISIONS OF FAIRY-LAND[81]

One, with her blue, faint eyes, could dream too much;
One, rosily sun-stained, wanted things to touch.

She met him on the stair with half a blush:
"How late you sleep!" he said. She whispered, "Hush!

"I read that painted book last night, and so
I dreamed about Prince Charming——" "Did you, though?

"Why, I was wide awake in time to see
All Fairy-land! I wish you'd been with me."

"What was it like?" "Oh, it was green and still,
With rocks and wild red roses and a hill,

"And some shy birds that sung far up the air,—
And such a river, all in mist, was there!"

"Where was it?" "Why, the moon went down on one
Side, and upon the other rose the sun!"

"How does one get there?" "Oh, the path lies through
The dawn, you little sleeper, and the dew."

Text from *St. Nicholas,* 1881

SOME MORNING ORDERS[82]

["]I say, mamma, are you awake?
The stars keep shining and the moon—
I can't help that. I want the cake
I didn't have last night, right soon.
The sun will make the river red
In just a few more hours!" he said.

"I dreamed the prettiest dream, about
Some crows with wings up in a tree!
I threw a stone and they flew out,
And so I caught me two or three
And tied them with your bonnet-strings!
—Please go and get me all my things.

"Put on your shawl—you'll have to go
Out by the well. The knife is there.
My wagon's in the garden, though.
The nails are—almost everywhere!
My blue balloon sailed to the sky,
You can't get it. You needn't try.

"The rock I left my hammer on
Is—where I left three walnuts too.
You'll find it, for it can't be gone.
We saw a bird there that was blue
One time, just years and years ago—
Before I was so old, you know.

"My ball rolled down the cliff that day
When I was good. But I'm afraid
It's in the river. Let it stay.
(I wish that cliff was never made.)
My fishhook's in the arbor, though,
Caught on that vine where grapes don't grow.

"My sled is—somewhere. You just look
Till you can find it, for, you see,
I'll want it—sometime. And my book
Is—all torn up—down by the tree
Where all the apple-blossoms grow—
Last summer, but not now, you know!

"Mamma, you're gone to sleep again!
I hear the clock keep striking four.
Somebody'll miss the morning train,
Don't make me call you any more.
I'm getting sleepy. Please to wake
And get me, first of all, the cake."

Text from Wide-Awake, 1881

OUT OF TUNE

Someone has told you that the moon is old?
(Do you not see to-night that it is new?)
It just pretends that it is made of gold;
It's made of—matter? (Matter means what's true.)

A rainbow is not sure enough at all?
The sky is nothing, only it looks blue?
Some night, you guess, the stars will have to fall
Down in the grass when everything breaks through?

Some things *are* pretty, but they will not stay?
Out on the cliff you saw the reddest rose,
The wind or something blew it right away—
That black rock lasts forever where it grows?

The butterflies are only worms with wings?
Without them they would not know how to fly?

And we are sinners? Girls should not wear rings
And gloves and sashes—for they have to die?

The sun shines sometimes, but it always rains
Forever, so you can't play in the sand?
Walnuts and berries spoil your hands with stains?
And—no one knows the way to fairy land?

Text from Wide-Awake, 1881

TRUMPET FLOWERS

They light the green dusk with their fire-like glow,
And the brown barefoot boys laugh out below.

The wind wakes in the grass and climbs the tree,
The wind—ah, what a trumpeter is he:

He blows them in the leaves above my head,
So low, so long, that he might wake the dead.

He blows them, till a child they cannot see
Hears them, and plays with that brown company.

Text from Youth's Companion, 1881

THE FIRST PARTY[83]

"It was just lovely, mamma, and my dress
    Was much the prettiest there, the boys all said,
They said, too, that I looked—my best. I guess
    These ribbons suited me. You see that red
You did not fancy lighted up so well.
Somebody told me I was quite a belle.

"I wish you didn't want me to wear white,
    With just a flower or two. Rose wears such things.
They're so old-fashioned. She was such a fright!
    I wish that I had fifty diamond rings—
I'd wear them all at once! I'd almost paint
Before I'd look like Rose. She's such a saint."

111

"I thought you were the best of friends." "We are—
     Only we hate each other! That is what
The best of friends do—in our school. How far
     Away you look. Forgive me. I forgot.
I've made you sad. *I'll* love the whole world too,
I guess, mamma—when I'm as old as you!

"Why don't you listen, mamma? You must be
     Thinking of Adam. Here's a bud he gave
You once in Eden—shut up here, you see,
     In this old book." "That grew upon a grave."
"Oh! I'll not touch it then. I wish that pearls
Would grow on trees—but not for other girls.

"Now, mamma, please to hear me to the end.
     The handsomest of all the boys last night
Looked like that picture of—your brother's friend.
     He hardly spoke to Rose. Oh, I'm not quite
An angel yet. I shall be, I suppose,
Sometime. I'm glad he hardly spoke to Rose.

"I wonder, mamma, did you ever go
     To a first party. And what did you wear?
How odd you must have looked! But tell me, though,
     About your dress. How many girls were there?"
"Fifty, perhaps." "There were some boys, I guess?"
"Yes, there was one." "And he was handsome?" "Yes."

"Where is he now, do you think?" "I do not know.
     (In some sweet foreign Country, it may be,
Among the palms.") "He might have written, though,
     In all these years." "He cannot write." "I see,
What a strange party! Fifty girls—oh dear!
And one boy—and he couldn't write! How queer!"

Text from *Youth's Companion*, 1882

LITTLE DRAGON'S-TEETH[84]

I thought you were my own two pretty boys
   You rosy, restless, yellow-headed things,
Born only to look sweet—and make a noise!
   (And to find out that butterflies had wings?—
   And, much I fear me, that the bees had stings?)
Or bring the broken buds of morning-glories,
In their blue season, to buy fairy stories!

But now I know that in some field so far,
   Three thousand years or more back through the light,
A ploughman broke the dark ground up for war,
   And scattered dragon's-teeth to left and right,
   That sprang up into soldiers mad for fight!
Yes, now I know—or take it all for granted—
You are the very fellows Cadmus planted!

Youth's Companion (1882)
Text from *Child's-World Ballads*, 1895

A PARTY IN A DREAM[85]

Strange, after five-and-twenty years, to keep
A tryst, made, somehow, in the shadow of sleep!

In the sad island-moon, here by the sea,
What still ship landed such a company?

Now, that I think, some of the girls wore white
With flowers.—Ah me, my heart! as well they might!

The boys—but, surely, long ago I read
That one in battle drooped his shining head.

And one, they said, had vanished through the sand,
A home-sick alien, in a palmy land.

One laughing, whispered: "After such a night
We shall not look well in the morning light;

"The boys would say——but it is time to go;"
And suddenly the cock began to crow.

"So, I, the only living one," I said,
"At dead of night have entertained the dead."

Queenstown, Ireland

The Independent (1883)
Text from *In Primrose Time*, 1886

A CHILD'S PARTY[86]

Before my cheeks were fairly dry,
   I heard my dusky playmate say:
"Well, now your mother's in the sky,
   And you can always have your way.

"Old Mistress has to stay, you know,
   And read the Bible in her room.
Let's have a party! Will you, though?"
   Ah, well, the whole world was in bloom.

"A party would be fine, and yet—
   There's no one here I can invite."
"Me and the children." "You forget—"
   "Oh, please pretend that I am white."

I said, and think of it with shame,
   "Well, when it's over, you'll go back
There to the cabin all the same,
   And just remember you are black.

"I'll be the lady, for, you see,
   I'm pretty," I serenely said.
"The black folk say that you would be
   If—if your hair just wasn't red."

"I'm pretty anyhow, you know.
   I saw this morning that I was."
"Old Mistress says it's wicked, though,
   To keep on looking in the glass."

Our quarrel ended. At our feet
    A faint green blossoming carpet lay,
By some strange chance, divinely sweet,
    Just shaken on that gracious day.

Into the lonesome parlor we
    Glided, and from the shuddering wall
Bore, in its antique majesty,
    The gilded mirror dim and tall.

And then a woman, painted by—
    By Raphael, for all I care!
From her unhappy place on high,
    Went with us to the outside air.

Next the quaint candlesticks we took.
    Their waxen tapers every one
We lighted, to see how they'd look;—
    A strange sight, surely, in the sun.

Then, with misgiving, we undid
    The secret closet by the stair;—
There, with patrician dust half-hid,
    My ancestors, in china, were.

(Hush, child, this splendid tale is true!)
    Were one of these on earth to-day,
You'd know right well my blood was *blue*;
    You'd own I was not common clay.

There too, long hid from eyes of men,
    A shining sight we two did see.
Oh, there was solid silver then
    In this poor hollow world—ah me!

We spread the carpet. By a great
    Gray tree, we leant the mirror's glare,
And graven spoon and pictured plate
    Were wildly scattered here and there.

And then our table:—Thereon gleamed,
    Adorned with many an apple-bud,

Foam-frosted, dainty things that seemed
   Made of the most delicious mud.

Next came our dressing. As to that,
   I had the fairest shoes! (on each
Were four gold buttons) and a hat,
   And the plume the blushes of the peach.

But there was my dark, elfish guest
   Still standing shabby in her place.
How could I use her to show best
   My own transcendent bloom and grace?

"You'll be my grandmamma," I sighed
   After much thought, somewhat in fear.
She, joyous, to her sisters cried:
   "Call me Old Mistress! Do you hear?"

About that little slave's weird face
   And rude, round form, I fastened all
My grandmamma's most awful lace
   And grandmamma's most sacred shawl.

Then one last sorrow came to me:
   "I didn't think of it before,
But at a party there should be
   One gentleman, I guess, or more."

"There's uncle Sam, you might ask him."
   I looked, and in an ancient chair,
Sat a bronze gray-beard, still and grim,
   On Sundays called Old Brother Blair.

Above a book his brows were bent.
   It was his pride as I had heard,
To study the New Testament
   (In which he could not spell one word).

"Oh, *he* is not a gentleman,"
   I said with my Caucasian scorn.
"He is," replied the African;
   "He is. He's quit a-plowing corn.

"He was so old they set him free.
   He preaches now, you ought to know.
I tell you, we are proud when he
   Eats dinner at our cabin, though."

"Well—ask him!" Lo, he raised his head.
   His voice was shaken and severe:
"Here, sisters in the church," he said.
   "Here—for old Satan's sake, come here!

"That white child's done put on her best
   Silk bonnet. (It looks like a rose.)
And this black little imp is drest
   In all Old Mistress' finest clothes.

"Come, look! They've got the parlor glass,
   And all the silver too. Come, look!
(Such plates as these, here on the grass!)"
   And Uncle Sam shut up his book.

The priestess of the eternal flame
   That warmed our Southern kitchen hearth
Rushed out. The housemaid with her came
   Who swept the cobwebs from the earth.

Then there was one bent to the ground,
   Her hair than lilies not less white,
With a bright handkerchief was crowned:
   Her lovely face was weird as night.

I felt the flush of sudden pride,
   The others soon grew still with awe,
For, standing bravely at my side,
   My mother's nurse and mine, they saw.

"Who blamed my child?" she said. "It makes
   My heart ache when they trouble you.
Here's a whole basket full of cakes,
   And I'll come to the party too.". . .

Tears made of dew were in my eyes.
  These after-tears are made of brine.
No sweeter soul is in the skies
  Than hers, my mother's nurse and mine.

Text from *Wide-Awake*, 1883

A CHILD'S CRY[87]
At Kilcolman Castle, March, 1883

I do not meet him in his place,
(Nor miss him), I, who came to meet
At his own hearth, and face to face,
A poet, world-beloved, whose feet
  Here, walking toward Westminster's gloom,
  Left daisies in their prints to bloom.

I do not miss him, though I look
From windows where he watched, and try,
Ah me, to think about his book!
There lie his hills, and there—the high
  Fair singer, whose divine old song
  Was—well, perhaps almost too long!

Hush! (Do I hear his grave, sweet words
To Walter Raleigh on the stair?)
"You hear some little Irish birds;
They're singing all at once out there,"
  The children said: "We made them fly
  Out of the ivy." No, not I.

It is—I tell you it might break
One's heart to hear it! Listen! Oh,
It is a child's cry, scared awake
By soldiers tramping to and fro;
  The baby, by its father's flight,
  Left—to the fire—at dead of night.

At dead of night it was. And still
(Oh, burning cradle, foolish tears!)
At dead of night——but, doubt who will,

I hear it, through three hundred years,
   And all the music Spenser writ
   Is as a whisper now to it!

Text from Youth's Companion (1883)

THE WATCH OF A SWAN

I read somewhere that a swan snow-white,
In the sun all day, in the moon all night,
Alone by a little grave would sit,
Waiting and watching it.

Up, out of the lake her mate would rise,
And call her down, with his piteous cries,
Into the waters, still, and dim:
With cries she would answer him.

Hardly a shadow would she let pass
Over the baby's cover of grass;
Only the wind might dare to stir
The lily that watched with her.

Do I think that the swan was an angel? Oh,
I think it was only a swan, you know,
That for some sweet reason, winged and wild,
Had the love of a bird for a child.

Text from Youth's Companion (1883)

THE CHRISTENING[88]

In vain we broider cap and cloak, and fold
   The long robe, white and rare;
In vain we serve on dishes of red gold,
   Perhaps, the rich man's fare;
In vain we bid the fabled folk who bring
   All gifts the world holds sweet:
This one, forsooth, shall give the child to sing;
   To move like music this shall charm its feet;
   This help the cheek to blush, the heart to beat.

Unto the christening there shall surely come
   The Uninvited Guest,
The evil mother, weird and wise, with some
   Sad purpose in her breast.
Yea and though every spinning-wheel be stilled
   In all the country round,
Behold, her prophecy must be fulfilled;
   The turret with the spindle will be found,
   And the white hand will reach and take the wound.

Text from *Atlantic Monthly* (1884)

AN IRISH FAIRY STORY

"Good mother, from your wayside hut,
   Wise with your ninety years,
Tell me a fairy story—but
   First wring out all the tears;
For I am hurt beyond the skill
   Of leech, hurt with a knife
That seems, in sooth, but slow to kill—
   Good mother, hurt with life!"

"My lady, sure you are but sad,
   Yet it's a merry day.
I'm not too wrinkled to be glad
   (And you are not yet gray).
It's long, long yet I hope to live,
   For God is good, I'm told,
And life's the best He has to give;
   I'm thankful to be old.

"Yes, God is good, I'm told. You see,
   I cannot read. But, then,
I can believe. He's good to me,
   He is, and good to men.
They say He sends us sorrow, too.
   The world would be too sweet
To leave, if this should not be true."
   ("The world the moth can eat.")

"He keeps my little cabin there
    Safe when the sea-wind blows.
When I was young he let me wear
    Upon my cheek a rose;
And then it was he sent a youth,
    The handsomest, you'd own,
On all the Irish coast. . . . In truth
    It's much I've lived alone,

"My lady, since that long black night
    His fishing-boat went down.
My boy that kept my heart so light
    Had work there in the town:
A lovely boy! Such gold-like hair,
    All curls!" (Her eyes grew dim.)
"Christ keep him. He is quiet there
    With daisies over him."

She hushed and turned to go inside.
    An earthen floor, ah, me!
A heap of straw (the door was wide)
    Was all that I could see.
Yet on the little window, low,
    A bright geranium grew;
"That's for my boy, he loved them so,
    He loved these thrushes too.["]

"Good mother——" "Sure but things go ill
    In our poor country. Yet
He gives me bread and shelter still,
    It's me He'll not forget."
We parted, for the light was low;
    I turned and looked around;
Lord of us all, can heart's-ease grow   *
    In such a plot of ground?

Text from *The Manhattan,* 1884

ON THE PIER AT QUEENSTOWN[89]

So, there were they, all going home,
In their long gloves and heavy rings,
Chattering of Paris, Venice, Rome,
The Alps—and certain other things.
(O Land where they and I were born,
Somehow I loved them, half in scorn.)

And there sat she—her cap of snow
No whiter than her head, her face
(A gracious one, I thought) bent low
In withering hands—there in her place,
While, careless of us all, she wailed
For one who—in the steerage—sailed.

And there, in that poor crowd, he sat:
(The widow's only son was he?)
I knew him, for he wore his hat
Low on his brow, that none might see,
Through the still sadness of his eyes,
His heart shake at his mother's cries.

A young man, tall, with dark, curled hair,
The rose of Ireland in his cheek,
And something stately in his air,
And Southern in his voice. To speak
The truth, he looked more proud than vain
Of blood the Armada brought from Spain.

Rough men with burdens passed her way,
With curse and jest. The ladies smiled
And stared. But still I heard her say,
Through many a sob, "My darling child!"
As from the Old World, fading through
The mist, he floated toward the New!

But when the boat had left the pier,
Where, with her head wrapped in her cloak,
She sat and moved not, I could hear

How, with his last long look, he broke
Into a farewell chant of pain
For this green isle of ruin and rain!

Text from *Irish Garland* (1884)

RACHAEL AT THE LODGE[90]

I know. It is the world-old wail,
  And through the window I can see
The waxen candles, that make pale
  The rose outside. Ah me, ah me!—
That light like this should ever fall
On lovers by yon grey sea-wall!

There lies Spike Island in the stars.
  Ah, many a mother's boy is there,
Loved once like hers, behind the bars:
  Who knows but he—she does not care:
Her dead child was a girl, they say,
The peasant folk who walk this way.

A girl! And, therefore, born to be
  At most, my lady's maid, and wait,
Meanwhile, here barefoot by the sea.
  Oh, sobbing keeper of the gate,
Is it sweet to serve and to be still,
In the high house there on the hill?

Or were it sweet to sail—and sleep
  Full fathom five below the cries
Of the wet gulls, perhaps, or keep
  Awake all night, with tearless eyes
Down in the steerage, but to see
How lone a stranger's land may be?

Can thoughts like these not make it sweet
  To miss her brown head from the sun,
Her singing from the birds', her feet
  From following—"Oh, my little one,

My darling, oh my darling!" she,
The unreasoning woman, moans to me.

The Wise-men's star, out of the East
   Is shining on her baby's bed.
(Comfort her, crucifix and priest!)
   Madonna-face and thorn-stabbed head
Watch from her wall. And yonder lie
The Heavens. And—still that cry, that cry!

Queenstown, 1884

The Independent (1885)

Text from *The Enchanted Castle*, 1893

IN PRIMROSE TIME[91]
(Early Spring in Ireland.)

Here's the lodge-woman in her great cloak coming,
   And her white cap. What joy
Has touched the ash-man? On my word, he's humming
   A boy's song, like a boy!
He quite forgets his cart. His donkey grazes
   Just where it likes the grass.
The red-coat soldier, with his medal, raises
   His hat to all who pass;
And the blue-jacket sailor,—hear him whistle,
   Forgetting Ireland's ills!
Oh, pleasant land—(who thinks of thorn or thistle?)
   Upon your happy hills
The world is out! And, faith, if I mistake not,
   The world is in its prime
(Beating for once, I think, with hearts that ache not)
   In Primrose time.

Against the sea-wall leans the Irish beauty,
   With face and hands in bloom,
Thinking of anything but household duty
   In her thatched cabin's gloom;—
Watching the ships as leisurely as may be,
   Her blue eyes dream for hours.

Hush! There's her mother—coming with the baby
　　In the fair quest of flowers.
And her grandmother!—hear her laugh and chatter,
　　Under her hair frost-white!
Believe me, life can be a merry matter,
　　And common folk polite,
And all the birds of heaven one of a feather,
　　And all their voices rhyme,—
They sing their merry songs, like one, together,
　　In Primrose time.

The magpies fly in pairs (an evil omen
　　It were to see but one);
The snakes—but here, though, since St. Patrick, no man
　　Has seen them in the sun;
The white lamb thinks the black lamb is his brother,
　　And half as good as he;
The rival carmen all love one another,
　　And jest, right cheerily;
The compliments among the milkmen savor
　　Of pale gold blossoming;
And everybody wears the lovely favor
　　Of our sweet Lady Spring.
And though the ribbons in a bright procession
　　Go toward the chapel's chime,—
Good priest, there be but few sins for confession
　　In Primrose time.

How all the children in this isle of faery
　　Whisper and laugh and peep!
(Hush, pretty babblers! Little feet be wary,
　　You'll scare them in their sleep,—
The wee, weird people of the dew, who wither
　　Out of the sun, and lie
Curled in the wet leaves, till the moon comes hither.)—
　　The new-made butterfly
Forgets he was a worm. The ghostly castle,
　　On its lone rock and gray,
Cares not a whit for either lord or vassal
　　Gone on their dusty way,

But listens to the bee, on errands sunny.—
    A thousand years of crime
May all be melted in a drop of honey
    In Primrose time!

Text from *St. Nicholas*, 1885

COURTESY[92]

An earthen floor, a thatch-roof, low and dark;
One little window with geraniums red;
An empty cage, sad for the wingèd lark;
A stranger guest, a sudden fire, and bread.

A blue-eyed peasant-girl; an open door,
And the old sea forever within call,
To whisper fairily of the Atlantic shore
Unto my servant's sister. That was all.

Queenstown, Ireland.   Text from *The Independent*, 1886

PRO PATRIA[93]
(From Exile.)

To stand on some grey coast, uncertain, lonely,
    As some new ghost wrecked on some other world,
This is to love my country—the One only!
    To watch the boats of strange-voiced fishers, whirled
Toward islands with strange names, and then to see—
Nothing that ever was before, ah me!

To watch weird women in great cloaks, for ever
    Crying strange fruits, who will not let you be;
Or shadows in black bridal veils, who never
    On earth may hope their plighted Lord to see;
Or feel some sandal-footed, vision-eyed,
Sad-hooded monk into your wonder glide.

More sad, to wake in some void morning, smitten
    With the sharp shadow-work of dark and dream,

Sick with a sorrow that was never written—
    No, not with heart's blood—and to hear the scream
Of the wan gulls along the hollow foam
Of alien seas—while blue-birds brood at home.

To think, if it be in the dew-dim languor
    Of the new year, of peach and apple-blooms
By the Ohio—and to start in anger,
    Almost, at glimmerings in the faëry glooms
Where the primroses hide and the young thrush
Makes songs about some old-world daisy's blush.

Or, if it be when gorgeous leaves are flying,
    Through all the mighty woods, where I was born,
To sit in immemorial ruin sighing
    To braid the gold hair of the Indian corn,
With my slave-playmates singing, here and there,
Ere they were sold to their new master, Care!

Yes, if it be the time when things should wither
    In our old places—(oh, my heart, my heart!)
Whence comes the evil wind that blows you whither
    It listeth?)—walking in a dream, to start
At this immortal greenness, mocking me
Alike from tower and tomb, from grass and tree:

This is to love my country! Oh, the burning
    Of her quick blood at the poor jest, the sneer,
The insolent calm question still, concerning
    Her dress, her manners! "Are you, then, so queer
At home—we mean no harm—as we have heard?"
This is to love my country, on my word!

Ah, so across the gulf they hiss and mutter:
    "Her sins they are as scarlet?" Had they been,
Whiter than wool they're washed! What of the utter
    Love of her million sons who died for sin
Not hers but theirs—who, from their common grave,
Would rise and die again were she to save!

The Boston Pilot (1886)
Text from *Irish Wildflower*, 1891

AT THE GRAVE OF A SUICIDE[94]

You sat in judgment on him,—you, whose feet
   Were set in pleasant places; you, who found
The Bitter Cup he dared to break still sweet,
   And shut him from your consecrated ground.

Come, if you think the dead man sleeps a whit
   Less soundly in his grave,—come, look, I pray:
A violet has consecrated it.
   Henceforth you need not fear to walk this way.

                              Text from *Atlantic,* 1886

A TRAGEDY OF THE NIGHT[95]
(At an Edinburgh Street-Crossing.)

She started suddenly from the moving mass.
   The wind sprang up and caught her by the shawl,
And held her like a thing that dared not pass—
   Then shook her for an instant. That was all.

Once beautiful and still almost a child!
   She wore her wet hair round her with a grace.
I saw the great eyes staring black and wild
   As the scared lamplight shuddered from her face.

Upon her track there followed such a cry:
   "Will you come back, or no?" was all it said.
"Will you come back, or no?" The Voice wailed by;
   On—to the Pit?—the girlish phantom fled.

Queenstown, Ireland.   Text from *The Independent,* 1887

AN IRISH WILDFLOWER[96]
(A Barefoot Child near——Castle.)

She felt, I think, but as a wild-flower can,
   Through her bright, fluttering rags, the dark, the cold;

Some farthest star, remembering what man
   Forgets, had warmed her little head with gold.

Above her, hollow-eyed, long blind to tears,
   Leaf-cloaked, a skeleton of stone arose. . . .
Oh, castle-shadow of a thousand years!
   Where you have fallen, is this the thing that grows?

Text from Scribner's Monthly, 1887

THE NIGHT COMETH[97]

Fold up the work wherein, hour after hour
   (Only to sew my shroud, then, was I born?),
I've wrought faint pictures, look, of many a flower
     And many a thorn.

Yea, many a flower. Some bridal blossoms; some
   Spell my dead children's names in their sweet way;
One blew in Eden ere the Snake was come;—
     And there are they.

Yea, many a thorn. Behold, my hand hath bled,
   Even in tracing them, so sharp were they,
On this long, shining garment. Did His head
     Wear such, that day?

I can but think me how, before the dew
   Melted in sunrise, and when noon was hot,
Till on the dusk my coffin's shadow grew,
     I rested not.

Working forever on this one white Thing!
   Why, of a truth, it should be fair to see
And sweet to sleep in. Love, you need not bring
     Your lamp to me.

Look you, the graveyard moon ariseth. So,—
   That light is for the blind. Now let me be.
Listen! The graveyard wind. There! I will go.
     It calleth me.

Text from Lippincott's Magazine, 1888

"WHEN SAW WE THEE"[98]

Then shall He answer how He lifted up,
  In the cathedral there, at Lille, to me
The same still mouth that drank the Passion-cup,
  And how I turned away and did not see.

How—oh, that boy's deep eyes and withered arm!—
  In a mad Paris street, one glittering night,
Three times drawn backward by his beauty's charm,
  I gave him—not a farthing for the sight.

How in that shadowy temple at Cologne,
  Through all the mighty music, I did wring
The agony of his last mortal moan
  From that blind soul I gave not anything.

And how at Bruges, at a beggar's breast,
  There by the windmill where the leaves whirled so,
I saw Him nursing, passed Him with the rest,
  Followed by His starved mother's stare of woe.

But, my Lord Christ, Thou knowest I had not much,
  And had to keep that which I had for grace
To look, forsooth, where some dead painter's touch
  Had left Thy thorn-wound or thy mother's face.

Therefore, O my Lord Christ, I pray of Thee
  That of Thy great compassion Thou wilt save,
Laid up from moth and rust, somewhere, for me,
  High in the heavens—the coins I never gave.

Text from Belford's Magazine, 1888

A NIGHT-SCENE FROM THE ROCK OF CASHEL, IRELAND[99]

And this was, then, their Cashel of the Kings,
  As babbling legends fondly call it; oh,
The Cashel now of—certain other things;
  Come, look by this blurred moon, if you would know.

From darkness such as hides the happier dead,
  On the wet earth-floor grows a ghastly flame;
A woman's wasted arm, a child's gold head,
  Shrink back into the wind-stirred straw for shame.

Through the half-door, down from the awful Rock,
  The death chill from some open grave creeps in—
The skeleton's fixed laugh is seen to mock
  The cry for bread below. Oh, shame and sin!

Warm only with the fire of its starved eyes,
  In one grim corner, crouches a black cat.
. . . Night moans itself away. The sun must rise.
  As it has risen—spite of this or that. . . .

And look! In meadows beautiful, knee-deep
  In bloom for many a shining mile around,
The undying grass is white with lambs and sheep
  And wandering cattle make a pleasant sound.

Cork (Queenstown), Ireland.   Text from *The Independent*, 1889

THE DANCE OF THE DAISIES[100]

So, my pretty flower-folk, you
Are in a mighty flutter;
All your nurse, the wind, can do,
Is to scold and mutter.

"We intend to have a ball
(That's why we are fretting).
And our neighbor-flowers have all
Fallen to regretting.

"Many a butterfly we send
Far across the clover.
(There'll be wings enough to mend
When the trouble's over.)

"Many a butterfly comes home
Torn with thorns and blighted,

Just to say they can not come,—
They whom we've invited.

"Yes, the roses and the rest
Of the high-born beauties
Are 'engaged,' of course, and pressed
With their stately duties.

"They're at garden-parties seen;
They're at court presented:
They look prettier than the Queen!
(Strange that's not resented.)

"'Peasant-flowers' they call us—we
Whose high lineage you know—
We, the ox-eyed children (see!)
Of Olympian Juno."

(Here the daisies all *made* eyes!
And they looked most splendid.
As they thought about the skies,
Whence they were descended.)

"In our saintly island (hush!)
Never crawls a viper,
Ho, there, Brown-coat! that's the thrush:
He will be the piper.

"In this Irish island, oh,
We will stand together.
Let the loyal roses go;—
We don't care a feather.

"Strike up, thrush, and play as though
All the stars were dancing.
So they are! And—here we go—
Is n't this entrancing?"

Swaying, mist-white, to and fro,
Airily they chatter,
For a daisy-dance, you know,
Is a pleasant matter.

Text from *St. Nicholas*, 1889

AN IDYL OF THE WAYSIDE IN IRELAND[101]
Near Clonmel Parish Churchyard, County Cork, 188—

Clonmel's sad church, unroofed, alone,
As sleepy as its dead,
Shivered through every leaf and stone—
For pity?—overhead.

They waited by the graveyard wall.
(Marsh-lilies down below
Were beautiful and strong and tall,
With room enough to grow.)

God gave to them—the wayside dust.
A woman old in youth
Leant on her empty hands.—We trust
He is the Way, the Truth.

A man, whose sins or woes had cut
Deeper than years can reach,
Wandered among the hedges, but
Showed us no sign of speech.

He broke dead thistles, bit by bit,
And stalks of leafless brier,
To make his brood, as it was fit,
A weird and thorny fire.

The broken cart, themselves had drawn
Along their aimless way,
Was in their midst, and, heaped thereon,
Their poor home-treasures lay.

That day their cabin's straw-roof, sweet
With its wild-waving bloom,
Had fallen, and they had turned their feet
From its one wretched room.

Yet where the fault? The landlord's? Mark,
He, too, has wrongs. Ah me,
These things lie deeper in the dark
Than eye of man may see!

FIGURE 14. *"The Distress in Ireland—Exterior of a Cabin"*

And there were children to light up
This picture strange and grim.
One, with a dimple for a cup,
Was catching moon-rays dim.

One, with a shadowy gipsy grace,
Danced in the dust, and one
Whirled a wild ball. One had a face
Christ would have wept upon.

One on its little head had quite
Enough of gold to buy
Bread, shelter,—yea, and raiment white
As souls wear in the sky.

Yet all were hungry, all disguised
In rags, all chilled with dew. . . .
Go, ask of Nature, oh, despised
Of men, to pity you!

Text from *Child's-World Ballads*, 1895

IN THE ROUND TOWER AT CLOYNE[102]
(C. L. P., OB. July 18, 1884.)

They shivered lest the child should fall;
   He did not heed a whit.
They knew it were as well to call
   To those who builded it.

"I want to climb it any way,
   And find out what is there!
There may be things—you know there may—
   Lost, in the dark somewhere."

He made a ladder of their fears
   For his light, eager feet;
It never, in its thousand years,
   Held anything so sweet.

The blue eyes peeped through dust and doubt,
   The small hands shook the Past;

"He'll find the Round Tower's secret out,"
   They, laughing, said at last.

The enchanted ivy, that had grown,
   As usual, in a night
Out of a legend, round the stone,
   He parted left and right.

And what the little climber heard
   And saw there, say who will,
Where Time sits brooding like a bird
   In that gray nest and still.

... About the Round Tower tears may fall;
   He does not heed a whit.
They know it were as well to call
   To those who builded it.

Text from *The Enchanted Castle*, 1893

A CHILD IN THE PARK[103]
St. Stephen's Green, Dublin, July, 1890.

You come to me with winged feet,
   Oh, sweet—too sweet!
"Mamma," you say; then, rosily shy,
   Away you fly. . . .

I send the wind upon his track
   To call him back.
I follow him with wild eyes wet;—
   Can he forget?

I was his mother years ago.
   Through bloom and snow
That glimmering head upon my breast
   Was warmed to rest.

Silk tassels blew from Indian corn
   Where he was born.
The Atlantic fireflies led him through
   The dusk and dew.

The slave's light songs had left the south;
    But that young mouth
Mocked them, till his dark nurse would weep
    Herself to sleep.

Those hands, once folded cold, so cold,
    With flowers to hold.
Drop bread into this old-world lake
    For swans to take.

To this green island, ruin-grey,
    He comes to play.
He leaves his moss-grown rest so deep,
    This tryst to keep. . . .

Oh, men who pass us in the dew,
    What if you knew!
With shaken heart and shroud-pale face
    You'd fly the place. . . .

My child, the world is sweet; but oh,
    We two must go—
We are not of it, Golden-head!
    We both are dead.

Text from *Irish Monthly,* 1891

THE COMING-BACK OF THE DEAD[104]

No, not the long-prest rose, the empty ring,
    The folded hand's cold glove,
The lonesome toy, or gold shorn hair can bring
    Your dead to you, O love!

They are not slaves to rise before the charms
    With which we could compel
Them to the beating breast, the yearning arms—
    I know their moods too well.

They come, they come! But never when you call.
    In their own time they start:

At hush of night when dreams begin to fall
  Upon the half-shut heart—

Look not for them. They do not love the dark,
  Nor travel by moonlight.
They keep to their own country till the lark
  Sings herself out of sight.

Then all at once they laugh into your face,
  Or blind you with a kiss,
Or catch you in a sudden glad embrace—
  My boy, it's you!—like this.

Text from *Irish Monthly,* 1891

A BID FOR THE CROWN JEWELS[105]
(An Incident at the Tower of London.)

Before the crown of England, he
  Stood, whistling low, with blue-eyed scorn.
(Oh, well,—they don't wear crowns, you see,
  There in the land where he was born!)

Then every jewel flashed its best;—
  Full in his face their fire was thrown;
And still the spirit of the West,
  Through all that glitter, held its own.

He turned his back on them, and shut
  The door behind him, whispering low:
"They are not worth a copper—but
  I wonder if they'd sell them, though.

"Ask those old fellows if they would,
  And then I'll buy some. Don't forget:
You know they'd like to, if they could;
  And, see—I have a shilling yet!"

. . . Years after, in a desolate hour,
  At dusk, his mother passed the place,
And all the grim and evil Tower
  Was flushed and lighted with his face.

Glad of its dimpled New-World guest
    The old-time prison seemed to be;
He was become—one of the rest!
    And loved by all the ghosts was he!

Tall regal women bent to kiss
    "That sweetest mouth on earth," they said.
Dark kings would ask him that or this;
    And Raleigh's hand was on his head.

Once, hearing sudden laughter there,
    She looked—the stars were sad and dim:—
The little Princes on their stair
    Were playing hide-and-seek with him!

Wide-Awake (1891)
Text from *Child's-World Ballads,* 1895

"THERE SHALL BE NO SEA THERE"[106]

Some sweetest mouth on earth, bitter with brine,
    That would not kiss you back, you may have kissed.
Counting your treasures by your night-lamp's shine,
    Some head that was your gold you may have missed.

Some head that glimmers down the unmeasured wave
    And makes an utter darkness where it was,
. Or, flung back in derision, lights some grave,—
    Some sudden grave cut sharp into the grass.

If so—There shall be no sea there . . . . And yet
    Where is the soul that would not take the sea
Out of the world with it? What wild regret
    In God's high inland country there must be!

Never to lift faint eyes in love with sleep
    Across the spiritual dawn and see
Some lonesome water-bird standing dream-deep
    In mist and tide. How bitter it would be!

Never to watch the dead come sailing through
    Sunset or stars, or dew of dusk or morn,

With flowers shut in their folded hands, that grew
   Down there in that green world where I was born. . . .

There shall be no sea there. . . . What shall we do?
   Shall we not gather shells, then, any more,
Or write our—names, in sand, as here, we two
   Who watch the moon set on this island shore?

Text from Irish Monthly, 1892

MY OTHER GODS

Into my dream, and bearing a still light,
   Not like the sun nor moon nor any fire,
Among my statues, One has come to smite.
   . . . Outside the frost was bitter on the briar.

Wide was my dream. One lay deep in dead grass,
   In some forgotten war, struck by a shell,
Hid in forlornest tropic woods one was
   And, over him, a bird tolled like a bell.

One only was left standing. Life was sweet
   About his mouth and in his eyes—but they
Had wandered from me. It may be, his feet,
   Even as the Preacher told me, were of clay.

The jealous God laid his still hands on this:
   A great and an exceeding bitter cry
Went up. I drained my heart out in one kiss.
   And turned and fell upon my face to die.

. . . Then, from my dream I broke, and on the stair
   I called you, and beside the moon-stilled sea
And in the shivering garden—everywhere,
   But, after that—you never answered me.

Cork, Ireland.
Text from The Independent, 1893

HIS ARGUMENT

"But if a fellow in the castle there
  Keeps doing nothing for a thousand years,
And then has—everything! (That isn't fair,
  But it's—what has to be. The milk-boy hears
The talk they have about it everywhere.)

"Then if the man there in the hut, you know,
  With water you could swim in on the floor,
(And it's the ground,—the place is pretty, though,
  With gold flowers on the roof and half a door!)
Works,—and can get no work and nothing more:

"What I will do is—nothing! Don't you see?
  Then I'll have everything, my whole life through.
But if I work, why I might always be
  Living in huts with gold flowers on them, too—
And half a door. And that won't do for me."

Text from The Enchanted Castle, 1893

A REPROACH[107]
(Addressed to Ireland.)

Beautiful, cruel Mother, you who sit
  Singing with voice of linnet, lark, and thrush,
Among the sorrows born of you! Is it
  Nothing to you, your children's crying? Hush.

Can rose-leaves cure the heart-ache, think you, Sweet?
  Are starving mouths with dews and perfumes fed,
That thus, with your wild brood about your feet,
  You give them blossoms when they wail for bread?

Text from The Enchanted Castle, 1893 ·

HEREDITY[108]

(On Seeing a Donkey Looking through a Ruined Castle-Window, in Ireland.)

Are name and fame, then, briefer than the dew? . . .
    Lord-lacquey in the livery of the king!
His sometime minister of justice, you
    Who weighed the world and—took what it would bring!

See (from oblivion),—banners rent away,
    Graveyard escutcheons wasted from the grass;
And yet, take comfort. Still, as in your day,
    My lord, your castle-window frames—an ass.

Text from *Child's-World Ballads,* 1895

A SWALLOW IN THE HALL OF MIRRORS[109]
At Versailles

About your palace, shadowy one, you flit,
    Dressed in dark plumes.
And, ah! your beauty—with the thought of it
    Each mirror blooms!

Lo, with a spirit's grace, you turn aside
    That small head, where
The crown of France, ashamed, was wont to hide
    In brighter hair.

I know. Remembrance keeps the dead awake
    With its sweet stings.
And drives the heart back for the bitter sake
    Of this world's things.

The children laugh, and cry: "A swallow!" Yet
    The voice I heard,
The face I saw! Ah, Marie Antoinette!—
    Ah, home-sick bird!

Text from *Child's-World Ballads,* 1895

A PRAYER TO OSIRIS[110]
(On a Sarcophagus at Edinburgh.)

"Guide thou my barque." So run the piteous words—
    How sad with faith!—upon this coffin-stone,
With the still wings of Egypt's mystic birds
    And strange bright creeping creatures overgrown.
Lord of a kingdom's souls—and flocks and herds!
    You started on the lonely voyage alone!

Would no dusk daughter of your languorous land,
    No palm-tree's sister with the desert's grace,
Leave for your sake her warm world's sun and sand
    And take beside you just a woman's place?
Or did you shake away the clinging hand
    And shut your blind eyes on the wistful face?

You thought to land—somewhere, in golden dew,
    Where the white souls of Nile's dead lilies float. . . .
What dark whim of your pilot-god drove you,
    O most forlorn! spite of the prayer you wrote,
To this grey isle of rock and heath, whereto
    The Scotch mist clings, dumb in your dead-man's boat?

Text from Child's-World Ballads, 1895

A SEA-GULL WOUNDED[111]

Ah, foam-born, beautiful! So looked, I know,
    The Mother of Love, when her caressing arm
Felt the stung blood stain its immortal snow,
    After the fight there on the plain. . . . What charm,
Of all the blind Greek gave to her, had she
That you have not—her sister of the sea?

And this young Diomed, who gave the wound
  With his first gun, if truth the bitter need
Be told (man's race is pitiless), looks round—
  His eye is used to blood—and sees you bleed.
Fly to Olympus, with your broken wing,
And Jove will laugh at you, fair, hapless thing!

Text from Child's-World Ballads, 1895

A WOMAN'S LAST WORD[112]

Promise me nothing. Men are mortal. I
  Loose from your heart my hand.
(The grave is deeper than the heavens are high.)
  My house—of Love—was builded on the sand.

Promise me nothing. That the heart will rain
  On eyes whose tears are done
And lips that will not kiss you back again
  For ever any more, I know, for one.

Promise me nothing. You but said "Till death,"
  Even with my wedding-ring.
Promise me nothing, lest with my last breath
  I make you promise—only everything!

Promise me nothing. One day you will buy
  Another ring, you know.
Then, if the dead walk in their sleep, must I
  Come, shivering, back to say—"I told you so"?

Text from Child's-World Ballads, 1895

CONFESSION

"I love no man alive," I said, "but you,"
Upon my wedding day. Well,—that was true.
(But in the midnight moon, the midnight rain,
A mist of dead men's faces blurs the pane.)

Text from Child's-World Ballads, 1895

ONE JEALOUS OF A ROSE

Ah, my rose rival, beautiful in May!
   I grant that I was withered then: and you,
Who mocked me with your beauty for a day—
   So, you are withered too?

You blew the poignant sweetness of your breath
   Into my face—you stabbed me with that thorn;
Ah me, you made me heart-sick unto death!
   Now, who is most forlorn?

You quite forgot the passion of the sun,
   The singing of the young wind of the West,
And many a tree-born lover, for the one
   Who wore you in his breast.

And now you are so old. . . . Did he not bring
   You, once in Enna, from some dew-dim dell,
To Proserpine (to soothe her lord, the King),
   Beside the gate of Hell?

Text from *Child's-World Ballads,* 1895

HEREDITY IN DEATH[113]

If I might choose, would I say just 'Good-night,'
   And slip from sleep to—Sleep, and let the sea
With all its waves and wild birds, wet and white,
   At dawn, keep calling me?

No, not in exile, not in exile, no.
   Leave my last tear—weep where I may the rest—
To fall at least where my own violets blow
   On my own country's breast.

There in his fields, a hundred years ago,
   One loved by many, by his slaves the best,
Who left his blood in my own heart to flow,
   Was found in awful rest.

They missed him. When the terror of the storm
   Had left them with its rainbow overhead,
They found him in the sun—that will not warm,
   For all our cries, the dead.

Bean-blossoms in the silk hair of the corn
   Were wet around him. The light songs of men
Who called him Master, fondly, died forlorn
   Among his reapers then.

O sacred head, crowned with your crown of fire,
   By God's own hand, in one great instant's space!
O happy eyes, before the light could tire,
   You saw Him face to face!

If I might choose, the wraith of that same flash
   Should find me somewhere in the summer dark:
When morning came I would not lift a lash,
   But—show the lightning's mark!

Text from Child's-World Ballads, 1895

A MISTAKE IN THE BIRD-MARKET[114]

A Persian in the market-place
   Longed for, and so took home, a wren.
Yes, his was but a common case;
   Such always are the ways of men!

Once his, the brown bird pleased him not;
   Almost he wished it would take wing.
He loosed the cage-door, and forgot
   The dark, unsinging, lonely thing.

Night came, and touched with wind and dew
   (Alone there in the dim moonshine)
A rose that at the window grew—
   And oh, that sudden song divine!

His children started from their sleep,
   Their Orient eyes with rapture lit;

Their pale young mother hid to weep;
   Their father did not care a whit.

He only heard the impassioned wail
   From that small prison overhead.
"My wren is but a nightingale!
   I'll wring its noisy throat!" he said.

Text from *Century,* 1898

HEART'S-EASE OVER HENRY HEINE[115]
(In Montmartre Cemetery at Paris.)

Here, with your leaf or two of literal laurel,
   (That rustles somewhat dryly, I suppose,)
One finds you silenced by the usual quarrel;
   And—oh, the irony of it!—a rose
   Out of your bosom, Henry Heine, grows.

If one may only pray for you, my brother,
   (Heart of the dead, yours was a ghastly wrong!)
Christ rest you in this grave, who in that other,
   In Paris there, awake in death so long,
   Shouted the world back your derisive song.

Well, up here in the sun, to-day, with beauty
   So dark of promise it might break her glass,
I saw a street child, one whose piteous duty
   To offer heart's-ease to the world it was—
   And, for your sake, I could not let her pass.

So, here is heart's-ease for you, bitter lover,
   O German poet in the German Land
Well known! and with it tears enough to cover
   The dust of all your woes—you understand?
   Reach me, in taking it, that hollow hand.

Heart's-ease, and for a heart of dust and ashes?
  Heart's-ease, and does the dead man care a whit? . . .
Into the empty eyes the old scorn flashes:
  About the mocking mouth the slow smiles flit:
  The still voice laughs, "Here I've too much of it!"

Text from Harper's New Monthly Magazine, 1899

THE COMING OF EVE[116]
And What Came of It

God gave the world to Man in the Beginning.
  Alone in Eden there and lord of all,
He mused: "There may be one thing worth the winning.
  (All else is mine.) When will that Apple fall?

"I weary of the Garden. Here are roses
  That bloom and die not. Oh, that they would die!
Without one thorn each bud its blush uncloses.
  (Perhaps the thorns will sharpen by and by!)

"In all this world of loveliness, I find not
  One flower whose face seems fair at all to see.
I might endure—even Paradise, and mind not,
  Were Some One here to wear a rose for me.

"Still, yonder fruit must mock me with its glitter!
  (The Woman—were there one!—might rob the Tree!)
It may be that the taste within is bitter,
  And this eternal sweetness tortures me."

He yawned himself to sleep. And then, (oh wonder!
  Oh beauty that made flower and star look dim!)
He woke, and lo! the Woman waited under
  The Tree—whereon the Apple grew—for him.

"What would my lord?" the Vision sighed. "Command me.
  (Heaven for his pleasure made me—from his side—
At least, not for my own!)" "You understand me?—
  I want yon Apple, Fairest!" he replied. . . .

Then, lo! the seraph's sword of fire above them!—
    And lo! all Eden blackened at their feet!
With none on earth and none in Heaven to love them,
    Save one another, life at once grew sweet! . . .

God gave the world to Man. With eyes entreating,
    The Woman said: "Hast Thou no gift for me?"
"Yea, Woman! In thy breast a Heart is beating!"
    The Father spake. "That is my gift to thee!" . . .

Eve—passing—left this gift to all her daughters.
    Is Man a wanderer from his home apart?
Do great winds hurl him over troubled waters?
    Faints he on sand? She follows with her Heart!

He goeth forth to battle and is wounded.
    She binds the wounds he dies from—or has made!
He sounds the seas. She sounds the deeps unsounded—
    The darker deeps from which he shrinks afraid!

She watches by the cradle, and so catches
    The first light of the soul, God's new-born star!
She watches by the grave—alone, she watches
    (Others forget) where death and silence are.

She helps her race as maid, as wife, as mother—
    With grace, with love, with sweetness, with her Heart! . . .
Yet women, sisters, helping one another,
    Most surely ye shall choose the better part.

She has her little wrongs. To bear or mend them
    Is what she—must! God gave the world to Man.
To her He gave—her troubles! He will end them!
    But, meanwhile, let her help Him as she can!

Date of Composition, 1900.
Text from *Hesperian Tree* 2, 1903

A SHADOWY THIRD

I
Heart and Eyes
(*In His Jealous Mood.*)

"Why, so—I cannot help it, if my eyes
Must wander and alight like butterflies
To rest, one wavering instant, here or there.
One only—of the many—need you care?

"Hearts have no wings wherewith to fly away.
My heart but asks beside your hearth to stay
Forever and forever. Shall it, then?
Tell me, most loved, most pitiless of men!"

II
Another Woman's Eyes[117]
(*In Her Jealous Mood.*)

"Beautiful eyes, indeed, beautiful eyes!
    (He must be growing blind to think them fine!)—
If on your wedding-day you had been wise,
    They might have—shed the tears you've wrung from mine.

["]I only wish they had. (But no, no, no.
    I'd rather weep whole seas of bitterest brine
Than let those beautiful eyes—he calls them so—
    Have one sweet tear that he has wrung from mine.")

Text from Hesperian Tree 2, 1903

A WOMAN'S "NO"[118]

HE: "'No', then?"
    SHE: "There is this comfort in it:
    I shall not see you growing old
And stout. Men do. But wait a minute:
    I'd like to say . . . the night is cold."

HE: "Why 'No?'"
    SHE: "The butterfly, in flying,
  Still wears a glory on his wing.
But, catch him—if it's worth the trying—
  And he is quite another thing."

HE: "Still, "No?'"
    SHE: "Have I not heard my mother
  Sobbing her heart out at his ways,
Because—my father, and no other,
  Was charming in his time, she says?

"It's 'No.' Because—the words of honey,
  Wherewith a lover gives a rose,
Are wormwood when one asks for money
  After one's married, I suppose.

(*Aside:* "It can't be that he means to leave me.)
  Just see the lightning, hear the rain.
You will be wet, and that would—grieve me."
    H[E]: "Good-night—and I must catch my train."

Text from *Hesperian Tree 2,* 1903

THE BROKEN WEDDING RING

Good Master Goldsmith, here is work for you.
  Look at my ring, my ring, my wedding-ring.
Broken, all broken! See. What shall I do?
  Don't mind the cost. I'll pay you—everything.

He said, "Till death." But I—I thought to rise
  With it upon my hand when death was done,—
To shine with it into God's very eyes,
  Where sun or moon or other light is none.

Not mend it, Master Goldsmith? But you must!
  How dare you trifle with so bright a thing!
All else is vanity, all else is dust,
  All—but my ring, my ring, my wedding-ring!

Text from *Midland Monthly,* 1907

AT THE PLAYHOUSE[119]
(With a Child.)

That is the king's son. He is sad
    Because—the king is dead, you see.
Why, some do think he is gone mad,
    And some that he pretends to be.

"What does he say?" What does he say?
    You ask it in a world where each
Poor man you meet, in some poor way,
    Knows—my Lord Hamlet's famous speech.

Your father does not know it, though?—
    He could not say a single word?
One says that to one's self, you know.
    There are more things—than you have heard.

And must you learn it? Yes, you must.—
    By heart, indeed. Nothing can save
You from it—but a little dust,
    And rose-leaves for a child's sweet grave.

You'd like a real ghost the best?
    (Be to the mock one reconciled.)
You're tired? *"He does not know the rest?"*
    Because—the rest is silence, child!

Text from *Midland Monthly,* 1907

A LEGEND OF THE DAFFODILS[120]
A Poem for the Easter-Tide

Most-joyous things, so wide awake,
    With all your golden heads uncurled!
Like laughter—after death—you break
    Out of the lonely under-world.

And Proserpine comes back with you,
    Remembering Enna's Vales, a-light
With all your bloom, when sweet with dew
    She clasped you in her apron white.

"Is it the flower-time of the year?"
   Down in the dark, she sighs, and still
From Hades and its Lord, in fear,
   Earth-sick, she wanders up, at will.

(Meantime, the dark god, on his throne,
   There in his kingdom of the dead,
Can wait upon himself, alone—
   So say the legends I have read.)

Sad, sad, when it is time to go
   Her yearning arms she softly fills
And warms all their immortal snow
   With daffodils—and daffodils!

Back to the world of shadows, through
   The bird-songs and the dawn, she flies. . . .
"I brought these daffodils for you,
   Because—I love you so!" she sighs.

"Where have you been?" he storms. . . .
   Ah, well, As any mortal woman might,
She crowns—and cheats!—the Lord of Hell
   With earthly flowers of living light!

Ah, pagan soul of mine, that yet
   Must haunt dead worlds of myth and dream,
So poignant with divine regret
   For shadow-gods!—how blind you seem!

Lo! Easter-morning lights the skies!
   Out of her sleep of dark and rain,
This is the time for Christ to rise
   From Spring's new-wakened world, again,

All-glorious from His yearly birth!
   Go meet Him on the sky-kissed hills
And crown the Lord of Heaven and Earth
   With daffodils—with daffodils!

Text from *Midland Monthly*, 1907

A NEW THANKSGIVING¹²¹

For war, plague, pestilence, flood, famine, fire,
  For Christ discrowned, for false gods set on high;
For fools, whose hands must have their hearts' desire,
  We thank Thee—in the darkness—and so die.

For shipwreck: Oh, the sob of strangling seas!—
  No matter. For the snake that charms the dove;
And (is it not the bitterest of all these?)
  We thank Thee—in our blind faith—even for Love.

For breaking hearts; for all that breaks the heart;
  For Death, the one thing after all the rest,
We thank Thee, O our Father! Thou who art,
  And wast, and shalt be—knowing these are best.

Text from *The Independent*, 1910

A BIRD WITHOUT A MATE

I shut my eyes on all things fair to see,
I shut my eyes on all things else, ah me!

But first I throw my window wide, and so,
"Good-night, my Soul—my poor sad Soul, now go."

I whisper with a voice ear hath not heard;
Then into space I loose the Mateless Bird:

The Mateless Bird, the Bird forlorn, forlorn,
That will not build a nest here in the thorn;

That will not warm a brood nor rest one night
In any moon, on any snow-stilled height. . . .

It takes the wind and flies. It leaves me deep
In all the warm forgetfulness of sleep

Among what ashes of spent worlds to flit,
Among what fire-scarred angels of the Pit;

Into what shroud-pale kingdoms of the dead
Its shadow follows it—I have not said.

I only know—the night is sweet and long—
That in the leaves, at dawn, Christ hears a song:

A song that makes Him homesick for the earth,
His baby-playthings, His young mother's hearth:

A song that makes Him thirst, by streams divine,
To drink once more the wells of Palestine.

I listen with Him; then reach out and take
My Soul into my breast again, and wake. . . .

Its wings are wet and heavy. Can it be
With rain, or with the salt-mists of the sea?

The scents of palms and lilies, such as grow
In God's own Garden, cling to them, I know.

I long to breathe them with this mortal breath;
I long, and dare not breathe them—they are death. . . .

My Soul—my poor sad Soul—one night, when I
Shut my blind eyes to sleep, and let you fly,

I shall not wake again to take you through
My window—shall I? Then, what will you do?

My Soul—my poor sad Soul—if I could know!
My Soul, my poor sad Soul—where will you go?

North Bend, Ohio   Text from *The Independent*, 1911

A DAFFODIL[122]

Look!—all the vales of all the world are bright
    With you, as that of Enna was of old!
One sees the flutter of her apron light,
    All overflowing with your dew-dim gold!

Oh, shining memory of Persephone!
    Loosed from the dark of Dis, in this her time,
The sadder for its sweetness, does not she
    Out of her under-realm, rejoicing, climb?

155

And should the Shadow-King, in anger, miss
   His fair, young, wandering Queen, as well he might,
Then let her take the lord of Hades this—
   For his dark crown—this flower of living light!

Text from The Independent, 1911

Piatt's Juvenilia (1857–61)

"THE INDIAN'S INQUIRY"

"It is a land of love and light,
A land of glory soft yet bright,
   And flowers forever fair—
For gold and gems I'll give thee these!
And music murmuring on the breze"—
   "Are any Spaniards there?"

"The rich light's wavy quiverings
Fall over birds whose restless wings
   Shed rose-hues on the air;
Their sweet songs thrill the spirit's dreams,
And fadeless woods and cold, clear streams"—
   "Are any Spaniards there?"

"Mountains with summits dim and high
Are seen against the far blue sky,
   And forests sweet and rare
Wave on their sides forever green,
And wandering deer are always seen"—
   "Are any Spaniards there?"

"The maiden that the hunter loves,
Close by his side all changeless roves,
   His fondest thoughts to share,
No sound of words they ever need,
In dark eyes all the heart they read"—
   "Are any Spaniards there?"

"Yes! in those lovely vales of rest,
Our brothers are forever blest,
   Far from the storms of care,
In scenes of splendid light enshrined,
With heaven around, heaven in the mind—
   Yes—there are Spaniards there!"

"A curse then on your land of light!
I'd rather dwell where clouds of night
    Eternal blackness wear,
Mid wailing winds and icy rain,
Than share a heaven—I say again,
    A heaven—with Spaniards there!"

Louisville Journal
July 20, 1857

THE MEMORIALS

"Starlight and sunrise—very sweet
    The olden airs come up again;
And yet the joy that used to beat
    Its golden plumes to each soft strain
    Is sunken in a gulf of pain.
Starlight and music still," she said,
And sadly bowed her aching head.
"Starlight and music still—but oh,
I miss the charm of long ago.
'Tis true, the night is fair as then,
    Ay, fair as even night can be;
And never did the eyes of men
    See lovelier things than now I see;
For, white clouds fly across the moon,
    Like *shadows* of the angel's wings;
And far and near the wind's low tune
    Seems what a blessed spirit sings
    When first 'tis free from fated things,
To dive among the purple spaces
    With soul's delicious dreaminesses,
And float into the vailed places
    Of Glory, heaven and hell confesses.

"What made the charm of long ago?
    The heliotropes were sweet, I know;
And some late roses round us there
    Seemed crimson cradles rocked in air;
Where moonbeams lay in silence deep,
    Like baby-fairies gone to sleep.
Yet these, I think, have little part
    In the arcana of my heart.

Ah, midnight hair of heavy sweeping,
    And short, curved lip and fair young brow,
And voice of song, whose ghost is keeping
    An echo in my bosom now;
And dark-blue eyes, and languid lashes
    That drooped with dreams from lids of snow,
Or rose with passion's fiery flashes—
    Ye made the charm of long ago.

"Once, when a buried hope was young,
    I saw a comet, up among
The cloud-world's awful wildernesses,
    With star-pearls in its golden tresses.
Those stars themselves were wondrous bright,
    If they had only burned elsewhere,
But pale in the supernal light
    Of that fierce comet's flashing hair.
And thus it was with thee. Thy face
Had many a rare and radiant grace,
Which, seen alone, had looked divine,
But in thy soul's transcendent shine,
Even they wore but the glow which clings
Around creation's dimmer things.

"Another charm of long ago
    Was from a darker eye than thine,
    Which had as wild a spell for mine,
And lip as sweet, and voice as low—
Ah, still that voice floats thro' my dreams,
And still its: '*Hear me, Norma!*' seems
To keep the old, half-murmurous sigh,
Which might have won it a reply.

"One severed curl—some faded flowers,
And memories of the vanished hours,
Are all that's linked with him or thee
Which now remains on earth for me.
The curl has shaded his dusk brow,
    The flowers have touched thy snowy hand
The visions of the hours come now,
    Like spectres from a fearful land.
I looked upon the curl to-day,
Whose raven coils before me lay,

And heard these words beside me there:
'His heart is blacker than his hair.'
Well—I do not know * * But—I'll keep the curl—
For—I prized it much—when a dreaming girl.
And they've said of *thee* * * But—I'll keep the flowers,
Tho' they grew in this poisoned world of ours.

"Starlight and music. Hush the strain;
The dead will not come back again
To wake the voice of their still guitars—
So, hush the strain, and shade the stars,
With the closed blinds from my weary sight,
For I cannot bear their haunted light,
Since the dead will not come back again;
   Though they are not held by the grave from me,
Tho' they walk the world and share its pain,
   Tho' their lips are red, and their eyes can see,
Yes, the breathing changed are doubly dead,
   But curls and flowers from the long ago
Are enchanted things, whose spells are shed
   Like the still, white leaves from the Flower of Snow.
Touch them—and the glitter of holy wings
   Fills the heart as thickly as angels fill
The air round a pictured God. And springs
   Gush over life's deserts with musical thrill,
Till we feel there is naught has such blessed powers
As our severed curls and our faded flowers."

The New York Ledger
June 30, 1860

"IF FREEDOM'S MIRACLE SHOULD FAIL"

They are alive, they are awake,
   Mount Vernon's, Ashland's, Marshfield's best!
The billows of our madness break
   Against the glory of their Rest.

Thronged by an army still and pale
   Who were the truest soldiers all
Whether they wore the sword and mail
   For battle-ground or Senate-hall.

They feel the curse, whose fiery breath
    Fills all the land, they fell and see,
For love of country, touched by death,
    Wakes grandest Immortality.

They wear the memory of their scars,
    They stand in awful calms of light,
Surrounded by a guard of stars,
    And warn us from the middle night.

They warn us, they whose souls were souls,
    Whose greatness God and man could trust;
Who saw the Right's sublimest goals
    Even while their eyes were vailed with dust.

"We left our flag of stars to *Time*—
    Ha! traitors, it is now half buried,
And *ye* would blast with nameless crime
    The wonder of the West and world.

"Before a hundred years of psalms,
    Of triumph psalms were chanted by
The armies of your pines and palms
    For a victorious Liberty—

"And while a blessing sunned the land,
    From where the South's flame-roses blow
Upon its fairest summer strand,
    To the gray North's extremest snow—

"And while the world was haloed by
    The glitter of your nation-fame,
Traitors and traitors! ye could try
    To sink your souls in gulfs of shame.

"Ye dare to dream of wars—but know
    Enough of blood blushed on the land
When barefoot armies stained the snow,
    To gain the glory ye would brand.

"If more ye claim, but tear apart
    The Union-bands we clasped in trust,
And crimson drops again will start
    From wounds ye buried with our dust.

"North—South—wash out your hatred-stains,
　Ere Hope's God-lifted face is pale,
For tyrants laugh and forge new chains
　If Freedom's miracle should fail."

The winds on every hallowed spot
　Take up the warning with a wail,
And ask the Powers of Darkness *what*
　"*If Freedom's miracle should fail!*"

Ingrates or madmen—ye who keep
　A hideous Fear loose in the land
Does not the question strike your sleep?
　Do ye not hear and understand?

Tho' I have sung a powerless rhyme
　Here in a land where Hope *is* pale,
God help the [land?] the world, and time
　[*"If Freedom's miracle should fail!"*]

Louisville Journal
March 20, 1861

☙ NOTES

1. Originally published in 1860, this poem anticipates some of the most distinctive features of Piatt's mature writing, in particular, her sophisticated and witty ironization of gender issues in polite society, and her pictorial approach to social behaviors such as the sex game.

2. The date in the title is the date of the battle, not the date of composition. The first battle of Bull Run (to the South, "First Manassas") was the Civil War's first major engagement and the North's first major defeat. The battle was fought so close to the Capital that civilians could ride out to observe it. Some brought picnic baskets. Given J. J.'s egregious romanticization of this proximity in "The First Fire," his celebration of the cozy comforts of home (*NWa* 29), Hanawalt's assumption that Sarah's irony in the last stanza is "unintended" (133) seems off the mark. It is true, however, that nineteenth-century reviewers read the poem straight. Years later, a *New York Times* reviewer would extol "Hearing" as "never surpassed in tenderness and simplicity" (July 15, 1886, 3), making it a striking example of Piatt's "either you will read or you will not read" dictum.

3. Piatt's love of the theatrical, presumably repudiated in this poem, remained central to her writing; and so did her sense that social behaviors were, effectively, roles men and women "played." This sense of artificiality made the "fancy ball" a key metaphor for her, reemerging again and again in poems that either reference dramas (Shakespeare's, in particular) or are in themselves mini-dramas. Variants: line 6: by] through; line 7: mock] match, and the moon] and moon; line 14: soft] cold; stanza 5 missing (*Galaxy* [1866]).

4. In 1864, Arlington National Cemetery was established on the site of General Robert E. Lee's former estate. In September 1866 the mass grave holding the remains of 2,111 unknown soldiers was sealed, an event Piatt's poem, first published in August 1866, appears to commemorate. Piatt's description of the Potomac in stanza 3 deftly echoes Spenser's famous refrain in "Prothalmion" (1596), "Sweet Thames, run softly, till I end my song," and lines from Milton's "Lycidas" (1637) on the "perilous flood." The final stanza places blame for the dead squarely on General Lee's shoulders. Variants: title: Arlington Heights (*HW*); subtitle: [At Arlington, Va., 1866.]; line 15: Sing tenderly; O river's haunted flood!] Sing tenderly, O river's haunted flood! (*WP*).

5. The popular song "Hear me, Norma" (stanza 4) was based on Vincenzo Bellini's opera *Norma* (1832). Piatt may be suggesting that like the opera's Druidic heroine, secretly involved in a liaison with the Roman proconsul of Britain, the speaker took a lover from among the enemy. This same man figures in a number of Piatt poems; typ-

ically he has given her a flower and he dies of a chest wound in the war. Also see "The Memorials," in the appendix.

6. This could be Piatt's response to J. J.'s "The Birthdays": "My fancy, love-created, goes / Lightly from passing year to year: / My little fairy maiden grows / To tender girl-hood dear. / A dreaming girl, as shy as dew / In dells of Fairyland apart, / Within your soul a lily grew— / A rose within your heart" (*NWa* 94). Piatt's last-stanza allusion to Psalm 23:2—"He leadeth me beside the still waters"—suggests that the interlocutor will get what he wants (an "Angel" wife) only when she dies. Variants: line 3: For] At; line 21: viler] darker (*WP, P1*).

7. Like Norma, Cleopatra also chose a lover, the Roman general Marc Antony, from among the enemy. After Octavius Caesar defeated their combined forces in the naval battle at Actium (31 B.C.E.), Antony committed suicide by falling on his sword, and Cleopatra committed suicide not long thereafter. Piatt's view of the tragic pair reflects the influence of Shakespeare's *Tragedy of Antony and Cleopatra* (1606), a drama that strongly appealed to many nineteenth-century women writers, Dickinson included. Variants: line 4: The blossoms you brought me to-day] The vase with the flowers which you gather'd to-day; line 21: broken into two half lines (*WP, SP, P1*).

8. Most of the key components of Piatt's emerging poetic of dramatic realism are at work in this poem: her use of words actually heard in conversation, her rootedness in experience, her individualized metrics, and her tendency to build her poems as dramatic situations rather than rely on apostrophe or dramatic monologue. Variants: title: The Little Puzzler (*H&H*); subtitle: Marian, 6 years old (*PCC, P2*); line 12: clear] clean (*P2*); line 16: Who does He pray to—when He has to pray?] Who does he pray to, and what does he say? line 17: drops are in] drops are there in (*H&H*).

9. An Irish reviewer praising this poem in the pro-Parnell *The Nation* (December 5, 1885) says it exhibits a "sarcasm to rival Swift's." The stereotypic "Jew" in stanza 3 may be meant to indicate one more way in which the children are corrupted by their society or, closer at hand, by the prejudices of their parents, or it may be evidence of Piatt's own anti-Semitism. If Piatt was anti-Semitic, it is the only negative social attitude she possessed that she never interrogates, suggesting that it was either very superficial or very deeply entrenched. In the last days of the war, Grant ordered the siege of Richmond, blocking all avenues of access into the Confederate capital. General Lee ordered the evacuation of the city on April 3, 1865. As they left, Confederate forces set fire to the city. Nine hundred buildings were burnt out and hundreds more were damaged. The poem exploits the children's confusion in order to blame Grant, against whom Piatt harbored a lifelong dislike, for the devastation of Richmond.

10. Variants: line 35: my own?] my own!; line 37: If such dark Fancies can play in despair like tragedy queens] And my dark fancies but play'd in despair like tragedy queens (*WP*).

11. Piatt summarizes 1869's major political events (all of them written up in *HW*): the opening of the Suez Canal; the completion of the transcontinental railroad in the United States; Spain's brief experiment with elective monarchy; the First Vatican Council, called to ratify the doctrine of papal infallibility; and—representing women's on-

going struggle for the franchise—the 1869 woman's rights convention in Saratoga, New York. The "Other" in stanza 10 is 1870; Louis Napoleon (1808–73) was emperor of France, 1852–70, and Sultan Abd-al-Aziz ruled the Ottoman empire, 1861–76. "[E]arth's beautiful Oppressed" (line 40) received gallant support from two influential male figures. George Francis Train (1829–1904), ardent advocate of Irish home rule, financier, eccentric, and racist, "chivalrously" floated the first issue of *The Revolution*, Susan B. Anthony and Elizabeth Cady Stanton's woman's rights newspaper, in 1868, and John Stuart Mill (1806–73), British philosopher-economist, published one of the century's strongest feminist tracts, *On the Subjection of Women*, in 1869. Despite this, Piatt is not especially sanguine that 1870 would bring much improvement in women's situation.

12. On January 28, 1871, after months of siege and famine, Paris fell to Prussian forces, bringing the Franco-Prussian war (1870–71) to an end. Piatt's passionate response to Paris's fall may have been conditioned by her response to the fall of Richmond (1865).

13. Grant is Piatt's primary target in this otherwise very cryptic poem. However, along with Grant, a formidable number of other West Pointers also served as generals in the Civil War, on both sides: Robert E. Lee (1807–70), William Tecumseh Sherman (1820–91), Pierre G. T. Beauregard (1818–93), George Brinton McClellan (1826–85), and James (Jeb) Stuart (1833–64). Jefferson Davis (1808–89), president of the Confederacy, also graduated from West Point. Piatt seems to have had a consistent distaste for book-generals.

14. Variants: line 2: And] But; line 22: will] shall (*Cap, VFI*).

15. This is among Piatt's most complex poems, turning on a quadruple reference to "Beatrice Cenci": (1) Beatrice Cenci (1577–99), the historical personage, daughter of Francesco Cenci (1549–98). She, her brothers, and possibly a lover murdered her father after he imprisoned her and her stepmother in a tower. Although it was widely believed that Francesco committed incest with his daughter, she and her fellow conspirators were put to death; (2) the famed portrait, attributed to Guido Reni, said to be of Beatrice Cenci, which hangs in the Barberini Palace and was much copied in the nineteenth century. It is one of these copies that the speaker presumably views in the store window; (3) Beatrice Cenci, the heroine of Shelley's verse drama *The Cenci* (1819); and (4) an imagined actress who plays Beatrice Cenci's role in the drama. The speaker identifies so strongly with the latter that she begins hallucinating her own presence on the stage. Only her child's question recalls her to "reality." Variants: subtitle added: [Seen in a City Shop-Window]; line 19: a] her; line 20 is not split (*VFI, P2*).

16. This poem provides stunning evidence of Piatt's sometimes uncanny ability to capture the visual effects of bourgeois emotional life, as the accompanying illustration demonstrates.

17. Unsigned. This is a companion piece to "A Lily of the Nile." Both exhibit Piatt's tendency to locate sites of romance (and self-destruction) in the south, suggesting they can be read allegorically. In Shakespeare's *Antony and Cleopatra*, the beset queen uses an asp or horned North African adder to poison herself.

18. By 1860, Daniel Boone's grave in Frankfort, Kentucky, was already a tourist site

complete with a fifteen-foot monument and a fence to protect it from souvenir-collecting vandals. See Kincheloe, "Through the Claude Glass" (72–77). "Dark and Bloody Ground" was a popular if inaccurate translation of the state's Shawnee name. Like "Beatrice Cenci," this poem engages multiple time frames: (1) the moment in which the poem itself is spoken; (2) the moment "many withered springs ago" when the speaker threw down the rose; (3) the moment "last winter" when she hallucinated her vision of Boone; and (4) Boone's own mythological time. The rose ties the latter three times together and in all likelihood is the same flower that the speaker gives back in "Giving Back the Flower." Piatt's ironic view of her "kinsman" strikingly contrasts with J. J.'s more conventional description of him in "The Birthdays," as the "Ulysses of the Indian wild" (*NWa,* 98). Piatt may also be parodying J. J.'s paean to the frontier spirit, "Farther" (see Bennett, in Haralson, 329–32). A note to line 7 cites Byron as the source for Boone's "homely generalship": "General Boone, backwoodsman of Kentucky— Byron." Variants: line 3: had] how; line 4: secured] seemed; line 7: homely] wildwood; line 8: troubled] border; line 15: A] Some; line 19: garments] garment (*Hesp2*).

19. Unsigned. The speaker echoes a question her husband asks. They are at a "fair seaside town" (possibly a South Carolina resort) and he is interrogating her about other vacationers, some of whom he thinks were her lovers prior to marriage. Of the first (the man with the scar), she says she knew him only "slightly." She admits to having had a relationship with the second, "the fellow . . . with the low Southern swagger," but it was broken off after his pursuit of another woman (an heiress). For all his air of chivalry, the former lover ended up a guerrilla raider in the Confederate forces—if not, as the husband suggests, a Klansman. Since the "heiress" turned out not to have any money, both are the "Mock-Diamonds" of the title.

20. In this dream vision, Piatt's speaker identifies her scene of temptation with that of Christ in the wilderness: Matthew 4:1–12, Mark 1:13, and Luke 4:2–13. However, just as the poem merges Christ and the speaker, so it seems at points to merge Christ with the tempter (Satan), making the conventional piety of the final stanza an uneasy resolution at best. A white dove traditionally represents the Holy Spirit. See also Matthew 14:25: "And in the fourth watch of the night, Jesus went unto them, walking on the sea," and John 11:44: "And he that was dead came forth, bound hand and foot with graveclothes." Stanzas 5–8 fuse two separate temptations: turning stones into bread and yielding to the desire for worldly power, see Matthew 4:3–9. The "Word" in the final stanza can be either the Bible or Christ (the Logos), or both.

21. Little Nell is the highly sentimentalized heroine of Charles Dickens's *The Old Curiosity Shop* (1841). She epitomizes the most salient traits of the Angel in the House— passivity, spirituality, goodness, etc.—making Piatt's reference to a "waxen saint" (line 11) a bitter jibe. Variants: line 10: ring] sing (*Cap*); line 22: the Doll] the darling (*P1*); line 37: And] And, and (*VFI*).

22. Goethe's *The Sorrows of Young Werther* (1774), the bible of late eighteenth-century European sentimental masculinity, set off a vogue for romantic suicide that swept Western culture. However the novel's most lasting impact may have been its domestication of romance. In *Werther's* most famous scene, the hero falls in love with the

unobtainable Charlotte while watching her distributing "bread-and-butter" to her younger siblings.

23. Variant: line 27: that] its (*VFI, P2*).

24. Variants: title: Her Well-Known Story; line 3: lovely] lonely (*Cap*); line 5: faded] withered; line 12: And] Then (*TNW, P2*).

25. Piatt's sphinx (stanza 5) represents a common conflation of two distinctly different figures from antiquity: the Greeks' winged monster with the body of a lion and the head and breasts of a woman, famous for its riddles, and the Egyptian sphinx, a pharonic symbol, with the body of a lion and the face of a man, which asked no riddles.

26. Except for the parenthetical clause in line 2, the first stanza is spoken by the speaker's daughter; the second is spoken by the same black nurse who appears in "The Black Princess" and other poems. The remaining stanzas represent the thoughts of the mother, a former Kentuckian now living across the Ohio River in Cincinnati. The nurse's nostalgia for prewar days is not necessarily a projection of the mother's own (presumably disavowed) nostalgia. Many Southern blacks found the reconstruction period a time of difficult readjustment. Stanza 3's treatment of the "old slave-music," as Piatt calls it elsewhere, is another matter. These "glad songs" were not lost, although white slave-holders such as Piatt did lose access to them. Variants: line 17: iron] leaden (*Cap, Ind*); line 30: moan] moon (*Ind*); line 32: forms] shapes (*Cap*); line 36: pretty] snowy (*Cap, Ind*).

27. For the sphinx, see note 25. The slave of the lamp (stanza 5) is the genie in the story of Aladdin; the slave of the ring is a married woman. The "Knight of the Pale Horse" (stanza 9) is death. Piatt's description of Jordan (stanza 10) echoes the spiritual "Michael, Row the Boat Ashore."

28. See the frontispiece. The Paris Commune (March 18–May 28, 1871) was Europe's first experiment in communism. Coming at the end of the Franco-Prussian War (see "Paris"), it was an insurrectionary government led by urban workers who destroyed a number of buildings including the Tuileries palace. Over seventeen thousand men, women, and children were executed by government forces following a three-month siege. The article accompanying the *Harper's* illustration focuses on women's role in the revolution, expressing abhorrence of their actions but sympathy for their plight (*HW* [July 8, 1871], 628). Variants: subtitle, Paris, 1871; stanza 8 is cut (*SP, P1*).

29. Variant: line 13: held] ours; line 26: "And" cut; the grass] the soft grass (*VFI*).

30. Variants: line 19: fair fall] Autumn (*SP, P1*); line 26: semicolon substituted for question mark (*VFI, SP, P1*). The effect of this latter variant is to turn the interlocutor's interrogation into the speaker's assertion. Unfortunately it is impossible to know who made this change.

31. Unsigned. Pro-slavery apologists liked to point to slave songs as evidence that the slaves were happy at their work, a position vehemently disputed by Frederick Douglass (1845) and W. E. B. Du Bois (1903). Writing nostalgically, Piatt appears to adopt a position between the two alternatives: singing was a form of self-comforting that gave the slaves (real) pleasure and a sense of freedom while they sang. As with "Over in

Kentucky," the really troublesome issue is the speaker's narcissism: *she* will never hear this music again.

32. The beautiful "he" in stanza 5 is probably Piatt's cousin James, the long-lost son of her paternal aunt, "Annie" Boone of New Castle, Kentucky. See "Aunt Annie." Variants: subtitle added: After the Civil War—in Kentucky; stanza 5 cut; line 6: Old trees before me by enchantment grew] Trees gray with moss and time before me grew; line 9: awful] golden; line 15: ah] oh; line 32: lifted] fevered; line 33: fading] fiery (*P2*).

33. Unsigned. Piatt's treatment of this well-known Aesop fable makes a very different point. The grapes are "sour" not because the fox cannot have what it wants, but because they are poisonous, as the "Fathers" discovered. The reference is probably to the Old South, which poisoned itself with what it most desired. Grapes reach full sweetness only after the first frost.

34. Unsigned. This poem is best read against "Prevented Choice," whose positive and highly conventional conclusion this later poem undoes, leaving it unclear in the end whether the "Lord" whom the speaker chooses is Christ or his dark double, Satan. These poems may have been inspired by Piatt's early infatuation with Byron.

35. Variants: title added; line 3: blindly] idly (*UAP&A*).

36. The second stanza alludes to *MacBeth* 5.5.24: "Life is but a walking shadow, a poor player / That struts and frets his hour upon the stage / And is heard no more. It is a tale / told by an idiot, full of sound and fury, / Signifying nothing." This speech was so well known in Piatt's day that she needed only to refer to the "Poor Player" to evoke the lines—and all their nihilism. The last stanza alludes to the Civil War. Variants: title: The Play; line 3: What if] Who cares if; line 9: wavering] waning (*Ind*).

37. Variants: subtitle: [Madam Cinderella Speaks] (*P2*); line 21: wines] wine (*VFI*, *P2*).

38. In a letter to Stedman (August 20, 1873), J. J. describes the death of Sarah's four-day-old infant from unknown causes (ECSP). It was her first such loss and she was inconsolable. Appearing in the *Ind* a scant three months after the baby's death, this poem supports J. J.'s contention that Piatt put her own experience directly into her poetry, here at a pitch of absolutely raw emotion. Line 13 alludes to John 20:15, words spoken by Christ to Mary.

39. Among Piatt's angriest poems, "We Two" may reflect her rage at having lost two children within a single year—the unnamed baby in 1873 and Victor, who died in a freak Fourth of July accident in 1874. The poem's imagery draws heavily on the Bible. See Psalm 91:5–6: "Thou shalt not be afraid for the terror by night, nor for the arrow that flieth by day, nor the pestilence that stalks in the darkness, nor the destruction that wastes at noonday"; Job 21:33, "The clods of the valley are sweet to him," spoken by Job of the wicked who are nevertheless favored by God; and Matthew 3:17, "and lo, a voice from heaven, saying, 'This is my beloved son, with whom I am well pleased,'" spoken by God at Christ's baptism. Clearly distinguishing between obedience to God's will and acceptance of it, Piatt identifies her speaker with Job as much as with Christ.

40. Variants: title: The Song No Bird Should Sing in Vain; line 20: It passed away— the window shut] It found and left my window shut; stanzas 2, 3, 4, and 6 cut (*TNW*).

41. Variants: title: Counsel; subtitle added: [In the South.]; line 2: pass] path (*DP*, *P2*); line 10: your] his (*P2*); stanza 4 cut (*P2*); stanza 6 is reworded throughout: Ah, tell the prophets in their graves, / Who ask of you such blood as this, / "I take Him, then, with swords and staves,— / I will not with a kiss!" (*DP*, *P2*).

42. J. J. calls this poem a "homely real ballad" in a letter to Stedman, May 10, 1874 (LCMP). Aunt Annie's son, James, left home when Piatt was about twelve. Considerably older than his bereft cousin, he appears in many of her poems as an early lover, suggesting, if nothing else, that he awakened her sexuality at this very vulnerable age. This poem took on terrible irony in July with the death of Victor, the living child mentioned in the poem. Variant: line 56: God] He (*SP*, *P1*).

43. Internal evidence in "A Butterfly's Message," and in the next poem, "The Favorite Child," makes it virtually certain that these two poems were written between July 4 and the beginning of August, when *VFI*, the volume in which they first appear, was reviewed in *SMo*. J. J. Piatt writes poignantly about the circumstances of Victor's death in a long letter to Stedman, August 2, 1874: "Today is Victor's birth-day; he would have been ten years old this morning. While I have been writing I have heard his poor mother, looking at his little relics in the room below (his clothes, his school-books, his little drawings and other tokens of his affection for her) crying and—crying as she does every day. His little grave (beside his baby-brother's made last August) is about four hundred feet back of our house on a little wooded hillside" (ECSP).

44. Piatt's four surviving children were, in birth order, Marian Prentice (1862–19?), Arthur Donn (1867–1914), Frederick (1869–1918), and Guy R. (1871–19?). Two more sons, Louis (1875–84) and Cecil (1878–1949) were born after Victor's death. Piatt's use of a four-beat line, parallel phrasing, riddle structure, and question-and-response are all evocative of traditional ballad devices, positioning the poem somewhere between a conventional nineteenth-century elegy, a lullaby, and a ballad lament. Variant: title: The Favorite of Five (*PCC*).

45. Unsigned. "Siempre," "always" (Spanish). Despite the unfortunate last line, this poem sheds interesting light on the lifestyle (and gender games) of the postbellum Ohio haute bourgeoisie. There is no hard evidence that Piatt committed adultery, but her female speakers often sound as if they had, in a quest for romance not unlike Madame Bovary's. J. J. Piatt's cousins, Abram Sanders Piatt, a Civil War general, and Donn Piatt (1819–1891), a lieutenant-colonel in the Civil War and an outspoken publisher of the *Cap* (see the illustration accompanying "A Coat of Arms"), built side-by-side castles one mile east of West Liberty, Ohio. Neither of the castle's towers faces south, but the remaining details in the poem all point to one of these buildings as the setting for this poem, most probably A. S. Piatt's Castle Mac-A-Cheek, a Norman-French style home, completed in 1868. In a recent travel brochure, Castle Mac-A-Cheek is described as sitting "atop a hill," having "a breathtaking view of the surrounding landscape"— the fertile Ohio valley—and an interior "decorated with elaborate woodwork and intricate frescoed ceilings." Portraits of J. J. and Sarah Piatt, along with Francis Bret Harte and Louise Kirby Piatt, Donn Piatt's wife, grace one of the ceilings in Donn's Castle Mac-O-Chee.

46. Piatt's submerged allusion to Columbus's discovery of the New World in the title points to her deeply entrenched skepticism respecting the afterlife. From the "'Indian's Inquiry'" (1857) on, Piatt questions the value of fantasies that allow people to rationalize suffering here and now for "rewards" that may or may not come later. See "Keeping the Faith," among her bitterest treatments of this theme. Variants: line 5: the] this; line 22: vacant] empty; line 26: the] this (*TNW, P2*).

47. In 1845, Lady Franklin's explorer husband, Sir John Franklin, disappeared while searching for the northwest passages. Twelve years later, she outfitted an expedition that successfully located his remains. For the nineteenth century she served as a popular symbol of wifely devotion. Variants: subtitle added: On her Death, 1875 (*P2*); stanza 2 cut; line 15: Into another world forever winding] To the great Peaceful Sea forever winding; stanza 4 cut; line 21: that] her; line 23: lain] laid (*TNW, P2*); stanza 6 cut (*P2*).

48. Variant: line 3: spreads] spread (*TNW, P2*).

49. Variant: line 12: did] would (*TNW, P2*).

50. Stanza 2 contains an allusion to I Corinthians 2:9: "But as it is written, Eye hath not seen, nor ear heard, neither have entered into the heart of man, the things God hath prepared for them that love him."

51. Variant: line 21: hopeless] hapless (*TNW, P2*).

52. This wittily sophisticated poem is of a piece with other poems focusing on dating games and male narcissism that appeared in *HB* in this period, making it a good example of Piatt's "niche" writing.

53. "Fred," in stanza 5, would be Piatt's second-oldest surviving son, Frederick. Variants: subtitle added: To Another Little Boy (*P1*); line 12: and] or (*TNW, PCC, P1*); line 15: the] with (*TNW, P1*), by] to; line 17: try] cry (*TNW, PCC, P1*); line 19: And] to (*TNW, P1*); can] will (*TNW*); line 26: said] say, would] will (*TNW, PCC, P1*); line 32: if it *is* true] though it be true; line 45: the] good (*P1*).

54. In ironizing faith, Piatt is once again critiquing one of J. J.'s more conventional renderings: "You'd have a Fairy Book, you said? . . . / I pray that from your eyes and heart? / Faith, the True Fairy, 'll ne'er depart!" ("To Grace at Christmas," *NWa*, 96). Denying the possibility of a "True Fairy," Piatt treats the South's "Lost Cause," Columbus's fabled Indies, the child's dream, and the Christian's heaven as interchangeable delusions. After his third voyage to the New World (1500), Columbus was sent back to Spain in chains, a fate typically treated as tragic by nineteenth-century artists but with cold realism by Piatt (see the accompanying illustration). Variant: title: Faith in Fairy-Land (*Cap*).

55. Signed S.M.B.: these are the initials of Piatt's maiden name, suggesting that the poem may have been written before her marriage. If so, then like "Waiting at the Party," it is of special interest as an anticipation of her later technique, in particular, the sting in the tail, upending the poem's direction.

56. Variants: title: A Lament of My Lady; line 13: me] the; line 17: can] may; line 19: wild] wildest (*Cap*); line 12: marble] statues (*CWB*).

57. The allusion in stanza 5 is to *Hamlet* 1.3.78, but Piatt seems to be reading Polonius's platitudinous advice ironically. The speaker has been far too "true" to herself

and insufficiently caring of others. The story of Rachel, wife of Jacob and mother of Joseph, is told in Genesis 29–30. In abolitionist literature, Rachel represents the archetypal grieving mother, and Piatt consistently draws on this tradition when writing social-protest poetry. Farman, in Stoddard, comments that "the Rachel-sorrow" never found "more powerful expression" than in Piatt's poetry (68). Variant: line 30: subtle] noble (*DP*).

58. Variant: title: Word of Counsel (*DP, SP, P1*).

59. The allusion to Wolsey's "killing frost" in stanza 6 comes from Shakespeare's *Henry VIII* 3.2.355; but the strawberries come from *Richard III* 3.4.33. Variants: line 4: go] go to; line 8: foreign] foreign thing; stanza 7 cut (*HB*).

60. Coat of Arms: a heraldic emblem signifying family lines. Beginning with Alfred (849–99), fourth son of Æthelwulf, king of Saxons in England, Piatt turns her poem into a tour de force of royal references, providing capsule biographies mixing contemporary figures like Queen Victoria, newly minted "Empress of India," with historical figures, such as the Holy Roman Emperors, and mythic ones, such as King Arthur. Good or evil, well known or barely known, real or fantastic, all these figures are part of her daughter's cultural lineage. Much of the poem's fun lies in identifying the references from the clues Piatt provides. For example, the "One—who was half a god, they say— / Cried for the stars, and died of wine" is Alexander the Great (356–323 B.C.E.), king of Macedon and conqueror of Greece, Egypt, and greater Persia. "Great Frederick, with his snuff" is Frederick II, or Frederick the Great (1712–86), king of Prussia, notorious for the snuff stains on his clothing, and so forth.

Some of the more obscure figures or subtler points may require glossing. It is worth noting, for example, that in a poem largely devoted to subverting the boundary between the historical and the high fantastical, Piatt is at some pains to redeem King Richard III of England (1452–85) from Shakespeare's rancorous portrait of him. Other glosses: Charles I (1600–1649), king of England, Scotland, and Ireland, was beheaded by order of Parliament at the direction of Oliver Cromwell (1599–1658), who became lord protector of England four years after the king's execution. Charles V (1500–1558) was Holy Roman Emperor (1519–58). Casting off his imperial responsibilities, he retired in 1556 to a monastery, where two years later he died. Philip the Handsome (1478–1506), king of Castile, was born in Belgium and laid claim to it. The Flemish people, Piatt seems to be suggesting, were not as entranced with Philip's beauty as history has been. As a young man, Philip was held prisoner in Ghent for three years, until his father and regent won his release. Like Frederick the Great, Peter the Great (1672–1725), czar of Russia, and Napoleon I (1769–1821), the emperor of France whom Piatt identifies by his defeat at Waterloo, were enlightened despots who brought many needed social and legal reforms to their countries. Frederick I, or Frederick Barbarossa (red beard) (c. 1125–90), was Holy Roman Emperor and king of Germany. While on the Third Crusade, Frederick was drowned in Cilicia. According to legend, however, he remained alive, sleeping in a cave until the day when he would restore his empire to its former greatness. Roland was the great French hero of the medieval Charlemagne cycle of *chansons de geste* (eleventh or twelfth century). Too proud for his own good,

Roland refused to sound his horn for help when outnumbered by Basques at the pass at Roncesvalles. After Roland's death, Charlemagne had his body and those of the peers carried back to France for burial. Aix-la-Chapelle was Charlemagne's birthplace and the northern capital of his empire. Piatt's familiarity with Roland may have come through Milton (*Paradise Lost*) since like him she incorrectly locates the scene of Roland's travail near the town of Fontarabia (now Fuenterrabía). It is also possible, however, since Charlemagne's "war" was intended to contain further ninth-century Muslim advances into Europe, that Piatt mis-cited Roland's place of death in order to take advantage of the poetic associations embedded in the name "Fontarabia." Piatt's daughter, Marian, attended a convent school in Cincinnati. "Madam" was her French teacher (see "Somebody's Trouble"). Presumably the latter would know how to act at the court of Louis XIV, *le Roi soleil*, but the intrusive, democratic cadre composing the Washington press corps would not. J. J.'s journalist cousin, Donn Piatt, was probably on Sarah's mind when she wrote stanza 12 (see the accompanying illustration). According to Piatt, stanza 17 alludes "to the Khedive's present to an American Lady." Ismail Pasha (1830–95), the khedive (viceroy) of Eygpt, was best known for his personal extravagance and for attempting to modernize his country. Piatt goes on to identify nations and peoples by their heraldic or cultural symbols: lilies (France), lions (England), stars (the United States), Damascus swords (the Ottoman empire), Spartan shields (ancient Greece), crescents (Islamic nations), crosses (the Christian West), Jason's "golden fleece" (Western symbol of heroic endeavor), and King Solomon's seal, the six-pointed star (Jewish symbol of wisdom). In the last stanza, Piatt's speaker provides a "coat-of-arms" for her daughter that theoretically embraces all mankind. Her "family tree" is the tree of the fruit of the knowledge of good and evil; the "sword of fire" is the flaming sword held by the cherubim whom God sets at Eden's gate to prevent Adam and Eve's return; and the serpent, of course, is Satan.

Variants: line 1: is old] is so old (*PCC, SP, P1*); line 31: the] that (*PCC, SP, P1*); line 33: smothered] murdered; line 38: France and Germany] Spain and Germany (*SP, P1*); line 53, can] could; line 58, sits] sat (*PCC, SP, P1*); stanzas 18 and 20 cut in *SP* and *P1*.

61. Sir Philip Sidney (1554–86) was a gallant in the court of Queen Elizabeth I and author of *Astrophil and Stella*, an Elizabethan sonnet sequence modeled on Petrarch. Viewed as the chivalric beau ideal in his own day, he capped his short career by dying nobly and senselessly in the battle of Zutphen in 1586. Sidney fits the pattern of Piatt's early romantic interests, treated with such self-mockery in the final stanza.

62. Piatt's note: *Stories from Homer,* by Rev. Alfred J. Church. Like Church, Piatt reduces Homer's epics, the *Iliad* and the *Odyssey* (8th century B.C.E.), to their key moments: the description of Achilles's shield, Hector's farewell to his wife and child, Priam's mourning for his dead son, and Ulysses's return to Ithaca, where his first act is to slaughter his wife's unwelcome suitors. In the final stanza, Piatt obliquely alludes to the Civil War. The allusion in line 19 is to *The Tempest* (1.2.50): "In the dark, backward and abysm of time." Variants: title: Their Heroic Lesson; subtitle added: (Learned from Homer.) (*TWG, P2*); line 5: know] knew; line 6: guessed] knew (*DP, TWG, P2*);

line 10: rather piteous] piteous after; line 11: Stole] Breathed (*TWG*, *P2*); line 18: rust] rest (*DP, TWG, P2*).

63. Piatt's note: September, 1878. Variants: no subtitle or note (*YC*).

64. Unsigned. Louis Napoleon (1856–79), was the son of Napoleon III and the equivalent of a "pop royal" in Piatt's day, his career from birth to death recorded, tabloid-style, in the newspapers. After the humiliating defeat of Napoleon III in the Franco-Prussian war, he and his family went into exile in England. "[B]orn heir to the imperial throne of France," as *HW* puts it (July 5, 1879), the prince joined the British army to give himself something to do and was ambushed and killed by Zulu warriors in 1879, hardly the end for which he was intended.

65. Variant: line 4: beat] best; line 20: watched her a] watched her in a (*P2*).

66. In stanza 3, cap and plume signify a young courtier; cap and bells, a jester or fool.

67. This poem appeared in the *AM* as one of a group, under the general title "Three Songs."

68. Raphael's pencil sketch of himself between the ages of twelve and fourteen suggests he was very beautiful as a young man. Piatt's last line pun on "Master" conflates the Renaissance artist with God.

69. Piatt is parodying J. J.'s "Firelight Abroad:" "There the young bride alights from charmèd air, / Into the real air, enchanted still, / Breathing a bower of roses evermore / Over her husband's dusty work-day toil—" (*Western Windows* 95–6). J. J.'s thinking on domesticity and its hearth-side delights seem to have been heavily influenced by the immensely popular *Reveries of a Bachelor* (1851), by the male sentimentalist Ik Marvell (Donald Grant Mitchell).

70. Variant: title: Reproof to a Rose (*DP, P1*); line 13: snows] snow (*P1*).

71. Variant: line 18: dread] weird (*YC*).

72. Under the title "Turned Away," this poem was originally printed in *AM* (February 1879) as one of three songs, along with "Engaged Too Soon" and a third poem, "Life and Death," not reprinted here.

73. The companion piece to "Turned Away," "The Mother's Thought" never appeared in *AM*; but it does appear in *YC* under the title "The Mother's After-Thought" (July 1879). My sense of the poems is that the Piatts probably sent the *AM* all four poems, split into two groups. For whatever reason, the *AM* did not care for "The Mother's Thought" and created its own division. The Piatts then sent the rejected poem to *YC* where it came out a few months later. From my perspective the Piatts had it right in the first place. Variants: title: Denied; subtitle added: (The Mother's After-Thought.); line 2: breathes] breathed; line 9: glimmer of] glimmering light (*YC*).

74. Piatt's note: Written after reading certain newspaper discussions as to the treatment of the "tramp." The missing word in line 7 is "impostor." *HW* and other middle-class periodicals waxed sentimental over the plight of starving women and children, but male tramps were viewed as a dangerous social problem on whom sympathy was wasted. See "Playing Beggars." The final biblical allusion may be to Isaiah 66:2: "All these things my hand has made, and so all these things are mine"; but it is also

suggestive of Jesus of Nazareth's deep identification with the poor and outcast. Variant: line 31: you] your (*TWG, P2*).

75. The biblical allusion in the last stanza is to Matthew 6:28: "Consider the lilies of the field, how they grow; they toil not, neither do they spin." Variant: line 2: Well, then—well] Louis? Well (*TWG, IG, P2*).

76. In Greek mythology, Cadmus was the son of Agenor and founder of the city of Thebes. He was told by the Delphic oracle to abandon his search for a missing sister and to follow a cow that he would meet until it lay down. On that spot he was to build his city. Variant: title: The Little Cowherd; line 15: moonlight's] moon's weird (*TWG, P2*)

77. Piatt's note: The pathetic little episode to which this piece refers is related in the third book of Virgil's *Aeneid,* lines 482–92, where the poet describes Aeneas meeting Andromache during his wanderings, after the fall of Troy, with his son Ascanius (also called Iülus). To the latter, Andromache gives some garments wrought by herself, and in presenting them she recalls her own boy Astyanax, who, in obedience to an oracle, had been thrown headlong from the walls of Troy and killed. This was after the death of Hector, his father, whose parting with Andromache—in which the child "headed like a star," together with "the horse-hair plume," is mentioned—forms one of the most famous passages in the *Iliad* of Homer. The passage in Virgil is literally as follows:— "Andromache, sad with the last parting, brings garments figured over with golden embroidery and a Phrygian cloak for Ascanius, and loads him with woven gifts, and thus speaks,—'Take these, too, my boy, and may they be to thee mementoes of my handiwork, and bear witness to the lasting love of Andromache, Hector's wife; take these last gifts of thy friend, O only image remaining to me of my Astyanax. Just such eyes, just such hands, just such features he had, and he would now be growing up in equal age with thee'" (*TWG*). Just as child death created solidarity among women from different social registers (see, for example, "The Prince Imperial" and "A Tragedy in Western Woods"), so, for Piatt, it created solidarity through time and story.

78. This poem had the dubious honor of being plagarized by Dorothea Moore in "Precocity," published in *The Chap-Book* (97). Even more interesting, the editor of the *Philistine,* a rival "penny magazine," gleefully caught Moore out. See *The Philistine* 3 (1897): 190. Whatever else, this contretemps points to the poem's popularity among nineteenth-century readers.

79. Variants: title: The Coming Out of Her Doll; subtitle: Young Girl-Graduate to Her Mother; line 10: One's Papa] Papa, he (*TWG, P2, TLE*).

80. The final stanza contains an allusion to Milton's "Lycidas": "The hungry Sheep look up, and are not fed" (line 125). Unlike Milton, however, Piatt is concerned with physical, not spiritual, starvation. Variants: line 18: furthest] farthest (*COD, TWG, P2*); line 37: they] these (*TWG, P2*).

81. Stanza 7 consists of a periphrasis for earth. Variant: line 11: sung] sang (*COD, TWG, P2*).

82. If one credits Katherine Tynan's memoirs of her visits with the Piatt family, this implied portrait of a Piatt son would fit any of them: wild, careless, and full of zest for

living. Tynan repeatedly calls the boys "very positive," finding their exuberance in strik-
ing contrast to the rather sad and faded demeanor of their parents, whom she describes
as "two little grey ghosts" forever walking about hand in hand or drifting off to write
poems (*Memories* 180).

83. The description in the last stanza points to James, Aunt Annie Boone's son. As
in so many of Piatt's mother-child dialogues, the mother's split consciousness between
time past and time present ironizes what she says in ways her daughter cannot com-
prehend. Variants: title: After Her First Party; line 1: lovely, mamma, and] lovely, and,
mamma; line 35: I guess] I'd guess (*TWG, P2*).

84. After killing the sacred dragon that guarded the spring of Ares, Cadmus plant-
ed the dragon's teeth, from which sprang the Sparti (sewn men), the ancestors of lat-
er Theban noble families. As soon as they were "born" the Sparti fell to killing one
another, making them a convenient figure for civil war both in the family and in the
nation at large. According to Tynan, among Piatt's sons, Fred and Guy were particu-
larly given to hostilities and did not speak directly to each other for years. Variants:
line 2: rosy] very; line 4: had] have; line 5: And, much I fear me] And to find out, too;
line 12: for] to (*YC*).

85. Variants: there are two additional stanzas (9 and 10) in the *Ind* version: "They
wore the rose out of the world, where I / Walk in the frosty leaves and know not why,
/ Yet, from the Blessed Islands, it may be / They brought some scent, some secret word
to me."

86. In a letter to a Mrs. Nixon or Pixous [?], written from "The Crescent," Queens-
town, Ireland, Piatt says of this poem's basic situation: "Here in exile, I can only feel a
far-away interest in the New Orleans Exhibition. But I belong, by birth, at least, to the
old South and once I had friends there. I sometimes amuse my children with stories
of my slave-playmates and find myself home-sick for the time when I was, as they seem
to imagine, 'a little negro myself!'" (March 4, [18]86, Miscellaneous Papers, Manu-
scripts and Archives Division, New York Public Library, Astor, Lenox, and Tilden Foun-
dations). The later addition of a subtitle ("In Kentucky, A.D. 185—") in *CWB* confuses
this picture but probably represents a typographer's error. Piatt's minimalist use of
dialect in this poem—written at a time when dialect poetry was all the rage—is worth
noting. The setting for the poem is her maternal grandmother's plantation. One of the
most interesting aspects of the poem is Piatt's handling of power relationships within
the plantation household. The white child has power by virtue of her white skin but
the cook ("the priestess of the eternal flame") has power by virtue of her position at
the top of the hierarchy for "house slaves," and "brother Blair" has the de facto power
that the slave community itself has conferred upon him as its spiritual leader. Insofar
as the white child is a child and a guest on the plantation to boot, she is subordinate
to the latter two adults, who claim to speak the will of "Old Mistress," the maternal
grandmother. Only the support of her nurse, who claims status equal to or greater than
that of the cook and brother Blair, can rescue her in this situation, acting as a conduit
for the dead mother's protecting love. Variants: subtitle added: In Kentucky, A.D. 185—;
line 34: By Raphael, for all I care] Ignotus, doubtless, tired and fair; line 36: to the out-

side air] just to take the air!; lines 54–55: leant the mirror's glare / And] let the mirror stare / While; lines 59–60: seemed / Made of the most delicious mud] seemed—— / Not made of most delicious mud; line 64: the plume the blushes of the peach] plume like blushes of the peach; line 80: guess] think; line 92: a-plowing] a-ploughin'; line 93: was] got (*CWB*).

87. Kilcolman Castle was acquired by the British poet Edmund Spenser (1552?–99) in 1589, a reward for state service. He returned to England in 1598 after rebelling Irish burnt the castle to the ground. Spenser's posthumously published treatise *A View of the Present State of Ireland* (1633) suggests that he had little sympathy for the Irish. See Kincheloe, "Through the Claude Glass," 118–23. Sir Walter Raleigh, poet and states-man, also held extensive lands in Ireland, where he and Spenser became close friends. Spenser's great nationalist allegory, the *Faerie Queen,* was still unfinished at his death; but Piatt would not be the only reader who failed to grieve over this. Variants: line 10: There lie his hills, and there—the high] . . . There lie his hills, his streams, the high; line 11: Fair] Far; line 15: some] the (*IG, EC*).

88. Variant: line 16: her] the (*COD, TWG, P2*).

89. After the defeat of the Spanish Armada in 1588, some of the sailors whose ships were destroyed took refuge in Ireland and were assimilated into the population. Pi-att's sensitivity to their "Southern" presence, expressed in stanza 4, again points to her own sense of double displacement. Variants: line 9: bent] but; line 11: While] And; line 31: But] Then; line 36: rain] sun (*YC*).

90. Piatt's note on Spike Island: Since disused as a prison for convicts. Stanza 4 al-ludes to *The Tempest* 1.2.396: "Full fathom five thy father lies." Variants: line 2: I] one; line 8: Ah] Oh!; line 17: Is it] Is't; line 24: a] the; line 25: can] will; line 26: brown] bright; line 27: birds'] bird's; line 28: following—] following?; line 35: wall] walls (*Ind*).

91. In *EC* and *PT,* this poem is accompanied by a lengthy explanatory note intend-ed (apparently) to de-politicize its subject matter:

"This piece was published in *St. Nicholas,* the New York Magazine for young folks, for May 1885, the following note by the Editor [Mary Mapes Dodge] at the time refer-ring to it:—'Mrs. Piatt's charming poem, "In Primrose Time," which appears on page 497 of this number, with its sympathetic glimpses of early spring in Ireland, will be appreciated by all the older readers of St. Nicholas. It will show, moreover, that to all classes in that green island across the sea, as also, we hope, to St. Nicholas readers ev-erywhere, the sweet yellow flower of the British Isles, that is so welcome a spring vis-itor, means much more than it did to that all too practical Mr. Peter Bell in Words-worth's well-known poem: "'A primrose by a river's brim / A yellow primrose was to him, / And it was nothing more.'" Mr. J. J. Piatt sends a letter to the Editor, accompa-nying Mrs. Piatt's poem, written from Queenstown, the Irish port which all the At-lantic steamers first "speak" on their eastward-bound trips, and the town to which the verses refer: In this he says: "The leaves of the primrose are soft, somewhat flannel-like in texture, and of a pale-green colour (they resemble mullein leaves in texture and colour); the flower is of a delicate light yellow. The primrose has always, I suppose, been a favourite early spring flower here. One day last spring it was used all over Great Britain to commemorate the anniversary of Lord Beaconsfield's death. I saw many ladies and gentlemen wearing it on the streets in Cork upon that day, and it was reported that so great was the demand for the flower in London that many orders for supplies were sent to France and Belgium." Mrs. Piatt's verses, of course, have no reference to any political sentiment associated with the primrose, but only to the "era of good feeling" it seems to bring in, and the delightful new heaven and earth of spring.'"

If Dodge could overlook "A thousand years of crime," Piatt did not. On the contrary, in one of her rare prose pieces, "A Handful of Irish Spring-Flowers" (*Hesp2* 110), she explicitly identifies Disraeli, or, as she calls him there, "the great 'English-Jew,'" and his "affection (or affectation?)" for the primrose. Since Disraeli was commonly referred to as the English Jew, Piatt's use of the sobriquet is not necessarily sarcastic. However, her parenthetical move from "affection" to "affectation" suggests not only contempt but a sharp awareness that Disraeli's famous preference for the spring flower was itself not innocent. Stanza 3 obliquely alludes to racial divisions in the United States. See n. 100 below. Variants: line 29: one] are; line 31: merry] many; line 46: toward] towards; line 49: How] Now (*PT, EC*).

92. Variant: title: The Wayside Courtesy (*EC*).

93. Latin title meaning "for the fatherland"; a patriotic expression connoting love of country. The biblical allusion in stanza 6 is to John 3:8: "The Wind bloweth where it listeth." Variant: title: America in Europe (*Pilot*).

94. Variant: line 6: come] yet (*TWG, P2*).

95. Tynan describes Piatt's method in poems such as this as follows: "She took an anecdote of someone or other and told the story in a poem. She did not even attempt any analysis of her subject. The pity or the passion of it was something quite external." However, Tynan's next observation, that a "child or a peasant could understand what she wrote," is a good deal more problematic (*Memories* 179). The "Pit" in the final line is hell (see "A Bird without a Mate). Variant: line 8: lamplight] lamplights (*TWG, P2*).

96. Variant: subtitle: near] by (*IW, EC*).

97. Variants: line 7: was] had; line 8: there] these; line 11: shining] shivering (*TWG, P2*).

98. Title: see Matthew 25. This poem takes Piatt's speaker as tourist to various European cities renown for their cathedrals and their religious artwork: Lille, Paris, Cologne, and Bruges. In each site she refrained from giving charity to the poor because she needed the money to pay entrance fees to sites where images of Christ and his mother could be viewed. The final lines are open to opposing readings—Piatt's guilt-ridden speaker wants Christ to preserve for her what she herself "never gave" (charity, or love); or, far more likely, the speaker sardonically acknowledges that she will receive in heaven precisely what she "gave" on earth (that is, the coins she *didn't* give, or "nothing"). This would fit with the chapter in Matthew, where the righteous are identified by their charity to the poor. Variants: lines 7, 8 11: capitalize "his," "him," and "his" respectively; line 18: to] must; line 20: thy mother] Thy Mother (*CWB*).

99. The Rock of Cashel, Ireland: a 306–foot-high rock in south Ireland, upon which

are the ruins of a cathedral, a chapel, and a round tower. Two major Irish defeats are associated with this site. It was here that the Irish chieftains of Munster submitted to Henry II of England in 1171; and here in 1647 that the forces of Cromwell burned fleeing townspeople alive after they had taken refuge in the fortress's interior. In attempting to take the measure of Piatt's politicization of this highly popular tourist site, Kincheloe usefully compares the poem to one by Piatt's Irish acquaintance Aubrey de Vere. Much influenced by Shelley's "Ozymandius," de Vere's highly romanticized and aestheticized portrait of "Royal and saintly Cashel" compares its ruins to those of Persepolis and Thebes but makes no mention of the Rock's current inhabitants or the horrendous conditions under which they live ("Through the Claude Glass," 110–16; also see "*Two Visions,*" 46–49). The sheep in the final stanza would be the property of loyalist landlords. See note 101. Variants: title: A Night-Scene at Cashel; line 6: wet] damp; line 17: Look] See (*EC*).

100. Splitting the Irish "garden" between "loyal" "high-born" roses (the Anglo-Irish Ascendancy) and common ox-eye daisies (the native peasantry), Piatt takes swipes at an aging Queen Victoria, no longer as "pretty" as she once was; at the Irish diaspora, that has sent many a butterfly "across the water"; and at the "troubles" themselves, as they were called. Variant: title: A Dance of the Daisies (*EC*).

101. Piatt was not alone in acknowledging that Irish landlords had troubles of their own. While passionately attacking the system, William Desmond O'Brien comments: "Whilst pleading the cause of the Irish tenants with whom all my nature is in sympathy, yet, from personal knowledge of Irish landlords, I feel sincere sorrow and sympathy for a majority of them as individuals. . . . Like the oligarchy of the Slave States, they inherited legal rights, which, however contrary to the laws of humanity, their education, customs and self-interest taught them to regard as just" (*Our Continent* 561). Given her background, Piatt knew what it meant to "inheri[t] legal rights . . . contrary to the laws of humanity," and this stanza may come out of such understanding.

102. Called "perfect after its kind" by Yeats, this elegy commemorates the death of Piatt's sixth child, Louis, who drowned in a boating accident in Cork Harbour. The family had presumably visited the round tower at Cloyne among many tourist sites in the area; and it is to this location that Piatt transfers Louis's death, turning it into a quest for secret knowledge. Round towers were stone structures built in the first century C.E. to provide protection against Viking raiders and they are extremely difficult to climb. In a letter to William Henry Venable, September 12, 1884, J. J. describes Louis's death in poignant detail. Louis and Cecil, who also came close to drowning, had gone out to sail in two "tiny yachts . . . of pine" that they had built the night before. "I am told," J. J. adds, in an image that may have helped inspire Sarah's "A Bid for the Crown Jewels," "they were last seen by our postman around 10:30 that day leaving our terrace gate, with their arms prettily about each other" (Mss 127, DCVMC). So the little princes are said by Shakespeare to have been found sleeping in the Tower of London when their murderers came on them (*Richard III* 4.3.11). The next three poems are also on Louis: "A Child in the Park," "The Coming-back of the Dead," and "A Bid for the Crown Jewels."

103. Piatt's nurse makes her last appearance in Piatt's poetry in stanza 5.

104. Variant: line 16: herself] himself (*CWB*, *Hesp2*)

105. Built in the eleventh century, the Tower of London was an ancient fortress and royal residence during the Middle Ages. By the time of Richard III, it had become a prison for the nobility, including his murdered nephews, Edward V and Richard of York, the two "young Princes" referred to in the final stanza. Raleigh was also kept in the Tower prior to his beheading in 1618—serving as the occasion for one of Piatt's grimmer jokes (stanza 7). In her memoirs, Tynan speaks of the Piatt boys' hyper-Americaness, presumably their response to their parents' "exile." Tynan's father apparently called them "Red Indians" (*Memories* 190). Piatt embraced the epithet and calls them "savages," albeit affectionately. It is worth noting that the two oldest boys, Donn and Fred, remained in Europe after their parents' departure. Marrying into the Sigerson family, Donn carried on his mother's radical politics, becoming an ardent supporter of Irish home rule. Donn's son was an active participant in the Gaelic revival. Piatt glosses the "old fellows" in stanza 4 as the Beefeaters.

106. The title comes from Revelations 21:1. The striking similarity between Piatt's image of a "lonesome water-bird standing dream-deep / In mist and tide," in stanza 4, and the famous epiphanic moment at the conclusion of Joyce's *Portrait of the Artist as a Young Man* (1916) may not be entirely coincidental. This was Tynan's favorite Piatt poem and she cites the relevant lines in her 1894 account ("Poets in Exile") as well as in later versions of her essay on them.

107. Piatt or J. J. prefaces *EC* with a note claiming that the "sympathy" which the poems evince toward "the people of that beautiful and interesting country [Ireland], should be understood to be simply a human not a national one," a position impossible to sustain if one looks at the volume's contents. *EC* not only includes "A Reproach" but "An Irish Wildflower," "In Primrose Time," "A Child's Cry," "An Irish Fairy Story," "His Argument," "A Dance of the Daisies," "A Night-Scene at Cashel," and "Last of His Line." The Piatts may have been attempting to deflect the negative criticism *IW* had received: "If Mrs. Piatt does not check a tendency evident in much of the contents of her new book to let politics, instead of poetry, get hold of her verse—well, she will be writing politics instead of poetry" (as quoted by Roberts xxiii). As is so often the case, the negative reviewer came closer to the mark than those more friendly to Piatt herself.

108. In a letter to Stedman, November 3, 1888, J. J. says that Sarah was uneasy publishing this poem under her own name since she feared some would view it as "unfeminine or unladylike" (ECSP). In this instance, J. J. was on the side of the angels and pushed the poem through. It is possible, however, that in his mind Sarah was incapable of being either unfeminine or unladylike and therefore, ipso facto, no poem of hers could be either. Piatt also wrote a longer version of this send-up of British aristocratic pretensions, "Last of His Line," which is also in *EC*. Piatt's note to line 3: J.P. [Justice of the Peace].

109. Versailles's famous Hall of Mirrors, in which the swallow-queen is helplessly trapped, is a fitting symbol for the imprisoning narcissism of the French royals, a nar-

cissism that made it impossible for them to feel/respond to the desperate social conditions of the French masses and resulted in the execution of Marie Antoinette (1755–93) and Louis XVI during the French Revolution.

110. Along with being cold and dreary (and thus, in climate, Egypt's antithesis), Edinburgh was the home of John Knox (1514?–72) and Scottish Presbyterianism. A stern Calvinist, Knox frowned on all forms of pleasure in general and on women in particular, including women rulers. (See Knox's *The First Blast of the Trumpet Against the Monstrous Regiment of Women.*) One cannot, in short, think of a more inappropriate resting place for this poor pharaoh than the Scottish city. The wit Piatt displays here is highly intellectual and, like her irony, far too subtle, one suspects, for many of her readers to get. Variant: subtitle: On a Sarcophagus Containing the Mummy of an Egyptian King, at Edinburgh (*Hesp1*).

111. Aphrodite, Greek goddess of beauty, was born of the sea foam produced when Uranus's testicles fell into the ocean after his gelding by Zeus. In classical times, the white dove was sacred to Aphrodite. Piatt has transferred this association to the white seagull. In the *Iliad* (5.295–364), the Greek warrior Diomedes accidentally wounds Aphrodite as she steps between him and Paris, whom she is protecting.

112. In a letter to Louise Chandler Moulton in which Piatt lashes out against second wives, she goes on to say that men, being creatures "of flesh and blood" and living very much "in the present," are incapable of remembering their dead wives (January 7 [1890], LCMP). It is astonishing that after so much time, Piatt's resentment of her stepmother and her contempt for her father were still so vivid. In an 1863 letter to James Russell Lowell, J. J. links the sadness in Sarah's poetry, evident from the beginning, with the "death of a tender mother . . . the loss of a beautiful and happy home, [and] her father's second marriage" (September 1, 1863, bMS Am 765, James Russell Lowell Papers, quoted by permission of the Houghton Library, Harvard University). Although Piatt is undoubtedly a dark, even morbid, writer, J. J.'s defense of her bleakness here and elsewhere also testifies to the difficulties writers like Piatt and Melville encountered when they tried to raise truly unpleasant issues. Nineteenth-century readers might be "sentimental" and weepy, but pessimism and bitterness were definitely "out."

113. Nowhere is Piatt's nostalgia for the Old South more evident—or more dismaying—than in this poem. It is possible that after having witnessed the brutality of poverty in Ireland, her own family's slave-holding came to seem relatively benign; but, like the "Old Slave-Music," the poem remains deeply troublesome. Piatt's note glossing "corn": the Indian maize.

114. This poem turns on the popular Persian fable of the nightingale who fell in love with a rose. The father's rage appears to result from the bird's singing to the rose rather than to him.

115. Heinrich Heine (1797–1856) was a German romantic poet. Traditionally, laurel or bay leaves have signified victory, whether in war, athletics, or the arts. Piatt glosses "Well known" in stanza 4 as Heine's expression regarding himself.

116. Written by request, to be read at the convention of the Federation of Women's Clubs in Marietta, Ohio, October 1900. In a long, frequently incoherent letter Piatt

wrote to her son, Guy, about 1893 or 1894, her frustration at her inability to control essential aspects of her life boiled over. She and J. J. had gone into "exile" in Ireland precisely because, despite endless efforts, he had failed to procure a steady job in the States. When a change in administration in Washington, D.C., forced J. J. out of the Irish position in 1893, the couple returned to their former hand-to-mouth existence. As Sarah put it in the letter to Guy, they had gone back to "waiting, waiting, waiting," hoping that something might come through (Oct. 21, [early 1890s?] PFP-Y). As expressed both in the letter and in this poem, Piatt viewed disempowerment as the principal effect of God's curse on Eve. For good or ill, he made men rulers of the world; and left women to pay the cost, usually in "tears."

117. This poem appeared independently in *CWB* in 1895.

118. Piatt may be parodying Elizabeth Barrett Browning's "The Lady's 'Yes,'" in this poem. Barrett Browning's poem asserts that real women (i.e., "ladies") will respond positively only to suitors who offer high-minded love. Piatt's poem suggests that both men and women play games and neither is to be trusted in the courtship relationship. Thematically this and a number of other late poems sound as if they might have been written earlier. See "A Shadowy Third."

119. Given the poem's tone, stanza 2 probably alludes to Hamlet's famous third soliloquy: "To be, or not to be" (3.1.56). The poem also includes other *Hamlet* chestnuts: "There are more things in heaven and earth, Horatio, / Than are dreamt of in your philosophy" (1.5.67) and Hamlet's last words: "The rest is silence" (5.2.369).

120. This poem is the first of Piatt's last set of poems, all of which deal with her struggle to reconcile her doubts about God and Providence with her "pagan" love of earth (conveyed through her allusions to the myth of Demeter and Persephone, or Proserpine), and with her faith in Christ. My own sense is that ultimately the pagan side won out, but this may be wishful thinking. Certainly, these poems, with their persistent emphasis on the heart-breaking beauty of the natural world, could be viewed as suggesting that, like Dickinson, Piatt preferred a tale told by "a warbling Teller" to one found in "an antique Volume— / Written by faded Men" (J1545).

121. This poem appeared in the Thanksgiving issue of the *Ind*, 1910, in the slot regularly reserved for legitimate expressions of gratitude. How many readers picked up on the "New" in the title and recognized the poem for what it really was can't be known. My hunch is most readers did not, making the poem a quintessential example of Piatt's ability to hone irony to the point where she could produce two totally opposing poems at once.

122. This is Piatt's last published poem. In its striking emphasis on light even in darkness it represents a rare moment of healing in her canon and a possible moment of acceptance in relation to the doubts that beset her through her lifetime. "Dis" is an alternative name for Hades, the place and the person.

❧ SELECTED BIBLIOGRAPHY

EDITIONS OF BOOKS BY SARAH PIATT

The Children Out-of-Doors: A Book of Verses by Two in One House. With J. J. Piatt. Cincinnati: Robert Clarke, 1885.

Child's-World Ballads: Three Little Emigrants: A Romance of Cork Harbour, 1884, etc. Cincinnati: Robert Clarke, 1887.

Child's-World Ballads and Other Poems. Second Series. Westminster, England: Archibald Constable, 1895.

Dramatic Persons and Moods, with Other New Poems. Boston: Houghton, Osgood, 1880.

An Enchanted Castle and Other Poems: Pictures, Portraits and People in Ireland. London: Longmans, Green, 1893.

The Gift of Tears. Cincinnati: Western Literary Press, 1906.

In Primrose Time: A New Irish Garland. Boston: Houghton, Mifflin, 1886; London and Edinburgh: Kegan Paul, 1886.

An Irish Garland. Edinburgh: D. Douglas, 1884; Boston: Houghton, Mifflin, 1885.

An Irish Wildflower, etc. London: T. Fisher Unwin, 1891; New York: Stokes, 1891, 1896; London: Longmans, 1894.

Mrs. Piatt's Select Poems: A Voyage to the Fortunate Isles and Other Poems. Boston and New York: Houghton, Mifflin, 1886.

The Nests at Washington and Other Poems. With John James Piatt. New York: Walter Low, 1864; London: Sampson Low, 1864.

Poems. 2 vols. London: Longmans, Green, 1894.

Poems: In Company with Children. Boston: D. Lothrop, 1877. Rpt., *A Book about Baby and Other Poems in Company with Children.* Boston: D. Lothrop, 1882.

That New World and Other Poems. Boston: James R. Osgood, 1877.

A Voyage to the Fortunate Isles, etc. Boston: James R. Osgood, 1874, 1877; London: Kegan Paul, 1885; New York: Houghton, Mifflin, 1886.

The Witch in the Glass, etc. Boston: Houghton, Mifflin, 1889; London: Eliott Stock, 1888, 1890; 2d ed., Boston: Houghton, Mifflin, 1890.

A Woman's Poems. Boston: James R. Osgood, 1871, 1878.

REVIEWS

"Art vs. Heart." Review of *A Voyage to the Fortunate Isles. Scribner's Monthly* 8 (August 1874): 501.

"Current Literature." Review of *A Voyage to the Fortunate Isles. Overland Monthly* 13 (September 1874): 295–96.

"Current Poetry." Review of *Dramatic Persons and Moods*. *Literary World* 11 (January 1880): 11–12.

"Five Books of Verse." Review of *A Voyage to the Fortunate Isles*. *The Critic* 5 (February 13, 1886): 80.

Howells, William Dean. "Recent Literature." Review of *A Voyage to the Fortunate Isles*. *Atlantic Monthly* 34 (July 1874): 104–5.

———. "Recent Literature." Review of *A Woman's Poems*. *Atlantic Monthly* 27 (June 1871): 773–75.

———. "Some New Books of Poetry." Review of *That New World*. *Atlantic Monthly* 39 (January 1877): 87–90.

———. "Some Recent Volumes of Verse." Review of *Poems in Company with Children*. *Atlantic Monthly* 41 (May 1878): 631–32.

"Linked Poets." Review of *A Voyage to the Fortunate Isles*. *The Nation* (December 5, 1885): np.

"Minor Notices." Review of *Enchanted Castle*. *Literary World* 24 (November 1893): 370.

"Mrs. Piatt's Poems: A Review of *That New World and other Poems*." *Scribner's Monthly* 14 (May 1877): 118–19.

"Mrs. Piatt's Poems." Review of *Complete Poems*. *The Literary World*. 25 (August 1894): 279.

"New Books." Review of *That New World*. *Appleton's Journal* (February 1877): 191.

"Notes on New Books." Review of *Complete Poems*. *Irish Monthly: A Magazine of General Literature* 22 (November 1894): 613–14.

"Poetry and Verse." Review of *Complete Poems*. *The Critic* 22 (October 1894): 257.

"Recent Poetry by Women." Review of *Dramatic Persons and Moods*. *Scribner's Monthly* 19 (February 1880): 634–35.

"Recent Verse." Review of *Three Little Emigrants*. *The Critic* 8 (September 1887): 137.

Review of *An Irish Garland* and *The Children Out-of-Doors*. *Academy* (March 21, 1885): 203.

Review of Mrs. Piatt's *[Select] Poems*. (*A Voyage to the Fortunate Isles and Other Poems*.) *Westminster Review*, n.s. 70 (July and October 1886): n.p.

Review of *Poems in Company with Children* by Mrs. S.M.B. Piatt. *Harper's New Monthly Magazine* 56 (March 1878): 628.

Review of *A Voyage to the Fortunate Isles*. *Academy* 709 (December 5, 1885): 369.

Review of *A Witch in the Glass*. *The Dial: A Monthly Journal of Current Literature* 9 (April 1889): 324.

Review of *A Woman's Poems*. *Harper's New Monthly Magazine*. 43 (August 1871): 460.

Scudder, Horace. "Recent Poetry." Review of *In Primrose Time*. *Atlantic Monthly* 59 (March 1887): 413.

Tynan, Katherine. "Mrs. Piatt's Poems" *Irish Monthly: A Magazine of General Literature* 14 (June 1886): 385–90.

Yeats, W. B. "A Bundle of Poets." *London Speaker*, July 22, 1893, 81–82.

ARCHIVAL COLLECTIONS

Bayard Taylor Collection, Division of Rare and Manuscript Collections, Cornell University Library

Dolores C. Venable Memorial Collection, Ohio Historical Society

Edmund Clarence Stedman Papers, Rare Book and Manuscript Library, Columbia University

Louise Chandler Moulton Papers, Library of Congress

Newberry Library, Chicago, Illinois

Piatt Family Papers, Manuscripts and Archives, Yale University Library

Piatt Family Papers and William Conant Church Papers, Berg Collection of English and American Literature; Richard and Elizabeth Stoddard Papers, and Miscellaneous Papers, Manuscripts and Archives Division, New York Public Library

W. D. Howells, Henry Wadsworth Longfellow, J. R. Lowell Papers, Houghton Library, Harvard University

PERIODICALS

Academy
Appleton's Journal
Atalanta
Athenaeum
The Atlantic Monthly
Bookman
Belford's Magazine
The Capital
Century
Cincinnati Commercial
The Cosmopolitan
Galaxy
Harper's Bazar
Harper's New Monthly Magazine
Harper's Weekly
Hearth and Home
Independent
Irish Monthly
Leslie's Magazine
Lippincott's Monthly Magazine
Louisville Journal
Mac-A-Cheek Press
Magazine of Poetry
Manhattan
Midland Monthly
Nation

New England Monthly
New York Ledger
Our Young Folks
Overland Monthly
Pilot
Potter's American Monthly
Putnam's
Scribner's Magazine
Scribner's Monthly
Spectator
St. Nicholas
Vindicator
Wide-Awake
Windsor Magazine
Youth's Companion

SECONDARY SOURCES

Alderman, Edwin Anderson, and Joel Chandler Harris, eds. *Library of Southern Literature.* Vol. 9. Atlanta, Ga.: Martin and Hoyt, 1907.

Bennett, Paula. "'The Descent of the Angel': Interrogating Domestic Ideology in American Women's Poetry, 1858–1890." *American Literary History* 7 (Winter 1995): 591–610.

———. "John James and Sarah Morgan Bryan Piatt." In Haralson, 329–34.

———. "Not Just Filler, Not Just Sentimental: Women's Poetry in American Victorian Periodicals, 1860–1900." In Price and Smith, 202–79.

———, ed. *Nineteenth-Century American Women Poets: An Anthology.* Oxford: Blackwell, 1997.

Burress, Marjorie. *It Happened 'Round North Bend.* Privately printed, 1969.

Colvert, James B. "Piatt, Sarah Morgan Bryan." In James et al. 3:63–64.

Cox, F. Brett. "'What Need, Then, for Poetry?' The Genteel Tradition and the Continuity of American Literature." *New England Quarterly* 67 (June 1994): 212–33.

Coyle, William, ed. *Ohio Authors and their Books: 1796–1950.* Cleveland, N.Y.: World, 1962.

Dowler, Clare. "John James Piatt: Representative Figure of a Momentous Period." *Ohio Archeological and Historical Society Publications Quarterly,* vol. 45, 1–26. Columbus: Ohio State Archeological and Historical Society, 1936.

[Farman, Ella]. "Mr. J. J. Piatt and Mrs. S.M.B. Piatt." In Stoddard, 56–74. Rpt. as "Poets' Homes—No. VI: Mr. J.J. Piatt and Mrs. S.M.B. Piatt." *Wide-Awake* (November 1876): 286–91.

Farnham, Christie. *The Education of the Southern Belle: Higher Education and Student Socialization in the Antebellum South.* New York: New York University Press, 1994.

Gray, Janet. "Race and Time: American Women's Poetics from Antislavery to Racial Modernity." Ph.D. diss., Princeton University, 1999.

————, ed. *She Wields a Pen: American Women's Poetry of the Nineteenth-Century.* Iowa City: University of Iowa Press, 1997.

Hagenbüchle, Roland, ed. *American Poetry: Between Tradition and Modernism, 1865–1914.* Regensburg, Germany: Verlag Frieddrich Pustet, 1984.

Hamilton, Gail (Mary Abigail Dodge). Review of *Poems by Two Friends* by W. D. Howells and John James Piatt. *National Era* 14 (February 16, 1860): 26.

Hanawalt, Jean Allen. "A Biographical and Critical Study of John James and Sarah Morgan (Bryan) Piatt." Ph.D. diss., University of Washington, 1981.

Haralson, Eric, ed. *Encyclopedia of American Poetry: The Nineteenth Century.* Chicago: Fitzroy Dearborn, 1998.

Herzberg, Max J. *The Reader's Encyclopedia of American Literature.* New York: Crowell, 1962.

Hollander, John, ed. *American Poetry: The Nineteenth Century.* 2 vols. New York: Library of America, 1993.

Howells, Mildred, ed. *Life in Letters of William Dean Howells.* 2 vols. Garden City, N.J.: Doubleday, Doran, 1928.

Howells, William Dean. "Editor's Easy Chair." *Harper's New Monthly Magazine* 135 (July 1917): 291–92.

————. *Literary Friends and Acquaintance.* Ed. David F. Hiatt. Bloomington: Indiana University Press, 1968.

————. "Recent Literature." Review of *Landmarks and Other Poems* by J. J. Piatt. *Atlantic Monthly* 9 (March 1872): 367.

————. "Recent Literature." Review of *Poems of House and Home* by J. J. Piatt. *Atlantic Monthly* 43 (April 1879): 546.

————. *Selected Letters.* 5 vols. Ed. George Arms et al. Boston: Twayne, 1879–83.

James, Edward T., et al., eds. *Notable American Women, 1607–1950.* 3 vols. Cambridge, Mass.: Belknap Press of Harvard University Press, 1971.

Kilcup, Karen L., ed. *Nineteenth-Century American Women Writers: An Anthology.* Oxford: Blackwell, 1996.

Kincheloe, Pamela J. "Through the Claude Glass: Nineteenth-Century American Writers and Monumental Discourse." Ph.D. diss., Southern Illinois University, Carbondale, 1997.

————. "Two Visions of Fairyland: Ireland and the Monumental Discourse of the Nineteenth-Century Tourist." *Irish Studies Review* 7 (1999): 41–51.

Kindilien, Carlin T. *American Poetry in the Eighteen Nineties.* Providence, R.I.: Brown University Press, 1956.

Leighton, Angela, and Margaret Reynolds, eds. *Victorian Women Poets: An Anthology.* Oxford: Blackwell, 1995.

Lowell, J. R. "Poems of John James Piatt." *North American Review* 107 (October 1868): 661–62.

Mainiero, Lina. *American Women Writers.* Vol. 3. New York: Frederick Ungar, 1981.

Melville, Herman. *Pierre or the Ambiguities.* Evanston, Ill.: Northwestern University Press, 1971.

Michaels, Larry R., ed. *That New World: Selected Poems of Sarah Piatt, 1861–1911.* West Liberty, Ohio: Mac-A-Cheek Foundation for the Humanities, Piatt Castles, 1999.

Michel, Nettie Leila. "Sarah M. B. Piatt." *Magazine of Poetry* 3 (July 1891): 279–85.

Moore, Dorothea. "Precocity." *Chap-Book* 5, no. 3 (1897): 97. See *Philistine* 3 (1897): 190.

Mott, Frank Luther. *A History of American Magazines.* 3 vols. Cambridge, Mass.: Harvard University Press, 1938.

Ninth Annual Announcement of the Henry Female College. Louisville, Ky.: Hull and Bros., 1859.

O'Brien, William Desmond. "Tenure of Land and Landlordism in Ireland." *Our Continent* 2 (November 8, 1882): 565.

Piatt, John James. "Biographical Sketch." In Piatt, ed., *The Poems of George D. Prentice,* i–xxxviii.

———. *Landmarks and Other Poems.* New York: Hurd and Houghton, 1872.

———. "The Morning Street." *Atlantic Monthly* 3 (February 1859): 150–51.

———. *Poems of Two Friends.* With W. D. Howells. Columbus: Follett, Foster, 1860.

———. *Western Windows and Other Poems.* Cincinnati: R. W. Carroll, 1868.

———, ed. *Hesperian Tree: An Annual of the Ohio Valley.* Cincinnati: George G. Shaw, 1900.

———. *Hesperian Tree: An Annual of the Ohio Valley.* Columbus, Ohio: S. F. Harriman, 1903.

———. *The Poems of George D. Prentice.* Edited with a Biographical Sketch. Cincinnati: Robert Clarke, 1876.

———. *Union of American Poetry and Art.* Cincinnati: Dibble, 1880.

"Piatt, Sarah Morgan (Bryan)." *National Cyclopaedia of American Biography.* Vol. 8. New York: J. T. White, 1926.

Piatt Castles. Travel Brochure. West Liberty, Ohio: Piatt Castles, n.d.

Price, Kenneth M., and Susan Belasco Smith, eds. *Periodical Literature in Nineteenth-Century America.* Charlottesville: University Press of Virginia, 1995.

Rable, George C. *Civil Wars: Women and the Crisis of Southern Nationalism.* Urbana: University of Illinois Press, 1991.

Review of *Recent Poems* by Edmund Clarence Stedman. *Harper's New Monthly Magazine* 56 (March 1878): 628.

Roberts, Jessica, ed. "The American Poetry of Sarah Morgan Bryan Piatt." Honors thesis. Dartmouth College, 1997.

Roller, Bert. *Children in American Poetry, 1610–1900.* Nashville: George Peabody College for Teachers, 1930.

Roller, David C., and Robert W. Twyman, eds. *The Encyclopedia of Southern History.* Baton Rouge: Louisiana State University Press, 1979.

Santayana, George. *The Genteel Tradition: Nine Essays.* Ed. Douglas L. Wilson. Cambridge, Mass.: Harvard University Press, 1967.

Shaw, John MacKay, ed. *Children in Poetry.* Vol. 6. Detroit: Gale Research, 1967.

Spengemann, William C., with Jessica F. Roberts, eds. *Nineteenth-Century American Poetry.* New York: Penguin, 1996.

Stedman, Edmund Clarence, ed. *An American Anthology, 1787–1900.* Boston: Houghton Mifflin, 1900.

———. *Poets of America.* Boston: Houghton Mifflin, 1886.

Steiner, Dorothea. "Women Poets in the Twilight Period." In Hagenbüchle, 169–90.

Stoddard, R. H. *Poets' Homes: Pen and Pencil Sketches of American Poets and Their Homes.* Boston: D. Lothrop, 1877.

Tardy, Mary [Ida Raymond], ed. *Living Female Writers of the South.* Philadelphia: Claxton, Remsen, and Haffelfinger, 1872.

Taylor, Bayard. *The Echo Club and Other Literary Diversions.* Boston: Osgood, 1876.

Terris, Virginia R. "Sarah Morgan Bryan Piatt." In Mainiero, 3:387–89.

Townsend, John Wilson. *Kentucky in American Letters: 1784–1917.* 2 vols. Cedar Rapids, Ia.: Torch, 1913.

Tynan, Katherine. *Memories.* London: Eveleigh Nash and Grayson, 1924.

———. "Poets in Exile." *The Critic* 21 (February 1894): 121–23.

———. *Twenty-Five Years: Reminiscences.* London: Smith, Elder, 1912.

Venable, Emerson. "Sarah Morgan Bryan Piatt." In Alderman and Harris, 4003–9.

———, ed. *Poets of Ohio: Selections Representing the Poetical Work of Ohio Authors from the Pioneer Period to the Present Day, with Biographical Sketches and Notes.* Cincinnati: Stewart and Kidd, 1912.

Watts, Emily Stipes. *The Poetry of American Women from 1632 to 1943.* Austin: University of Texas Press, 1978.

Willard, Frances E., and Mary A. Livermore, eds. *American Women: Fifteen Hundred Biographies.* 2 vols. New York: Mast, Crowell, and Kirkpatrick, 1897.

Wilson, Charles Reagan, and William Ferris, eds. *Encyclopedia of Southern Culture.* Chapel Hill: University of North Carolina Press, 1989.

☙ INDEX OF POEM TITLES AND SOURCES

PAULA BERNAT BENNETT is a professor of English at Southern Illinois University at Carbondale. She is the author of *My Life a Loaded Gun: Female Creativity and Feminist Poetics* (1986) and *Emily Dickinson: Woman Poet* (1990). She is the editor of *Nineteenth-Century American Women Poets: An Anthology* (1998) and coeditor, with Vernon Rosario, of *Solitary Pleasures: The Historical, Literary, and Artistic Discourses of Autoeroticism* (1995). She is a fellow at the Bunting Institute, Radcliffe College, and an NEH–American Antiquarian Society Fellow.

Typeset in 10/13 Minion
with Minion display
Designed by Dennis Roberts
Composed by Jim Proefrock
at the University of Illinois Press
Manufactured by Thomson-Shore, Inc.

University of Illinois Press
1325 South Oak Street
Champaign, IL 61820-6903
www.press.uillinois.edu